BRITISH SPORTING LITERATURE AND CULTURE IN THE LONG EIGHTEENTH CENTURY

Sport as it is largely understood today was invented during the long eighteenth century when the modern rules of sport were codified; sport emerged as a business, a spectacle, and a performance; and gaming organized itself around sporting culture. Examining the underexplored intersection of sport, literature, and culture, this collection situates sport within multiple contexts, including religion, labor, leisure time, politics, nationalism, gender, play, and science. A poetics, literature, and culture of sport swelled during the era, influencing artists such as John Collett and writers including Lord Byron, Jonathan Swift, and Henry Fielding. This volume brings together literary scholars and historians of sport to demonstrate the ubiquity of sport to eighteenth-century life, the variety of literary and cultural representations of sporting experiences, and the evolution of sport from rural pastimes to organized, regular events of national and international importance. Each essay offers in-depth readings of both material practices and representations of sport as they relate to, among other subjects, recreational sports, the Cotswold games, clothing, women archers, tennis, celebrity athletes, and the theatricality of boxing. Taken together, the essays in this collection offer valuable multiple perspectives on reading sport during the century when sport became modern.

British Literature in Context in the Long Eighteenth Century

Series Editor: Jack Lynch, Rutgers University, Newark, USA

This series aims to promote original scholarship on the intersection of British literature and history in the long eighteenth century, from the Restoration through the first generation of the Romantic era.

Both "literature" and "history" are broadly conceived. Literature might include not only canonical novels, poems, and plays but also essays, life-writing, and belles lettres of all sorts, by both major and minor authors. History might include not only traditional political and social history but also the history of the book, the history of science, the history of religion, the history of scholarship, and the history of sexuality, as well as broader questions of historiography and periodization.

The series editor invites proposals for both monographs and collections taking a wide range of approaches. Contributions should be interdisciplinary but always grounded in sound historical research; the authoritative is always preferred to the merely trendy. All contributions should be written so as to be accessible to the widest possible audience, and should seek to make lasting contributions to the field.

British Sporting Literature and Culture in the Long Eighteenth Century

Edited by
SHARON HARROW
Shippensburg University of Pennsylvania, USA

ASHGATE

© Sharon Harrow and the contributors 2015

All rights reserved. No part of this publication may be reproduced, stored in a retrieval system or transmitted in any form or by any means, electronic, mechanical, photocopying, recording or otherwise without the prior permission of the publisher.

Sharon Harrow has asserted her right under the Copyright, Designs and Patents Act, 1988, to be identified as the editor of this work.

Published by
Ashgate Publishing Limited
Wey Court East
Union Road
Farnham
Surrey, GU9 7PT
England

Ashgate Publishing Company
110 Cherry Street
Suite 3-1
Burlington, VT 05401-3818
USA

www.ashgate.com

British Library Cataloguing in Publication Data
A catalogue record for this book is available from the British Library

TThe Library of Congress Cataloging-in-Publication Data has been applied for.

ISBN 9781472465085 (hbk)
ISBN 9781472465092 (ebk – PDF)
ISBN 9781472465108 (ebk – ePUB)

Printed in the United Kingdom by Henry Ling Limited,
at the Dorset Press, Dorchester, DT1 1HD

*For my brothers Z, Mikey, Aram, Joseph,
who have made fun a sport and a pastime.*

Contents

List of Figures   ix
List of Contributors   xiii
Acknowledgements   xv

Introduction: Playing by the Rules   1

PART I   CONTEXTS

1   "Wholesome recreations and cheering influences": Popular Recreation and Social Elites in Eighteenth-Century Britain   19
Emma Griffin

2   Olympism and Pastoralism in British Sporting Literature   35
Jean Williams

3   Sporting with Clothes: John Collet's Prints in the 1770s   55
Patricia Crown

PART II   SPORTS

4   The Uses and Transformations of Early Modern Tennis   83
Alexis Tadié

5   Archery in the Long Eighteenth Century   105
Linda V. Troost

6   Jockeying for Position: Horse Culture in Poetry, Prose, and *The New Foundling Hospital for Wit*   125
Donald W. Nichol

PART III   PEOPLE

7   Boxing for England: Daniel Mendoza and the Theater of Sport   153
Sharon Harrow

8   Rehearsing Leander: Byron and Swimming in the Long Eighteenth Century   179
Jack D'Amico

Bibliography   195
Index   215

List of Figures

Cover	*The Meeting of Parties, or, Humphries & Mendoza Fighting for a Crown.* (1788). Courtesy, The Lewis Walpole Library, Yale University.	
I.1	Trade card of James Figg. © Trustees of the British Museum.	2
I.2	William Hogarth. *Second Stage of Cruelty* (1751). Courtesy, The Lewis Walpole Library, Yale University.	9
3.1	Robert Laurie after John Collet. *The Rival Milliners* (1772). Mezzotint. Courtesy, Colonial Williamsburg Foundation.	56
3.2	John Collet, after. *Shop-Lifter Detected* (1778). Mezzotint. Courtesy, The Lewis Walpole Library, Yale University.	57
3.3	John Collet, after. *The Female Fox Hunter* (ca. 1780). Mezzotint. Courtesy, The Lewis Walpole Library, Yale University.	58
3.4	Joshua Reynolds. *Lady Worsley* (ca. 1776). Oil on canvas (Harewood House, Yorkshire). Courtesy, Lord Harewood. Photo: courtesy, Bridgeman Art Library.	59
3.5	John Collet, after. *An Officer in the Light Infantry driven by his Lady to Cox Heath* (ca. 1770). Mezzotint. Courtesy, The Lewis Walpole Library, Yale University.	61
3.6	John Collet, after. *Miss Tipapin Going for All Nine* (ca. 1778). Mezzotint. Courtesy, Yale Center for British Art, Paul Mellon Fund.	62
3.7	John Collet, after. *Miss Wicket and Miss Trigger* (1778). Mezzotint. Courtesy, The Lewis Walpole Library, Yale University.	63
3.8	John Collet. *Modern Love: Courtship* (1763). Oil on canvas. Courtesy, Colonial Williamsburg Foundation.	66
3.9	John Collet. *Modern Love: Elopement* (1763). Oil on canvas. Courtesy, Colonial Williamsburg Foundation.	66
3.10	John Collet. *Modern Love: Honeymoon* (1763). Oil on canvas. Courtesy, Colonial Williamsburg Foundation.	67
3.11	John Collet. *Modern Love: Discordant Matrimony* (1763). Oil on canvas. Courtesy, Colonial Williamsburg Foundation.	67
3.12	J. Goldar after John Collet. *The Canonical Beau, or Mars in the Dumps* (1768). Courtesy, The Lewis Walpole Library, Yale University.	70
3.13	John Collet, after. *An Actress at her Toilet, or Miss Brazen just Breech't* (1779). Mezzotint. Courtesy, The Lewis Walpole Library, Yale University.	73
3.14	John Collett, after. *The Female Bruisers* (1770). Mezzotint. Courtesy, The Lewis Walpole Library, Yale University.	74

3.15	John Collet, after. *A Morning Frolic, or the Transmutation of Sexes* (1780). Mezzotint. Courtesy, The Lewis Walpole Library, Yale University.	76
3.16	Richard Newton. *Wearing the Breeches* (1794). Etching. Courtesy, the Whitworth, The University of Manchester.	77
4.1	M. de Garsault. *Art du Paumier-Raquetier, et de la Paume* (Paris: chez Saillant and Nyon, chez Desaint, 1767). Pl. 3. Shelfmark: (Vet) 1773 b.19. Courtesy, the Bodleian Library, University of Oxford.	89
4.2	Denis de la Marinière. *La Maison academique, contenant les jeux du picquet, du hoc, du tric-trac, du hoca, de la guerre, de la paulme, du billard, du palle-mail, divers jeux de cartes, qui se joüent en differentes facons ... & autres jeux facetieux & divertissans* (Paris: chez Etienne Loison, 1659). Frontispiece. Shelfmark: Jessel F.760. Courtesy, the Bodleian Library, University of Oxford.	96
4.3	Jean-Baptiste Oudry. *Bataille Arrivée Dans le Tripot* (1649–1657), illustration for *Le Roman Comique* de Scarron. Courtesy, Paris, Musée du Louvre, D.A.G. Photo (C) RMN-Grand Palais (Musée du Louvre) / Thierry Le Mage.	98
5.1	Thomas Waring. *Senior, shooting on Blackheath with the Royal Toxophilites in spring 1789* (after Joseph Slater, engraved by James Heath). Published March 2, 1789, by Joseph Slater. Image courtesy, the Heath-Caldwell Family Archive.	109
5.2	John Russell. The Prince of Wales (later George IV) in the uniform he designed for the Royal Kentish Bowmen (1791). Oil on canvas, 250.2 x 180.3 cm. Royal Collection Trust / © Her Majesty Queen Elizabeth II, 2015.	111
5.3	The Fairlop Oak with a meeting of the Hainault Foresters (engraved by Cook). Frontispiece for the January 1794 issue of *The Sporting Magazine*. Image courtesy, HathiTrust Digital Library.	112
5.4	Archery at Hatfield, depicting the Marchioness of Salisbury and members of the Hertfordshire Archers (engraved by Cook, after Richard Corbould). Illustration for the November 1792 issue of *The Sporting Magazine*. Image courtesy, HathiTrust Digital Library.	115
6.1	*The Jockey Club*, frontispiece, Edward Ward, *The History of the London Clubs, or, the Citizens' Pastime...*, part 1 (London: J. Bagnall, 1709). BL: 10349.bbb.25. © The British Library Board.	138
6.2	Detail of plate VI, 3rd state, William Hogarth, *A Rake's Progress*, 1734/35. Author's copy.	139
6.3.	Detail of plate II, 4th state, William Hogarth, *A Rake's Progress*, 1734/35. Author's copy.	140

6.4	Frontispiece, *The New Foundling Hospital for Wit*, vol. 6 (London: John Almon, 1773). Author's copy.	146
7.1	James Gillray. Portrait of Daniel Mendoza (1788). Etching and aquatint. © Trustees of the British Museum.	154
7.2	George Cruikshank. *Killing no murder. As performed at the Grand National Theatre* (1809). Print. © Trustees of the British Museum.	172

List of Contributors

Patricia Crown is emerita professor of eighteenth- and nineteenth-century art and women's and gender studies at the University of Missouri-Columbia. Her chapter was originally published in *Eighteenth Century Life* (February 2002). Several of her publications include: "Clothing the Modern Venus: Hogarth and Women's Dress," in Elise Goodman (ed.), *Studies in Eighteenth Century Art and Culture* (University of Delaware Press, 2001); and "Hogarth's Working Women: Commerce and Consumption," in Bernadette Fort and Angela Rosenthal (eds.), *The Other Hogarth: The Aesthetics of Difference* (Princeton University Press, 2001).

Educated at SUNY, Buffalo, after some peripatetic years teaching in Naples, Berkeley, Beirut, Dalian, and Rabat, **Jack D'Amico** returned to Buffalo as a professor and administrator at Canisius College. The author of *The Moor in English Renaissance Drama* (University of South Florida Press, 1991), D'Amico enjoys swimming and includes among his academic interests related to Byron and swimming an early essay on leisure in More's *Utopia* and a recent study on aquatic spectacle in the Roman theater at Pausilypon, Naples.

Emma Griffin is professor of history at the University of East Anglia and author of four books, including *England's Revelry: A History of Popular Sports and Pastimes, 1660–1830* (Oxford University Press, 2005) and *Blood Sport: A History of Hunting in Britain* (Yale University Press, 2007).

Sharon Harrow is professor of English at Shippensburg University of Pennsylvania. She is the author of *Adventures in Domesticity: Gender and Colonial Adulteration in Eighteenth-Century British Literature* (AMS Press, 2004) and of articles and reviews on eighteenth-century women writers, empire, and pedagogy. While completing her dissertation in Ithaca, New York, she trained as a boxer.

Donald W. Nichol is professor of English at Memorial University of Newfoundland. His edition of *The New Foundling Hospital for Wit* was published by Pickering and Chatto in 2006. He edited *Lumen*, vol. 31 (Montréal: Les Presses de l'Université de Montréal, 2012), the proceedings of the 2010 conference of the Canadian Society for Eighteenth-Century Studies. He saw Northern Dancer win the Queen's Plate in 1964.

Alexis Tadié is professor of English literature at the University of Paris-Sorbonne and a senior research fellow at the Institut Universitaire de France. He is the author of *Sterne's Whimsical Theatres of Language* (Ashgate, 2003) and the editor in French of *The Life of Opinions of Tristram Shandy, Gentleman* and of *Gulliver's Travels* (Gallimard, 2012). He has written about sports and recently coedited *Sport, Literature, Society: Cultural Historical Studies* (Routledge, 2013).

Linda V. Troost, professor and chair of English at Washington & Jefferson College, earned an AB from Smith College and a PhD from the University of Pennsylvania. She has published scholarly articles and essays on a wide range of topics, including British musical theater, Robin Hood, and Jane Austen. She edits two journals—*Eighteenth-Century Women*, an annual for AMS Press, and *Topic: The Washington & Jefferson College Review*. With Sayre Greenfield, she edited *Jane Austen in Hollywood* (University Press of Kentucky, 1998), the first book on the Austen film boom, soon to be available in Chinese.

Jean Williams is professor of Sports History and Culture at the International Centre for Sports History and Culture, De Montfort University, Leicester. She has written on the history and cultural context of sport, including Jeff Hill and Jean Williams (eds.) *Sport and Literature: A Special Edition of Sport in History* 29, no. 2 (2009). She is currently completing *Send Her Victorious: A History of British Women Olympians 1896–2012* with Manchester University Press.

Acknowledgements

The project has taken many shapes over the course of many years. Initially, I had planned to include a section of material intended to introduce the reader to primary sporting texts. After years of research and hundreds of pages of material, I concluded that I had been endeavoring to write two books in one. During the course of that research, I discovered a rich community of scholars interested in the literature and culture of sport, and I am enormously grateful to have found such intellectual camaraderie.

I read a version of Chapter 7, "Boxing for England: Daniel Mendoza and the Theater of Sport," at Sporting Life: An Interdisciplinary Symposium on the Cultures of Sport in the Eighteenth and Nineteenth Centuries held at the University of Paris-Sorbonne in March 2014. I extend my warm gratitude to the organizers and participants for sharing their perspicacious conversations about sport. Thanks to Alexis Tadié, Danny O'Quinn, Donna Landry, Marius Kwint, Phil Dine, John McLeod, Frans DeBruyn, John Whale, Alexander Regier, Simon Bainbridge, and Supriya Chaudhuri. A special thanks goes to Alexis and Danny for organizing the symposium.

I have presented numerous conference papers on the subject of sport, and I am indebted to the generosity of those eighteenth-century scholars who have strengthened my writing with their sharp insights. I owe special debts of gratitude to Jack Lynch, Nora Nachumi, Kirsten Saxton, Mary Peace, Alison Conway, Brycchan Carey, and Kevin Berland, all of whom supported this project with their good ideas and great wit. Without the intellectual and emotional support of Kirsten and Nora, I would not have finished this book. Thanks to Cedric Reverand and Don Mell for their encouragement. I have found the Women's Caucus of the American Society for Eighteenth-Century Studies to be a source of support, and I am pleased that sport and gender has become a subject of playful inquiry among my peers, including Devoney Looser (aka Stone Cold Jane Austen).

I thank members of Shippensburg University English Department for their intellectual fellowship, especially Carla Kungl, Shari Horner, Michael Bibby, Rich Zumkhawala-Cook, Cathy Dibello, Laurie Cella, and Neil Connelly. I am indebted to the university, and especially to Dean Jim Mike, for providing material assistance for my research. Thanks to Jim Schaeffer in the Computing Technology Center for his help with all things technical. I am grateful to my students for their enthusiasm for the subject matter. It has been a genuine pleasure to share my writing and publishing experiences with them. Jayda Coons assisted me with some early transcriptions, for which I thank her.

I thank Kirsten McDonald at the Lewis Walpole Library at Yale University and Marianne Martin, visual resources librarian at the Colonial Williamsburg Foundation for their gracious assistance with images. At Ashgate, I thank

Ann Donahue for making the publishing process both rewarding and pleasurable. I appreciate her enthusiasm for the subject matter. I am grateful for the careful work of production editor Kathy Bond Borie. Jack Lynch's assistance during the editorial process with Ashgate was invaluable.

For forever engaging my interest in boxing, I thank Danny Akers, who is an extraordinary trainer. In the broadest sense, I am grateful to Nancy Siegel, Kate McGivney, Fran Stewart, Mary Stewart, and Cathy Balascio for friendship and support. I owe an immeasurable debt to Kathleen Parvin for her skillful assistance in my preparation of the manuscript. Her prestidigitation and cheerful correspondence were sustaining. My parents, Carol and Bob Bernstein, and Ken and Liz Harrow have been a source of endless support. I have especially enjoyed and am grateful to Liz and Ken for serious and silly help with words. Thanks for all of the encouragement. I spent endless, joyful hours talking out ideas and sentences while walking with my big, wonderful dog, Muddy. He listened with enthusiasm, and he curled up next to me when we got home to write. I am beholden to my husband, Brian Butzer; his genuine interest in my work, his emotional generosity, and domestic prowess made hours of work at home possible and pleasurable.

Introduction
Playing by the Rules

The essays in this interdisciplinary collection demonstrate the ubiquity of sport to eighteenth-century life, the variety of literary and cultural representations of sporting experiences, and the evolution of sport from rural pastimes to organized, regular events of national and international importance. The long eighteenth century stands out as an important period in the literary and cultural history of sport for a number of reasons: many modern rules of sport were codified; sport emerged as a business, a spectacle, and a performance; and gaming organized itself around sports. A poetics, literature, and culture of sport swelled during the era. As the broader culture modernized, sport, too, became modern. Scholars have approached such far-reaching literary and cultural changes from a variety of critical perspectives. Taken together, the essays in this collection reflect the intricate and integral role sport played in the rapidly expanding world of eighteenth-century England.

Why was this period so ripe for the evolution of sport? Changes to the political, religious, and social milieus facilitated the development and popularity of sports and sporting culture. The long eighteenth century begins in 1660 with the restoration of Charles II to the throne. His loosening of the tight Puritan strictures that had fettered social life resonated culturally as well as politically. Charles II reinstated sports and theater, though the crown still controlled the theater (which often included sporting performances). With the licensing of official patent theaters came the development and expansion of illegitimate theaters and entertainments. Sport benefitted from its consanguinity with theater, and sporting performances often occupied many of the same venues as did legitimate entertainments.[1] No longer primarily festivities based upon a religious calendar, sporting events were staged regularly, and often in commercialized, specialized sites. Sport arose as both subject and theme in poems, plays, novels, satires, prints, tracts, treatises, and in specialized newspapers. Print culture advertised and dramatized sport, which became a national, not just a regional, activity. And the market supplied what people demanded: sports events, celebrities, scandals, reporting, literature, art—in sum, a culture of sport spread by mass marketing. This social climate receptive to sports and popular entertainments permeated the country. Wider social developments, such as urbanization, improved transportation, increased literacy, as well as the possibility of income and time for leisure activities, all favored the expansion of sport.

The rise of the public sphere, which facilitated public discourse and debate on culture and politics, and the increase in literacy contributed importantly to sports' expansion. In the early decades of the eighteenth century, the flourishing

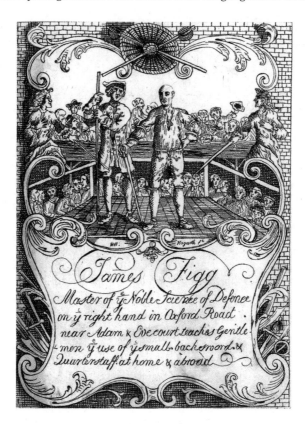

Figure I.1   Trade card of James Figg. © Trustees of the British Museum.

of popular periodicals such as the *Tatler* and the *Spectator* in addition to other mass market print facilitated debates about sport and culture.[2] Periodicals were often communally read, discussed, and disseminated at the newly fashionable coffee and chocolate houses that sprung up all over London, which had become a sporting mecca. Sport was popularized by multiple genres. In 1719, famous artist William Hogarth may have designed the business card for James Figg, the first professional fist/cudgel/sword fighter to open a sporting amphitheater (Figure I.1).

As the "Master of the Noble Science of Defence," Figg is on stage, framed by a sober and cheerful-looking crowd. The whole composition suggests order. *The Daily Journal* claimed that by 1724 adverts for blood sports (bareknuckle boxing, cockfighting, bear- and bullbaiting, for example) were published daily. And, though it was published only once a year, the *Racing Calendar* was initially issued in 1727, marking the first official sporting release. That same year, a match between Figg and another fighter, Ned Sutton, attracted thousands of spectators, including Prime Minister Robert Walpole, writers Jonathan Swift and Alexander Pope, and actor Colley Cibber.[3] Figg also arranged for the first international boxing exhibition between an Englishman and an Italian fighter. George I and the Prince of Wales both attended. These examples illustrate the way that the literary, artistic, political, and sporting worlds began to overlap.

Periodicals reported such activities, widening public discourse about sports and other pastimes. Journalists, moralists, civil servants, and sportsmen were keen to debate the definition and ideology of public recreation. An excerpt from the *Tatler* (1709) reveals the complex web of behaviors deemed deleterious to the nation:

> The present Grandeur of the *British* nation might make us expect, that we should rise in our Publick Diversions, and manner of enjoying Life, in Proportion to our Advancement in Glory and Power. Instead of that, take and survey this Town, and you'll find, Rakes and Debauchees are your Men of Pleasure; Thoughtless Atheists, and Illiterate Drunkards, call themselves Free Thinkers; and Gamesters, Banterers, Biters, Swearers, and Twenty new-born Insects more, are, in their several Species, the modern Men of Wit.[4]

The manner in which people spent their leisure time was hotly contested. Virtue and vice, true and false wit, national shame and pride were figured as opponents, and they remained central to discourses about sports and pastimes throughout the century. As the public sphere expanded, so too did the conversation about the definition, benefits, and dangers of sport.

༄ ༄ ༄

Widespread disagreement about the role of sport in English culture had occupied the minds of kings, religious leaders, journalists, and ordinary people. During the seventeenth century, varied sporting events took place mostly at fairs, festivals, and in local villages. Rural labor and leisure were structured around the religious calendar. Numerous traditional ways that people disported themselves included May-games, hunting, wrestling, leaping, cudgeling, running, fencing, bowling, swimming, bearbaiting, bareknuckle boxing, cockfighting, and juggling, to name only a few.[5] The shape and value of such public diversions formed an important part of the culture wars that contributed to the Civil War of 1642–1651. The royalty and royalist gentry promoted traditional sports and pastimes, whereas Puritans suppressed them. Battles over virtue and vice, legitimacy and illegitimacy were staged in sporting fields and arenas, and they were debated by politicians. Sport was alternately considered salubrious or deleterious to both the physical and social body.

Of course, the relationship of royalty to sport influenced such debates. James I (1603–1625) endorsed sport as practice of noble virtues. He particularly enjoyed hunting and apparently thrilled to hunting's sanguinary nature: "The kill excited him greatly and he delighted in plunging his legs into the beast's steaming entrails (a ghoulish habit that may have had something to do with the belief that stag's blood would strengthen weak limbs)."[6] While James's ritual had to do with his own physical shortcomings, the debates about Sunday sports stemmed from differences in religious beliefs between Puritans and almost everyone else. In 1617 James issued his *Book of Sports*, which sought to legitimize post-Church sports on Sundays, including "dancing, either men or women; archery for men, leaping, vaulting, or any other such harmless recreation, [and] May-games, Whitsun-ales, and Morris-dances; and the setting up of May-poles and other sports therewith used."[7] There were some notable exceptions of "unlawful games," such as bullbaiting, bearbaiting, and (oddly enough) bowling. James argued that sports readied men for war and diverted energy away from insalubrious activities such as drinking. He called for "lawful" entertainments; when, he asked, would "the common people have leave to exercise if not upon Sundays and holy days, seeing they must apply their labour and win their living in all working days?"[8]

Charles I (1625–1649) reissued his father's book in 1633 to the dismay of Puritans. That same year, Puritan William Prynne published his *Histrio-Mastix: The Player's Scourge; or, Actor's Tragedy*, a tome of complaints against the vices attendant upon theater, Sunday sports, and most popular forms of recreation. Objectors pitted sports against religious devotion, arguing that recreation should not replace worship, especially on Sundays. There were several exceptions, as illustrated by Prynne's hyperbolic syllogism:

> [If] Tilting Barriers, Jousts, and such like martial feats * * * with a hundred such like laudable exercises, favoring both royalty, valor, and activity * * * were now revived instead of effeminate, amorous, wanton dances, interludes, masques, and stage-plays, effeminacy, idleness, adultery, whoredom, ribaldry, and such other lewdness would not be so frequent in the world as now they are.[9]

Prynne and other Puritans like him accused certain sports of causing lewdness and laziness, riot and ribaldry, irreligion and intemperance. Moralists grouped together sports with a host of scurrilities, including whoring and dissolution. One writer, Richard Baxter, warned of "Voluptuous Youths that run after Wakes, and May-games, and Dancings, and Revellings, and are carried by the Love of sports and pleasure, from the Love of God, and the care of their Salvation, and the Love of Holiness, and the Love of their Callings; and into idleness, riotousness and disobedience to their Superiors."[10] Here, sports and pastimes foster rebelliousness and endanger hierarchy. Within such an authoritarian regime, might some religious objections, then, have served as convenient cloaks for fears of social unrest and public protest? As early as 1638, Public Record Office papers and contemporary histories record the use of football matches to mask public protest against land enclosure and drainage, or as a cover for food riots, among other things. Such clever maneuverings spanned the century. Some protests were quite large indeed, given that (by the end of the century, at least) a football match could number between 500–1000 people per team.[11] Neil Tranter has argued that the eventual codification of sport also served as a means of social regulation by ritualizing and containing working class violence.[12] It is certainly convincing to think that some viewed the commercialization of physical combat as a cultural way to contain the energies of a huge, disenfranchised laboring class.

The restoration of Charles II to the throne invigorated sport in England. Restoration libertinism reversed many Puritan restrictions on public morality; pleasure was not merely endorsed by but was modeled by Charles II who, as Birley asserts, "kept himself fit for work and sex by intense athletic activity: riding, hunting, swimming and tennis."[13] He enjoyed other sports as well, such as ice skating and yachting. Sports benefited from the Restoration ethos of cultural, intellectual, and social expansiveness. Charles II's support for science and the arts led to the founding of the *Royal Society*; the same intellectual climate concerned with classification and natural history also produced sports treatises and manuals. Restoration and eighteenth-century writers adapted neoclassical principles to represent sport as an art, a science, and a legitimate subject to be classified. Writers who took sport as their subject sometimes anatomized bodies. Sport also inspired one of the founding members of the *Royal Society*, John Evelyn, to engage in intellectual exercises about motion, wheels, and running. Many writers turned to math and science to explain and optimize the performance of sports such as golf, wrestling, and fighting.

The Restoration had so changed the public mood about sport that, by the reign of George I, even the corpulent Prime Minister Robert Walpole styled himself a sportsman. He was well known as an avid huntsman, an activity he advertised to "demonstrate political nonchalance," according to Birley.[14] Some have claimed that sporting events could themselves determine calendars, rather than the other way around. For instance, Walpole "hunted on one week-day and also on Saturdays—a practice which is said to have influenced Parliamentary time-tables and inspired the notion of the week-end, reputedly an English invention."[15]

Royal patronage allowed public sports to flourish. Even boxing—never a legal sport—survived because magistrates hesitated to challenge aristocratic backers. In the late eighteenth century, the Prince of Wales (the future George IV) and the Bon Ton were keenly interested in sports, which shaped sports' high profile. The Prince of Wales was one of the most important sports patrons of the Regency Era. While he certainly advanced sports, he was widely satirized by caricaturists such as James Gillray for indulging his many appetites; he was as well-known for illicit pastimes as he was for political affairs. He was so closely associated with sports that even the Regency Crisis was satirized in a print as a boxing match staged in the House of Commons between Richard Humphries and Daniel Mendoza (see cover illustration.) The boxing match is an allegory for several debates: the ethics of a prince assuming an ill king's authority, the balance of power between Parliament and the monarchy, and obedience versus usurpation.

The use of sports as a metaphor for political, national, or moral concerns was not unusual. Debates about the nature of sporting events continued throughout the century. Popular periodicals like the *Tatler* and the *Spectator* published essays about sport alongside news and reports of cultural goings-on about town.[16] In one such essay in 1710, Richard Steele (under the nom de plume Isaac Bickerstaff) opened with an epigraph from Virgil's *Aeneid*: "What Myrmidon or what Dolopian, / What soldier even of the harsh Ulysses, / could keep from tears in telling such a story?"[17] The author then meditates on a crowing cock outside of Bickerstaff's window. He personifies the bird, imagining that a cosmopolitan "tall black gentleman, who frequents the coffeehouses" has brought him an avian-penned letter. The bird pleads with Bickerstaff to intervene in the blood sports, or "inhumane barbarity" common to "Shrove Tuesday." Cockfighting at the time was ubiquitous and popular. Often, Shrove Tuesday, the day before Ash Wednesday, was marked by those excesses that were given up for Lent. Having read the plea, the cosmopolitan gentleman indicts England's reputation as a nation that participates in such activities: "What would a Turk say, ... should he hear, that [blood sports are] ... common entertainment[s] in a nation which pretends to be one of the most civilized of Europe?"[18] Bickerstaff is equally vexed by England's reputation as a sporting nation on the world's stage:

> I thought what this gentleman said was very reasonable; and have often wondered, that we do not lay aside a custom which makes us appear barbarous to nations much more rude and unpolished than ourselves. Some French writers have represented this diversion of the common people much to our disadvantage, and imputed it to natural fierceness and cruelty of temper; as they do some other entertainments peculiar to our nation: I mean those elegant diversions of bull-baiting and prize-fighting, with the like ingenious recreations of the bear-garden. I wish I knew how to answer this reproach which is cast upon us, and excuse the death of so many innocent cocks, bulls, dogs, and bears, as have been set together by the ears, or died untimely deaths only to make us sport.[19]

The essay depicts such bloody "performances" as a menace to England's social temperament and global reputation. Readers are cautioned away from sports that debase the English character and transform a civilized nation into a savage one.

Anxiety about the corrupting forces of violence was only one arm of a body of neoclassical thought that vilified but mostly venerated sport. Steele's reference to the *Aeneid* reminds readers that sport and theater have a long, storied history. As far back as the Elizabethan era, English theaters and blood sports arenas often shared the same physical space. Viewed as a form of theater, sport was often subject to criticism similar to that of theater proper. For instance, Steele's essay moves from a critique of blood sport to a critique of tragedy. Blood sports are properly those of the rabble, Bickerstaff allows, but they share the "same savage spirit" as upper-crust entertainments, such as the English theater and, more specifically, tragedy: "I must own, there is something very horrid in the public executions of an English tragedy. Stabbing and poisoning, which are performed behind the scenes in other nations, must be done openly among us, to gratify the audience."[20] This essay and one written two years later, in an issue of the *Spectator* that deals with poetics and the theater, invoke French critic Rene Rapin to address similar concerns about the staging of executions. (Steele means staged executions in the theater rather than from a hanging-tree, though of course there are compelling parallels.)

Both Steele and his coeditor Joseph Addison worry that audience delight at staged executions denigrates England's reputation as a civilized nation. Addison invokes John Dryden, Poet Laureate during Charles II's reign, to legitimize Rapin, who connects sports to theater to make the point:

> Rene Rapin,—whom Dryden declared alone "sufficient, were all other critics lost, to teach anew the rules of writing," said in his *Reflections on Aristotle's Treatise of Poetry*, translated by Rymer in 1694, "The English, our Neighbours, love Blood in their Sports, by the quality of their Temperament: These are *Insulaires*, separated from the rest of men; we are more humane ... The English have more of Genius for Tragedy than other People, as well as by the Spirit of their Nation, which delights in Cruelty, as also by the Character of their Language, which is proper for Great Expressions."[21]

Sport, then, is categorized as staged tragedy and as the illegitimate half-brother of proper theater. Addison brings Aristotle's poetics to bear on theatrical spectacle, which for him encompasses both sport and tragedy. On a deeper level, Rapin's final sentence illustrates an English attitude that language itself had national character and was a national concern. Nearly 80 years later, the editors of *The Sporting Magazine* showed the same pride in a national language, and they viewed sport as the ideal vehicle to express that sentiment.

Apprehension over sport and theater often stemmed from the belief that public diversions could be pure and legitimate or corrupt and illegitimate. That dichotomy persisted throughout the long eighteenth century. In 1724, the *Daily Journal* warned against the social ills resulting from bellicose sporting events:

> The sober part of town express great concern at the scandalous advertisements that are almost every day publish'd, for calling raw tradesmen out of their shops, students from their books, apprentices and hired servants, and even his Majesty's soldiers from their duty, to attend at the rude and savage diversions of the Bear-Garden, where prophaneness reigns triumphantly, vollies of the most dreadful oaths being pour'd out incessantly, and picking of pockets practic'd openly with impunity: The citizens are also under great grief to observe the minds of too many of their young sparks turn'd, and entertain'd with these idle amusements, and the grand question become[s], *Who fights?* Instead of *Who trades?*"[22]

The writer is apparently more concerned that sport corrupts the social body by diverting young men from the sober and salubrious business of trade than he is that blood sports are inherently cruel.

By midcentury, the Society for the Reformation of Manners became vocal in their objection to cruelty in sporting entertainment; some historians have viewed this social development as evidence of England's civilizing process. Richard Holt discusses the shifting attitude over sport in relation to a larger change toward public spectacles of violence or cruelty.[23] Toward the end of the century, he claims, the organization and regulation of sport helped constitute a transformation from traditional revels toward what spectators today consider "modern" sport.

The excesses of early festivals—gambling, drinking, sex, blood sports—diminished as the era underwent what Elias called "the civilizing process." One good example of this change, Holt says, is the gradual diminishment of public fighting.[24] Fighting was indeed a lightning rod for controversies over public and private morality. The issue of cruelty in sport was visible in artistic prints as well as in periodicals (Figure I.2). For instance, in the first plate of Hogarth's *The Four Stages of Cruelty* (1751) part of the caption reads: "Learn from this fair Example—You / Whom savage Sports delight, / How Cruelty disgusts the view, / While Pity charms the sight."

Advertisements for a cockfight and a boxing match at Broughton's Amphitheatre form part of the backdrop to the *Second Stage of Cruelty*, in which the anti-hero Tom Nero viciously beats a horse. The overturned coach is further evidence of a topsy-turvy world of violent disorder. In this world, sadistic men sport with life. Objections to the public disorder surrounding boxing matches prompted efforts to prevent bouts from being staged:

> Prize-fighting could be readily restrained under the law, either as a breach of the peace or an unlawful assembly, and though many matches were winked at—some were partly protected by their influential patrons, and others were accompanied by crowds too large for the resources of local constables—successful interventions against intended prize-fights were often reported in the newspapers of the first half of the nineteenth century. Boxing was not infrequently the cause of accidental deaths and serious maulings, a circumstance which incurred for it much public disfavor.[25]

To many, boxing was considered objectionable not because of the violence inherent to the sport but because of the excesses attendant upon large crowds. Gambling, drunkenness, and dissolute behavior were the ill consequences of rural festivals and urban sports alike, according to moralists.[26]

But while some writers warned against sport as the degradation of English identity, others valued sport's gruffness, particularly as a foil for French or Italian effeminacy. One suchlike example is a response to the importation of Arab stallions to breed with English racehorses. The April 1739 volume of the *Gentleman's Magazine* proclaimed, "Our noble breed of horses is now enervated by an intermixture with Turks, Arabians and Barbs, just as our modern nobility and gentry are debauch'd with the effeminate manners of France and Italy."[27] The writer metaphorizes horse breeding to express his fear of cultural miscegenation, using a common rhetorical gesture and parlance. Like other contemporary texts, the *Gentleman's Magazine* and the *Tatler* used sport as a metaphor for gendered nationalism as well as a measure of civilization. Thus Steele's invocation of Virgil's epic poem about a man's struggle with outside forces and internal emotions was an apt frame for his fictionalized plea to tame England's savage spirit. Steele's reference to the *Aeneid* is suggestive of Olympic Games, ancient boxing, and blood sports even more brutal than contemporary cockfighting or bearbaiting. Such activities appealed to a cultural ethos that valued classical ideals, even when

Figure I.2 William Hogarth. *Second Stage of Cruelty* (1751). Courtesy, The Lewis Walpole Library, Yale University.

those ideals needed to be refined to better represent contemporary Britain, her sports, and her athletes.

The classical and neoclassical ideal of a patriotic warrior made fit for battle by vigorous sports training is clearly figured as masculine. However, women participated in many sports, from foot races to boxing.[28] Women were especially active cricket players and horse racers. There were, of course, restrictions as to class and dress. Gendered clothing sometimes accommodated and sometimes confined movement. In an ironic incident, a woman's hoopskirt prevented her from drowning following a sailing accident, her otherwise restrictive clothing having been transformed into a life jacket.[29] Women did seriously compete in and participate in a number of athletic pursuits. Toward the end of the century, social theorists such as Mary Wollstonecraft and Erasmus Darwin encouraged physical activity as a means of cultivating a strong body and mind.[30] Popular opinion was sufficiently auspicious that an 1803 edition of *The Sporting Magazine* published a laudatory letter from the Duke of Dorset on the subject of a women's cricket match, one of whose participants was the Countess of Derby:

> Let your sex go on, and assert their right to every pursuit that does not debase the mind. Go on, and attach yourself to the athletic, and, by that, convince ... all Europe how worthy you are of being considered the wives of plain, generous, and native Englishmen.[31]

Thus women could participate in sport because a patriotic ethos prevailed over patriarchy's restrictions on women's activities.

The Duke of Dorset's letter is an example of the admiring tone characteristic of much late eighteenth-century sports writing. Violence in sport had been mitigated by rules, and criticism of fighting decreased the more fighting was depicted as patriotic and martial. Moreover, by the Regency Era, sports writing had begun to distinguish itself as a genre, and in the last quarter of the century, sports writing proliferated. Adrian Harvey locates the emergence of specialized sporting literature at the turn of the century with the publication of the *World*, *The Sporting Magazine*, the *Racing Calendar*, and later, at *Bell's Life in London*, for example. He writes: "Between 1793 and 1815 the press transformed the sporting culture, effectively rendering it national."[32] By the 1770s, daily media expanded rapidly, and according to Dennis Brailsford, "there was already almost complete press coverage of the country, with nearly 150 newspapers being published outside London."[33] Horse racing was one of the most well attended of sporting events, and it received the most media attention. In 1787, the *World* offered sports news, and the founding of *The Sporting Magazine* in 1792 gave rise to the first professional sports journalist. *The Sporting Magazine* was extremely popular. Carl Cone writes that

> *The Sporting Magazine* ... and the *Weekly Dispatch*, a Sunday newspaper begun in 1801, attracted a wide and influential readership among people of all ranks in life. Thus, the noblemen and gentlemen who governed England and the press which published sporting news tied the sporting life intimately to the public life of the nation. Even the more staid press, the London *Times* or *Blackwood's Magazine*, began to take notice of sporting events and personalities.[34]

This expansion of newspapers and magazines resulted in a small triumph of secularism over Sundays: "Newspapers began to appear on Sundays, as well as on weekdays, in spite of numerous complaints and questions in the House of Commons. Indeed, the first newspaper with sporting leanings, *Bell's Weekly Messenger*, appeared as a Sunday publication in 1796, and within a few years was selling 6,000 copies weekly."[35] Throughout the century, sport consistently engendered debates about morality. The witty, robust prose of sports writing—shot through with political, nationalistic, and gendered thought—could keenly address topical, contemporary subjects.

Scholars of sport have covered a lot of this ground, although inconsistently and with some lacunae. A number of valuable social histories followed Robert Malcolmson's 1973 trailblazing *Popular Recreations in English Society 1700–1850*, which took the kind of cultural materialist, Marxist approach spearheaded by E.P. Thompson in his 1963 book *The Making of the English Working Class*.[36] A number of other valuable histories of recreation, leisure, and sport in relation to class conflict, nationalism, and commercialization of culture followed Malcolmson's, including, for instance, Richard Holt's *Sport and the British*, John Hargreaves's *Sport, Power, and Culture: A Social and Historical Analysis of Popular Sport in Britain*, Thomas Henricks's *Disputed Pleasures: Sport and Society in Pre-Industrial England*, and Derek Birley's *Sport and the Making of Britain*.[37] The study of sport developed alongside other studies of popular culture, which challenged traditional master narratives of social, cultural, and literary history by taking seriously subjects that had previously been considered beneath academic notice. Literary critics and historians began to examine the lives, writings, and activities of the working class poor, of women, and of minority groups; the creation of academic programs such as women's studies, African-American studies, or ethnic studies, and eventually of cultural studies, for example, attest to the scholarly sea change in the 1970s. Sport tended to fall into the category of popular culture or cultural studies, but sport studies flagged for several decades.

Our millennium has seen a resurgence of interdisciplinary, critical attention to sport. Sport is emerging as one of the most compelling and playful areas of academic inquiry. Ten years ago, a call for papers about sport at the American Society for Eighteenth-Century Studies Annual Meeting received nearly no responses. But, in the past few years alone, several major conferences have been devoted to the topic, including international meetings at the University of Paris-Sorbonne, the University of London, and Rice University. The International Centre for Sports History and Culture at De Montfort University in Leicester, England (established in 1996), has hosted important conferences on sport, has an impressive faculty of sports scholars, and has forged connections with international centers for the study of sporting culture. Publisher attention to sport has increased; as an example, Routledge's series "Sport in Global Society—Historical Perspectives" has published over 100 titles. Important explorations of a specific sport (such as Kasia Boddy's *Boxing: A Cultural History*), of sport history (such as Adrian Harvey's *The Beginnings of a Commercial Sporting Culture in Britain: 1793–1850*, or Emma Griffin's *England's Revelry: A History of Popular Sports and Pastimes 1660–1830*), or of sport and literature (such as Gregory M.

Colon Semenza's *Sport, Politics, and Literature in the English Renaissance*) have been published by both scholarly and popular presses.[38]

Perhaps because sport permeated so many aspects of life during the eighteenth century, it has been difficult to categorize sporting literature and culture as an academic field of study. Arguably, the largest body of work on sport has been produced by historians,[39] and they tend to view literary works skeptically. In *Sport and the Literary Imagination: Essays in History, Literature, and Sport*, Jeffrey Hill discusses the "longstanding reluctance on the part of historians to take up 'literature' seriously."[40] On the whole, the field of literary studies has been more receptive to multiple sorts of texts as both products and producers of culture. Indeed, Hill notes that "the most systematic applications of this perceived fluidity of literature and history are to be found in the New Historicist tendency of American literary/historical studies."[41] He is right. In the 1980s literary studies turned toward the interdisciplinarity characterized by new historicism and cultural studies.[42]

For eighteenth-century studies, such a turn was made self-consciously. In 1987, *The New 18th Century: Theory, Politics, English Literature* marked a transition toward "an interdisciplinarity that would attempt to interrupt the established divisions among disciplines and remap the territory of the production of knowledge about the eighteenth century."[43] The book's editors, Felicity A. Nussbaum and Laura Brown, were responding to traditional literary scholars' claims that texts dealing with popular culture, feminism, or scholarship that was theorized (and therefore seen as political) did not legitimately belong in the field of literary studies. Nussbaum and Brown responded by arguing that "If eighteenth-century literary studies is to forge such a theoretically informed interdisciplinarity, it will have to become more skeptical about the traditional boundaries of the disciplines, largely formed in the nineteenth century, which confine the approaches and investigations of the eighteenth."[44] In the decades that have followed, disciplinary boundary crossing has opened up the possibility for the study of subjects like sport, so that rules, advertisements, tracts, diaries, fiction, and poetry, for example, can be read together in an effort to gain an expansive understanding of the subject.

The critical articles in this collection engage with sport from a variety of perspectives. Several essays offer a sweeping sense of sport and its impact on British cultural life, while others focus on a particular sport, celebrity, or facet of sport. In "'Wholesome recreations and cheering influences': Popular Recreation and Social Elites in Eighteenth-Century Britain," Emma Griffin reexamines elite attitudes toward popular recreations, particularly during the late eighteenth and early nineteenth centuries. Her study of a wealth of primary material revises previous historians' claims that pastimes were represented by the gentry with increasing rancor. Her chapter valuably grounds the reader by offering a sense of attitudes toward sport over time. Jean Williams's "Olympism and Pastoralism in British Sporting Literature" examines the influence of classical texts and of the Cotswold Games on eighteenth-century representations of Olympism. Noting the centrality of pastoralism to sporting discourse, Williams situates writing about Olympic festivals within larger debates about the role of sport in English society.

Patricia Crown's chapter "Sporting with Clothes: John Collet's Prints in the 1770s" further animates the period through a critically appreciative reading of the artwork of John Collet. Crown examines the numerous images of women playing sports to illustrate not only women's extensive participation but to reveal ways that sporting clothes challenged gender conventions.

Several chapters address specific sports, such as archery, tennis, horse racing, swimming, and boxing. The design of women's sporting clothes forms part of the subject of Linda Troost's "Archery in the Long Eighteenth Century." Troost offers a broad view of women archers at the end of the eighteenth century. Her descriptions of mixed-set competitions, societies, uniforms, and rules of play are set in the context of archery's historical significance as a symbol of England. Thus she widens readers' understanding of women's involvement in archery and of the sport as a symbol of the nation. Alexis Tadié's chapter "The Uses and Transformations of Early Modern Tennis" argues that tennis came to England via France, and therefore writing about the sport should be read in relation to the exchange of ideas evident in text and practice. Tadié reads literal and metaphoric representations of tennis in a fascinating range of texts from treatise to novels, poems, and plays. Reading sport from a literary perspective, Don Nichol's chapter "Jockeying for Position: Horse Culture in Poetry, Prose, and *The New Foundling Hospital for Wit*" examines the eponymous satirical publication in the years between 1768 and 1773. Nichol establishes the symbolic significance of the horse, with an emphasis on literary depictions by writers such as Jonathan Swift and Henry Fielding. Contextualizing satire, poems, and images in relation to the Jockey Club, Nichol illustrates the many uses aside from racing to which horses were put.

The enduring importance of sport to literature is developed with a singular focus in Jack D'Amico's chapter on Byron and swimming. In "Rehearsing Leander: Byron and Swimming in the Long Eighteenth Century," D'Amico posits Byron's literal swim across the Hellespont against the poet's literary depiction of swimming. D'Amico explains Byron's motivation for the swim as a theatrical rehearsal of the ancient legend of Leander. In so doing, he underscores the long-standing relationship between literary depictions and physical practices of swimming. I also aim to punctuate the kinship between sport and text. "Boxing for England: Daniel Mendoza and the Theater of Sport" argues that boxing literature played a central role in shaping English attitudes toward sport and theatricality, as well as discourses of nationalism and ethnicity. As the heavyweight Champion of England, Mendoza turned his Jewishness and fame to account on many stages and in a boxing manual and memoir, all of which the chapter situates along the literary and cultural trajectory of sports literature across the century.

For some of the contributors, interest in sporting literature, culture, or history developed out of participation in a particular sport. Jack D'Amico is a swimmer; Alexis Tadié is a tennis player; Linda Troost competed on her college intramural archery team and participates in longbow archery when she visits Renaissance Fairs; I trained as a boxer. Taken together, the primary material and scholarly essays pose a number of questions: Why is the eighteenth century distinctive in terms of the growth of sport? How did people disport themselves? Who participated in sports? Who watched sports? What were the rules? What forms of expression were employed to represent sports? How did the representation of sport literature and culture develop into an art and a business? This book offers the words and images of players, spectators, commentators, moralists, journalists, historians, literary critics, artists, and enthusiasts, in the hope that readers will continue to explore the evolution of sport over the course of the long eighteenth century and into their own.

Notes

[1] Two valuable studies of illegitimate theater are Jane Moody, *Illegitimate Theatre in London, 1770–1840* (Cambridge: Cambridge University Press, 2000); and Marc Baer, *Theatre and Disorder in Late Georgian London* (New York: Oxford University Press, 1992).

[2] See Derek Birley, *Sport and the Making of Britain* (New York: Manchester University Press, 1993), 104–6, on *The Tatler*, *The Spectator*, and sport.

[3] Birley, *Sport and the Making of Britain*, 109.

[4] Richard Steele, "No. 12, From Thursday, May 5, to Saturday, May 7, 1709. May 5," *The Tatler*, Volume 1, 1899, NewYork/ Hadley & Mathews/ 156 Fifth Avenue/ London: Duckworth & Co/ 1899).

[5] Joseph Strutt's *Sports and Pastimes of the People of England* (1801) is a valuable tome of sporting information, though he provides the least amount of material about the eighteenth century. See also the foundational twentieth-century history of sport by Robert Malcolmson, *Popular Recreations in English Society 1700–1850* (Cambridge: Cambridge University Press, 1973).

[6] Birley, *Sport and the Making of Britain*, 77.

[7] Quoted in Malcolmson, *Popular Recreations*, 11. For a smart reading of the literary and cultural significance of the *Book of Sports*, see Gregory M. Colon Semenza, *Sport, Politics, and Literature in the English Renaissance* (Newark: University of Delaware Press, 2003), especially chapter 3, "Performative Interpretations: The Literary Context of the *Book of Sports* Controversy," 85–114.

[8] Birley, *Sport and the Making of Britain*, 80.

[9] "William Prynne, from *Histrio-Mastix: The Player's Scourge; or, Actor's Tragedy*," *The Norton Anthology of English Literature*, Norton Topics Online, "The Early Seventeenth Century: Topics: Civil Wars of Ideas: Texts and Contexts," accessed 22 July 2012, http://www.wwnorton.com/college/english/nael/17century/topic_3/prynne.htm.

[10] Malcolmson, *Popular Recreations*, 7.

[11] See Malcolmson, *Popular Recreations*, 37–40, and 114–15. He includes some fascinating PRO reports. See also Birley, *Sport and the Making of Britain*, 115.

[12] Neil Tranter, *Sport, Economy and Society in Britain 1750–1914* (Cambridge: Cambridge University Press, 1998), 32–3, 37, 44, and chapter 4, "A Conspiracy of the Elites?" Also informative is Richard Holt, *Sport and the British: A Modern History* (Oxford: Clarendon Press, 1989), chapter 1, "Old Ways of Playing." Holt discusses factors other than urbanization that contributed to the rise of sport during the eighteenth century, including the role of violence.

[13] Birley, *Sport and the Making of Britain*, 88.

[14] Birley, *Sport and the Making of Britain*, 107.

[15] Birley, *Sport and the Making of Britain*, 107.

[16] Both *The Spectator and The Daily Courant*, Britain's first daily newspaper (11 March 1702), were published by Samuel Buckley. The next daily paper did not come onto the scene until 1719 (*The Daily Post*). While there was some news in *The Spectator*, its focus was culture, morality, wit, and learning.

[17] Richard Steele, "Tuesday, Feb. 14, to Thursday, Feb. 16, 1709–10," *The Tatler*, Volume 3, No. 134 (1899; Project Gutenberg, 2010), http://www.gutenberg.org/files/31645/31645-h/31645-h.htm#No_134. For a translation of the epigraph, see Allen Mandelbaum, *The Aeneid of Virgil: A Verse Translation* (New York: Bantam Books, 1981), Book 2, lines 9–11, https://books.google.com/books?id=AOWeCAAAQBAJ&pg=PT3&dq=Allen+Mandelbaum,+The+Aeneid+of+Virgil:+A+Verse+Translation&hl=en&sa=X&ei=q6GBVaHmNIq1ggTxiIOYBA&ved=0CB4Q6AEwAA#v=onepage&q=Allen%20Mandelbaum%2C%20The%20Aeneid%20of%20Virgil%3A%20A%20Verse%20Translation&f=false.

[18] Steele, "Tuesday, Feb. 14, to Thursday, Feb. 16, 1709–10."

[19] Steele, "Tuesday, Feb. 14, to Thursday, Feb. 16, 1709–10."

[20] Steele, "Tuesday, Feb. 14, to Thursday, Feb. 16, 1709–10."

[21] Joseph Addison, "No. 44, Friday, April 20, 1711," *The Spectator: A New Edition Reproducing the Original Text both as First Issued and as Corrected by its Authors, Volume 1* (London: George Routledge and Sons, 1881), http://www.gutenberg.org/files/12030/12030-h/SV1/Spectator1.html#section44.

[22] "Boxing and Prizefighting," *Early Eighteenth-Century Newspaper Reports: A Sourcebook*, ed. Rictor Norton, last modified 31 December 2005, http://rictornorton.co.uk/grubstreet/boxing.htm.

[23] Holt, *Sport and the British*, chapter 1, "Old Ways of Playing."

[24] Holt, *Sport and the British*, 29–30. He continues: "First the nobility were prohibited from dueling and gradually an educated rejection of all kinds of public fighting became widespread" (31).

[25] Malcolmson, *Popular Recreations*, 145.

[26] See Emma Griffin's chapter in this collection, "Wholesome recreations and cheering influences': Popular Recreation and Social Elites in Eighteenth-Century Britain." Griffin shows that such objections were rare compared to the general approval of sports as beneficial to society.

[27] Quoted in Birley, *Sport and the Making of Britain*, 110.

[28] For an insightful discussion of class, gender, and sport, see Betty Rizzo, "Equivocations of Gender and Rank: Eighteenth-Century Sporting Women," *Eighteenth-Century Life* 26, no. 1 (2002): 70–93.

[29] Dennis Brailsford, *A Taste for Diversions: Sport in Georgian England* (Cambridge, UK: Lutterworth Press, 1999), 147. See chapter 7, "Sporting Women."

[30] Brailsford, *A Taste for Diversions*, 143.

[31] Brailsford, *A Taste for Diversions*, 156.

[32] Adrian Harvey, *The Beginnings of a Commercial Sporting Culture in Britain: 1793–1850* (Burlington, VT: Ashgate, 2004), 31. See chapter 3, "Sex Sport and Sales: The Sporting Press," for a discussion of the way newspaper coverage changed the nature of sporting activity and organization.

[33] Brailsford, *A Taste for Diversions*, 10.

[34] Carl Cone, *Hounds in the Morning: Sundry Sports of Merry England* (Lexington: University Press of Kentucky, 1981), 19. *The Sporting Magazine* ran from 1792 to 1836, and there are complete holdings available at many public and research libraries. Several

years are available in full text online through Google Books. Cone's *Hounds in the Morning: Sundry Sports of Merry England* is the fullest in-print collection of excerpts from the magazine.

35   Brailsford, *A Taste for Diversions*, 11.

36   Robert Malcolmson, *Popular Recreations*; E.P. Thompson, *The Making of the English Working Class* (New York: Vintage Books, 1966). For a clear review of twentieth-century historians' use of popular culture in the study of leisure, see Emma Griffin, "Popular Culture in Industrializing England," *Historical Journal* 45, no. 3 (2002): 619.

37   Holt, *Sport and the British*; John Hargreaves, *Sport, Power and Culture: A Social and Historical Analysis of Popular Sports in Britain* (Cambridge: Polity Press, 1986); Thomas S. Henricks, *Disputed Pleasures: Sport and Society in Pre-Industrial England* (New York: Greenwood Press, 1991); Birley, *Sport and the Making of Britain*.

38   Kasia Boddy, *Boxing: A Cultural History* (London: Reaktion, 2008); Harvey, *The Beginnings of a Commercial Sporting Culture in Britain: 1793–1850*; Emma Griffin, *England's Revelry: A History of Popular Sports and Pastimes, 1660–1830* (Oxford: Oxford University Press for the British Academy, 2005); Semenza, *Sport, Politics, and Literature in the English Renaissance*.

39   A notable exception is the American-based Sport Literature Association, though it is not period specific. It is "an international organization devoted to the study of sport in literature and culture," publishes a journal entitled *Aethlon*, and holds an annual conference. The *Sport Literature Association* home page, accessed 2 January 2014, http://www.uta.edu/english/sla/index.html.

40   Jeffrey Hill, *Sport and the Literary Imagination: Essays in History, Literature, and Sport* (Oxford: Peter Lang, 2006), 20. His first chapter, "The Historicity of the Text: A Historian's Reading," is an astute and valuable review of the academic subject of sport in Britain, mostly for historians. He specifically addresses sport literature as a field of academic study.

41   Hill, *Sport and the Literary Imagination*, 28. See also Jeffrey Hill and Jean Williams, "Introduction," *Sport in History* 29, no. 2 (2009): 127–31, for a concise, sharp discussion of the use of literature in historical studies of sport. Hill and Williams point out that "historians in Great Britain have been less inclined to include 'literature' in their portfolio. In this respect the subbranch of sport history has been no exception, and for the most part it has been left to those in sociology and cultural studies to open up the field of representations in sport. The chief purpose of the present edition is, therefore, to point a way that might lead to a greater emphasis on 'creative' writing in the study of sport history. As far as the present content is concerned that creativity is limited to written texts: novels, mainly, but also travel writing, poetry, popular magazines and online forms, along with some visual sources" (128).

42   A valuable introduction to the aims and methodologies of Cultural Studies can be found in Simon During, *The Cultural Studies Reader* (London: Routledge, 1993).

43   Felicity A. Nussbaum and Laura Brown, eds., *The New 18th Century: Theory, Politics, English Literature* (Routledge, 1988), 21.

44   Nussbaum and Brown, *The New 18th Century*, 21. The transition of the journal *The Eighteenth Century: Theory and Interpretation* marks a similar shift of focus in eighteenth-century studies. The publication's webpage says, "Contributors give voice to a range of cultural and national traditions, and represent not only a number of disciplines but testify to the significance of cross-, inter-, and multi-disciplinary work in twenty-first century scholarship." *The Eighteenth Century* home page, accessed 2 January 2014, http://ecti.pennpress.org/home/.

PART I
Contexts

Chapter 1
"Wholesome recreations and cheering influences": Popular Recreation and Social Elites in Eighteenth-Century Britain

Emma Griffin

It has often been recognized that the response of social elites to the sports and pastimes of their poorer neighbors has waxed and waned with the centuries. The rise of hostility during the sixteenth and seventeenth centuries and the more benign attitude of Restoration rulers have both been well documented.[1] But the extent to which the more relaxed attitude of the Restoration continued into the century that followed has attracted considerably less attention. In order to find any discussion of elite attitudes towards popular recreation over the long eighteenth century, it is necessary to turn back to the 1970s and early 1980s, and inevitably much of this literature bears the preoccupations of that time.

Robert Malcolmson offered the most comprehensive account of attitudes to recreation in eighteenth-century Britain in his *Popular Recreations in English Society*.[2] This text positioned the history of popular pastimes in a Marxist framework and argued that industrialization first weakened, and then fatally undermined, the recreational calendar of old. In constructing this narrative, Malcolmson drew particular attention to a complex of forces—the rise of Evangelicalism, the American War of Independence, the French Revolution, and (above all) the complex of technological and economic changes known as the industrial revolution—and their role in fashioning a more hard-line view about the propriety of popular pastimes. And although more than four decades have passed since Malcolmson first formulated this thesis, it continues to cast a shadow over subsequent interpretations of popular recreation in this period. Of course, a number of scholars sought to point out the limitations of Malcolmson's account, but disagreement turned largely upon the outcome of middle-class endeavors to suppress or reform traditional recreations, rather than on the existence of a reforming impulse.[3] As Hugh Cunningham so succinctly wrote, "That many popular sports came under increasing attack in the late eighteenth and early nineteenth centuries has never been disputed. What has been disputed is the effectiveness of this attack."[4]

In this essay, I want to revisit this narrative. It is not my intention to consider the practice of popular recreation, which undoubtedly was affected by the rapid urbanization and industrialization that occurred at this time. In this essay I want to focus instead on the intellectual context. For many years, historians have quietly assumed that industrializing Britain witnessed a sharp increase in the volume and intensity of elite criticism of the sports and pastimes of the poor. I believe it is time to revisit that assumption. In what follows, I shall survey a wide range of sources in which social elites commented on the customs and pastimes of their poorer neighbors, and I will offer a new outline of elite attitudes towards popular recreation over the long eighteenth century.

ૡ ૡ ૡ

Our account should, of course, start with the Restoration of Charles II to the English throne in 1660. This event and the spontaneous outburst of popular rejoicing it prompted have been well documented.[5] The jubilant celebrations, the distribution of beer, bread, and meat, the loyal processions, and joyful bonfires lit to mark the King's return were painstakingly recorded by observers grateful to be witnessing such events. Of course, there were political undertones to the rapid reappearance of the old festive culture at the King's return in May 1660. As an astute observer at Oxford, Anthony Wood, noted, the maypole had been set up in order "to vex the Presbyterians and Independents," and his account of the maypolers' motivation was surely not incorrect.[6] Communal feasting and drinking, dancing around maypoles and traditional sports implied a rejection of the values of the Protectorate, a return to the supposed harmony and community of the pre-Civil War years. Little wonder, therefore, that the loyalists took such great pleasure in describing the restoration of such events.

What is perhaps most remarkable, however, is the degree to which this tolerance with respect to the sports and pastimes of the little people endured long after the excitement and novelty of the Restoration had passed. Feasting, drinking, and reveling could quickly degenerate into the kind of behavior that local communities were not inclined to tolerate. The suspension of censure in the politically charged climate of the early 1660s provided no guarantee for their long term security. Yet as life settled back into its ordinary groove, most of those writing about popular customs continued to assert that rustic amusements were considerably less harmful than the puritan zeal which had once harassed them. Even as those years of puritan zeal passed into the distant past, social elites clung to the notion that the poor should be permitted to enjoy their customary diversions.

Within little time, the view that rustic mirth was something to encourage was firmly entrenched. White Kennet, a late seventeenth-century antiquary writing about the "laudable Custom of Wakes," made pointed remarks about the "nice Puritans" who "began to exclaim against [wakes] as a Remnant of Popery."[7] Meanwhile, William Stukeley complained about the loss of sports in the early eighteenth century, "since the last age had discourag'd the innocent and useful sports of the common people, by an injudicious zeal for religion, which has drove them into worse amusements."[8] The vigor with which the godly had set about reforming popular festivities, and the descent into chaos following the outbreak of the first Civil War in 1642, had discredited attempts to interfere in popular recreations. It was not the most momentous consequence of the wars of the 1640s; nevertheless, civil conflict had set the stage for the ideological rehabilitation of popular amusements.

Even the parish dedication feasts, one of the primary targets of the traditional festive calendar for seventeenth-century reformers, were reconsidered in a more generous light at the Restoration. According to one late seventeenth-century historian, wakes were "kept in many Places at this Day" in spite of the recent attempts to reform them. They were celebrated by "holding up the Custom of Sports, Pastimes, and Feastings amongst Friends and Neighbours."[9] Most commentators, though not unaware of the risks of drunkenness and brawling that tended to accompany such "feastings," believed they were beneficial rather than otherwise. William Borlase marshaled all the traditional arguments in favor of parish feasts when he advocated their preservation by pointing to their role "for civilising the people, for composing differences by the mediation and meeting of friends, for increase of love and unity by these feasts of charity, and for the relief and comfort of the poor."[10] Most commentators were a little more measured. Wakes were typically seen more simply as harmless, rustic fun: "public assemblies, accompanied with friendly entertainments."[11]

Not least offensive to seventeenth-century reformers had been the opportunities that wakes and revels provided for sexual encounters. In the early eighteenth century, by contrast, the mixing of the sexes was viewed with considerably more indulgence. Eustace Budgell, a regular contributor to the *Spectator*, believed "Love and Marriage are the natural Effects of these anniversary Assemblies," and that for this reason wakes ought to be encouraged.[12] In similar vein, Sir Thomas Parkyns believed that even "naturally carping Criticks can't help allowing, that of all Exercise Wrestling is the most useful to all sorts of men.... For the most Part our Country Rings for Wrestlings, at Wakes and other Festivals, consist of a small party of young Women, who come not thither to choose a *Coward*, but the *Daring, Healthy* and *Robust* Persons, fit to raise an Offspring from."[13] Sir Thomas's interest was no doubt unusually enthusiastic: his will of 1740 bequeathed one guinea to be annually wrestled for, "for ever," so that "the Manly Art of Wrestling and Healthful exercises of [Boxing] may be kept up after my decease."[14] Nonetheless, his faith in the benefits of physical exercise received less energetic approval from other quarters.

Along with the manliness, good neighborhood, and marriages that sports and revels encouraged among the poor, a number of other benefits were thought to accrue to the nation if social elites allowed the poor to enjoy their traditional recreations. In the early eighteenth century, these too received more careful attention, recent civil strife having perhaps invested the Roman idea of bread and circuses with greater poignancy. In the *London Magazine* it was argued to be "a prudential Policy in a Government to regulate the Pleasure of the People, and have their publick Games and Spectacles such as may allure their Minds to Virtue, or inure their Bodies to Strength and Activity." By the revival of "antient manly and innocent Sports," the Country Gentlemen would make their tenants "brave and good subjects."[15] An essay printed in the same paper two years earlier had speculated on the consequences of banishing diversions: the common people would become "dull and spiritless," it was decided, and "addict themselves to less warrantable Pleasures." In contrast, the prospect of forthcoming festivals "[made] them dispatch their Business with Pleasure and Alacrity."[16]

Of course, no matter how much eighteenth-century writers might esteem the public benefits of popular amusements, the disorder so often associated with such assemblies could hardly be ignored. Wakes had been roundly condemned as occasions for drunkenness and profanity in the seventeenth century, and the stoutest advocate of tradition could not defend drunkenness and profanity, even in the more relaxed moral climate of the Restoration. Yet the potential for drunkenness and disorder was now approached with far greater pragmatism than previously. Christmas, Sunday recreation, and wakes, feasts, and revels were all, it was freely acknowledged, liable to abuse by the "loose and sensual." But they were generally beneficial for the "vertuously inclin'd," and for this reason, ought to be preserved.[17] As one writer in the *Gentleman's Magazine* argued, there was "sufficient Reason for [wakes] being reform'd, but not (as Women and Puritans would have it) abolished."[18] So far as the least favorable qualities of recreation were addressed, reform rather than suppression was the solution proposed, and this was a very much more measured response to the one that had dominated seventeenth-century discourse.

This more compromising attitude is illustrated in the work of the early-eighteenth-century antiquary Henry Bourne, a Newcastle clergyman and author of one of the earliest works devoted to popular customs. His purpose was both to describe certain popular traditions as well as to advise which were superstitious or sinful and ought consequently to be dispensed with. His heading for a chapter on New Year's Day ceremonies indicates how he approached these two priorities: "The New-Year's-Gift, an harmless Custom. Wishing a good New-Year, no way sinful. Mumming, a custom which ought to be laid aside."[19] These judgments, in common with those of the many other customs described, were established from religious principles. New Year's gifts and wishes, despite their heathenish origins, were (according to Bourne) harmless so long as they were not "used superstitiously or with obscenity and lewdness." Mumming, however, involved cross-dressing, and that was opposed to the word of God.[20]

It has been observed that Bourne's censorious tone places his work in the tradition of earlier complaint literature, and it is certainly true that Bourne had little sympathy for many of the popular customs he described.[21] Yet there were some significant differences between Bourne and his puritan predecessors. Despite his unease towards some popular customs, Bourne took great care to indicate the many others which were lawful: bonfires at Midsummer Eve, for example, were "Tokens of Joy to excite innocent Mirth and Diversion, and promote Peace and good Neighbourhood, they are lawful and innocent and deserve no censure." Elsewhere he concluded that "when the common Devotions of the Day are over, there is nothing sinful in lawful Recreation," when discussing the playing of handball during Easter week.[22]

Bourne was clearly ambivalent about popular recreation. Although he accepted that recreation might be "lawful and innocent," he was wary of the tendency of popular assemblies to degenerate into "Drunkenness and Luxury" or "Drunkenness, Rioting and Wantonness"—of recreation to become "scandalous, and sinful and abominable."[23] But his solution to this was vigilance, not repression. This discrimination placed him apart from most earlier critics of popular customs, many of whom had doubted that spending time at play could ever be consistent with the dictates of Christianity. Consider Richard Baxter, a Suffolk clergyman who resigned his living in 1662, just before the introduction of the Act of Uniformity. His *Christian Directory*, first published in 1673, restated the standard objections to recreation of seventeenth-century reformers. He advised that all sports are unlawful which "really *unfit* us for the *dutys* of our *Callings* and the service of *God*" and which "take up any part of the *Time*, which we should spend in greater works." Baxter did not prohibit all recreation—"no doubt but some *sport* and *recreation* is *lawful*"—but he did list 18 conditions which rendered it unlawful.[24] Clearly, such arguments came very close to denying that wakes, revels and most traditional sports could ever be permissible, and their authors' claims to the contrary were without real substance.

Above all, Bourne reminds us that elite attitudes to popular pastimes can rarely be distilled to one single viewpoint. Just as there had always been defenders of recreation in the late sixteenth and early seventeenth centuries, so did hard-line views about the sinfulness of recreation live on long after the fall of the Protectorate. Hostility towards popular recreation, however, was increasingly confined to the margins of debates about leisure. A range of arguments about the lawfulness of recreation had long existed, but the civil wars and Restoration decisively altered the relationship between them, discrediting overly zealous attempts to interfere in popular recreations and placing arguments in favor of sports firmly in the ascendant.

Significantly, those who did hold reservations about popular amusements took considerable care with the way in which they expressed those reservations. One writer in the *Gentleman's Magazine* who was keen to remedy the abuses at wakes nevertheless found it necessary to claim that "for a Sort of civil and political Reasons, as well as out of my natural Candor and Humanity, I am no Enemy to the Recreations of the Populace."[25] Another writer reassured readers that he was "very far from pretending, that all Diversions should be suppressed."[26] A tract advising servants admitted "the first Thing commonly thought on by Youth is Recreation and Pleasure: A Degree of which (if the Recreation be lawful) cannot reasonably be objected to."[27] Protestations of goodwill towards the "recreations of the Populace" are to be found in almost all discussions of popular traditions, and are telling indicators of how far the parameters of the debate had changed since the middle of the seventeenth century. A diversity of views continued to be expressed, and many remained uneasy about the practice of popular recreations. But the scales, which had long been weighted against recreation, had finally tipped the other way, and the assertion that play might be beneficial rather than otherwise admitted.

And it is in this context that we should understand the attack on popular recreation that is supposed to have emerged in the late eighteenth century. It is certainly true that the end of the century was a period of flux, with manifold developments in the political and economic spheres. Yet despite the upheavals that occurred around this time, the view that the poor were entitled to enjoy some measure of lawful recreation continued to find widespread support, and the advocates of recreation comfortably outnumbered those who were opposed.

This is not to deny the existence of those who dissented. Yet most of the complaints about popular recreation came from the pens of the political economists, who were exercised primarily by the extent to which sports and pastimes drew workmen from their proper labors and thereby undermined economic growth, rather than those who were interested in sports *per se*. One finds, for instance, the novelist and reforming magistrate Henry Fielding observing that "Besides the actual expense of attending these places of pleasure, [there is] the loss of time and neglect of business."[28] Yet even the political economists sometimes failed to convince the wider public of their case. John Clayton, in his ominously entitled *Friendly Advice to the Poor*, complained about the "Manufacturing Work-folks" of Manchester and their too-frequent "Play-days."[29] Yet Clayton's views were pilloried in Joseph Stot's response to the *Friendly Advice*, published just one year later. Stot's *Sequel to the Friendly Advice* poured scorn on Clayton's account of the supposedly dire consequences of the "Desire in Men to spend their time in Play or Pleasure."[30]

Criticism of the time-wasting inherent in popular recreation also surfaced occasionally in the metropolitan newspapers. Popular sports were criticized in one London paper, since "on these occasions the poor do not only suffer from the loss of a half or whole day's labour ... but also spend as much as they can earn in another day, or perhaps two, and besides, disqualify themselves by intemperance for working on the next."[31] Another argued that "however Diversions may be necessary to fill up those dismal Chasms of burdensome Time among People of Fortune, too frequent Relaxations of this Kind among the Populace, enervate Industry."[32] In the *Gentleman's Magazine* it was argued that cricket "upon days when Men ought to be busy ... [is] mischievous in a high Degree. It draws Numbers of People from their Employments.... It propagates a Spirit of Idleness."[33] In reality, however, one has to search the columns of the newspapers long and hard for commentary of this kind. Each of these contributions to the newspapers was isolated and failed to solicit any kind of supportive response. The topic was left untouched for years at a time.

It should also be recognized that most of this hostile commentary occurred during the middle years of the eighteenth century, and so predated the American

War, the French Revolution, the rise of evangelicalism, and other forces supposed to explain them by a considerable margin. By the end of the eighteenth century, the discussion about the time-wasting inherent in popular recreation had largely worked itself out. By this point, even the political economists were appearing decidedly more relaxed about public amusements. Adam Smith, for example, suggested that the state should promote the "frequency and gaiety of public diversions" as a counterattraction to religious sects.[34] In fine, although it is certainly possible to locate some criticism of popular pastimes in eighteenth-century Britain, the suggestion that these views were widespread, or that they gathered momentum in the final years of the century, is unconvincing.

For most of the eighteenth century, what is more striking than either hostility towards or support for recreation is the indifference towards it. Henry Bourne is a landmark figure in the history of folklore studies because his *Antiquitates Vulgares*, as the title suggests, was devoted to the popular, rather than considering it in passing. Prior to Bourne, no more than a handful of works concerned with popular customs had been published. Those late seventeenth-century antiquaries normally classified as the earliest students of folklore—Robert Plot, White Kennet, and Thomas Blount—had displayed only a cursory interest in popular custom. The antiquary and early archaeologist John Aubrey took a more sustained interest, but then, as Hutton has noted, Aubrey was a "thoroughly eccentric" figure.[35] Subsequent to Bourne, almost nothing devoted to the study of popular traditions (beyond a new edition of his own work prepared by John Brand) was published until the nineteenth century. Local historians and antiquaries displayed the most sustained interest in customs, though many of these did not study popular traditions, and others surveyed them only very superficially, often from the armchair rather than the village green.

The experience of E. Rowe Mores in attempting to compile parochial histories of Berkshire is instructive. In 1759, Rowe Mores sent out a list of 20 queries to correspondents in several Berkshire parishes who had offered to assist him in the compilation of a parochial history of the county. The questions addressed the usual areas of antiquarian concern—the age, fabric, location and so forth of the parish church, parish boundaries, local manors, gentry seats, and buildings of significance, but numbers 14 (what wakes, parish feasts, doles, or processions are observed in the parish and on what days?) and 17 (what particular games, sports, customs, proverbs, or peculiar words and phrases are used in your parts?) addressed the practice of popular custom. The parsons and rectors were often reasonably well informed about the celebration of dedication feasts, but all of the respondents proved woefully ignorant of popular games, customs, and speech. In most cases, no response to question 17 was supplied; a few others admitted their ignorance:

> [seventeen] none that I know of ...
> from fifteen to the end, are unanswered, because not in the power of ...

there is nothing contained in these questions [fourteen to eighteen] which can be answered by me ...
I know of no particular game used by the parish ...
I have nothing, Sir, to transmit to you under any of these heads [seventeen to twenty].[36]

Others with nothing to report claimed more confidently that there were no local sports. At Bisham, it was communicated "there are no games or diversions used here," and at Newbury, there was "little or nothing of this kind."[37] Only one correspondent provided any information about sports, customs or proverbs. This was one Richard Forster from Shifford, whose contribution amounted to the following: "our sports are foot-ball, wrestling and cudgelling, *ludi quidem, sed nonnunquam feria ducant in mala* (but sometimes indeed games on holy days lead to mischief)."[38]

In sum, this set of writers, sufficiently interested in their local community to assist in the preparation of a parochial history, knew almost nothing about the sports and pastimes popularly played in their village. It throws unexpected light on Peter Burke's influential argument that a novel gulf opened up between elite and popular culture between 1500 and 1800, suggesting that, in these Berkshire villages at least, such a cultural separation had indeed occurred by the eighteenth century.[39] And it also provides an important context for understanding eighteenth-century debates about popular recreation. Despite a few writers who formulated careful recommendations about when popular recreation was "innocent" and when it was not, most recreation tended to take place beyond the commentators' gazes, and local elites generally had no more than a very superficial interest in or knowledge of these plebeian events.

As the eighteenth century rolled into the nineteenth century, local historians and folklorists began to carve out popular pastimes as an area in which they had especial interest and expertise. The eighteenth-century county histories had been often wholly concerned with elites, and attention to the activities of the working people was extremely limited. In the nineteenth century, chapters on customs became more frequent in both county and urban histories. As Christopher Clarkson, the historian of Richmond, observed, it was necessary to include a chapter on customs, "it being equally the duty of the historian to describe the local customs of a place, as well as its antiquities."[40] Indeed, the nineteenth century was the first period of sustained intellectual interest in popular customs and recreations as it was the first time that scholars felt any sense of "duty" (in Clarkson's words) towards popular customs. Yet despite the emergence of new interest in popular culture, the content of this literature changed relatively little. Amusements for the people, it continued to be argued, were both good and necessary. Traditional recreations and celebrations promoted social harmony and reinforced bonds of deference and duty between the different levels of a hierarchical society, and it took a brave soul to recommend that they ought to be suppressed.

A particularly nostalgic view of traditional festivities was presented by the antiquarian John Throsby in his *History and Antiquities of Leicester*. He provided his readers with a description of a disused Easter Monday custom of the town in which "young and old, and those of all denominations" participated. In the old days, the morning of Easter Monday had been spent in "various amusements and athletic exercise," and so "in the greatest harmony the spring was welcomed." Throsby continued by relating the custom of dragging a dead cat around the town from the tail of a horse "in zig-zag directions" before hounds were set on the trail. Though this is hardly to modern tastes, it was, Throsby remembered, "a scene, upon the whole, of joy, the governing and the governed in habits of freedom, enjoying together an innocent, recreating amusement, seeming to unite them in bonds of mutual friendship, rather than to embitter their days with discord and disunion."[41]

Throsby was certainly presenting an idealized view of relations between the rulers and the ruled here, but his belief that public festivities promoted social harmony and reinforced bonds of duty and deference was not eccentric. Stebbing Shaw, the historian of Staffordshire, presented similar arguments when describing a disused civic ceremony held annually at Lichfield on Whitsun Monday— the "Whitsun bower." Following an elaborate ceremony and banquet for the corporation, the town diverted itself with "bear and bull baitings, interludes, flying chain, legerdemain practitioners, wild beasts &c." Shaw then reflected, "uncouth as these amusements may be deemed by our modern refined tastes, they had their charm and their utility ... and they afforded an opportunity of all ranks of people to assemble and spend their time in innocent mirth and hilarity."[42]

In the nineteenth century, there was less nostalgia for the mixing of classes that was presumed to have occurred during traditional festivities in the past, but the belief that some measure of recreation was beneficial to the populace did not diminish. Rather than romanticized as occasions of social mixing, popular custom was embellished with homely touches in order to reinforce its wholesome and harmless nature. In the Cotswolds, John Dunkin fondly described the Whitsun ales as "one of the most entertaining in the country."[43] In Cheshire, George Ormerod believed that the annual wakes were "the most lively and picturesque, and the best known of [the] village customs."[44] At Berwick-upon-Tweed, diversions at Easter afforded "much amusement to the young children, servant girls, and young lads.... The whole together may be called a *sportive fair*."[45] The historian of Derbyshire, Stephen Glover, noted the county's many fairs "devoted to amusement and jollity," and described a "very elegant rural ceremony" at Tissington.[46]

The growing number of chroniclers of popular customs provided several romantic images of popular rusticity. The unknown female writer who wrote under the pseudonym Jehoshaphat Aspin thought that the May customs still observed in some parts of the country were celebrated with "mirth and jollity." She added that an Essex variation of a traditional ballgame was "frequently productive of much pleasantry."[47] Guy Fawkes was an innocent "festive diversion" in the view of one anonymous writer.[48] Edward Moor, the rector of Great Bealings in Suffolk and a scholar of the county's popular dialect, observed "a variety of recreations tending to excite innocent gaiety among our young people" in that county.[49]

By the nineteenth century it had become increasingly rare for any writer to condemn the right of the laboring poor to enjoy some periods of recreation. As the Reverend John Bowstead informed his readers, "To the man, who earns his bread by the sweat of his brow, these seasons of relaxations [wakes] are especially useful; they refresh him after his toil; they brace him up for future exertion."[50] Antiquaries and historians were more likely to be concerned by the absence than by the abundance of recreation for the laboring population. J.S. Henslow, a clergyman from Suffolk making an enquiry into the condition of the laboring poor, argued that leaders needed to make an effort "to restore to the labouring classes the power of thus enjoying themselves in active and innocent amusements."[51] Rev. J. Giles, in Oxfordshire, regretted that "the people in general have so few opportunities of meeting together for recreation after their daily labours, or for the healthy games and pastimes in which our fathers so much delighted."[52] Robert Southey thought that "the want of holidays breaks down and brutalises the labouring class."[53] The belief that some kind of recreation was both good and necessary for the laboring poor was echoed throughout the early decades of the nineteenth century. "Wholesome recreations and cheering influences" were regarded as both right and proper for the ordinary working people of Britain.[54]

This is not to argue that criticism of recreation did not exist, for it certainly did. But debate centered on what was "wholesome" and what was "cheering" and rarely attempted to challenge the principle that some measure of recreation was to be encouraged. Furthermore, those who criticized any element of the recreational calendar often found their views the subject of criticism. In the county of Derbyshire, the wakes attracted the attention of no fewer than three different local historians. The first to comment was the Reverend James Pilkington. He had little to say about the wakes beyond the fact that they encouraged the "lowest class of people" to spend money they did not have, leaving them "distressed throughout the remainder of the year." But returning to the wakes two decades later, John Farey decided that Pilkington had been "rather too severe in condemning [the] Wakes." The wakes, Farey thought, were "rather beneficial than otherwise." This was so because the holiday season was accompanied with the cleaning of cottages, the whitewashing of rooms, and the purchase of food and new clothes. It all encouraged a spirit of economy and helped to "keep alive feelings and principles, which otherwise the Poor-Law system might utterly extinguish."[55] Finally, Stephen Glover entered the fray. Writing about the Derbyshire wakes a few decades on, he "[inclined] to the opinion ... that upon the whole, the good arising from occasional festivity and a little domestic pride among the poor, considerably counterbalances the evil."[56] The balance of opinion was clearly in favor of the wakes rather than otherwise, and there are no grounds to conclude from exchanges of this sort that popular recreation was now under attack.

A yet more direct exchange of views took place in 1824 between a national and a local newspaper. A number of letters and editorial comments about the vicious character of the Leeds Races published in the *Leeds Mercury* in 1823 and 1824 eventually provoked a lengthy response in favor of public amusements in the

Morning Chronicle, which in turn produced a defense of the original statements in the *Leeds Mercury*. The defense made by Edward Baines, editor of the *Mercury*, of his paper's original condemnation of the races is telling. His rival editor at the *Chronicle* had "quite mistaken our disposition," he wrote, "if he imagines that we are hostile to the innocent recreations of the working classes. So far from being hostile towards them, they have our warm approbation."[57] The difference, Baines continued, was that the *Leeds Mercury* limited their approbation "by the bounds of humanity and morality." Even at the *Mercury*, therefore, they were ready to encourage warmly most popular sports and recreations and the *Chronicle's* denunciation of the paper was quite unjustified. Criticisms of the recreations enjoyed by the masses had, it is clear, to be couched in the most inoffensive of terms.

And so discussion continued, with opinion dividing often along rather predictable religious and political lines. Decisions about when play was disorderly were of course subjective; the "bounds of humanity and morality" to which Baines referred were not clearly marked, and it was the drawing of these boundaries that distinguished one writer from the next. The adherents of the dissenting religions were particularly restrictive in their definitions of acceptable recreation. They tended to have very little sympathy for rustic amusements, and many doubts about whether public amusements could ever be consistent with the dictates of Christianity. One writer in the evangelical *Monthly Magazine* agreed that "poor folks, who work hard all the rest of their time, should now and then have a bit of diversion," but continued, "how ardently were it to be wished, that their diversions could be so contrived for them, as that they might at the same time be innocent!" It was a problem to which she had no solution.[58] Other dissenters tended to display considerably greater interest in preventing sinful recreation than in providing innocent alternatives. Rev. Aulay Macaulay thought the idleness, intoxication, riot, and "other abuses" at wakes rendered it "highly desirable to all the friends of order, of decency, and of religion, that they were totally suppressed."[59] Similarly, Rev. John Whitaker thought few could be entrusted to feast, owing to the "contagious viciousness" of crowds; together they acted "with irreligion and folly ... [and] wickedness and absurdity enter."[60] Neither had anything more to say about recreation.

But hard-line prescriptions of this kind remained on the defensive, hardly more popular than they had been at the Restoration. For the most part, writers took considerable care to underline their support for popular pastimes. Anything that went beyond advising the reform of certain elements of the recreational calendar was likely to prove controversial. An anonymous pamphlet published in 1827 complained about the "strong prejudices" that existed "against any arguments which may be advanced with the view of demonstrating the evil tendency and mischievous effects of our popular amusements.... Nothing, indeed, seems to excite more apprehension and alarm in some minds."[61] Though perhaps overstated, this writer's complaint was not entirely without foundation, for any overenthusiastic criticism of the people's pastimes was likely to attract a studied response.

This was certainly the experience of the Reverend George Burder, author of a pamphlet entitled *Lawful Amusements* in which he argued that only walking, riding, reading, music (though not singing), occasional enjoyment of company, and visiting the poor and sick were acceptable amusements. An anonymous pamphlet was promptly published in which every part of his argument was refuted.[62] In a similar vein, the *Edinburgh Review* drew attention to a recently published sermon entitled *The Drama Brought to the Test of Scripture, and Found Wanting*. In a response entitled "Public Amusements—the Pretensions of the Evangelical Class," the *Review* promised to expose the erroneousness and misapplication of [the evangelicals'] zeal." It complained:

> [T]heir zeal in denouncing the amusements of society as replete with danger and sin, is abundantly notorious.... They have long assumed the right (under what authority we have yet to discover) of reprobating the customary recreations of life, and of branding those who participate in them as enemies to God and of true religion.[63]

The *Edinburgh Review* did not represent elite opinion any more than the evangelicals did; it was a conservative periodical, with religious and political biases of its own. The point simply is to indicate the open-ended nature of discussion, the lack of agreement, and the failure of the evangelicals to carry the wider public with them. As we have already seen, there had always been criticism of certain elements of popular recreation, and the same was no less true at the turn of the nineteenth century than at any other time. Yet it is doubtful whether this period witnessed sufficient change, in either the quantity or nature of complaints, to support the view that decades of goodwill towards popular pastimes were now overturned. Complaints should be seen as part of an ongoing discussion about which recreations were acceptable, or "innocent," and which were not, rather than set apart as the emergence of new pattern of thought.

By the early nineteenth century, the appearance of a number of books devoted to describing popular customs for a middle-class readership suggests that more careful observation of popular recreations by the leisured elites was becoming established. Joseph Strutt's *Sports and Pastimes of the People of England*, published in 1801, was the first of many nineteenth-century works devoted to popular sports. It went through several editions, and inspired a small number of imitators.[64] The Radical printer William Hone also made a significant contribution to the study of popular customs with his series of books: *The Every-Day Book*, *The Table Book*, and *The Year Book*. Large sections of the later books were based upon the contributions of readers, which suggests that local elites were more aware of popular customs than had been the case when Rowe conducted his research in Berkshire in the mid-eighteenth century. The early nineteenth century also witnessed the emergence of studies in local dialect. Some of the dialect dictionaries published in the first quarter of the nineteenth century were particularly well informed, often containing substantial research on custom, superstition, and sports as well as language.[65]

In the two decades subsequent to the publication of Malcolmson's *Popular Recreations*, a number of scholars sought to challenge the idea that popular recreations were fatally undermined during the late eighteenth and early nineteenth centuries. But they have done so by claiming that most customs and recreations proved remarkably resilient to attempts to suppress them, rather than by challenging the existence of an ideologically inspired "attack." A careful reexamination of elite commentary on popular recreations around the turn of the century suggests that the idea of a decisive shift in attitudes towards the traditional pastimes of the poor in late eighteenth-century Britain does not appear to be so well grounded as has long been assumed. Quite to the contrary, the late eighteenth century, and particularly the first half of the nineteenth century, saw not ever more hostility towards popular recreation but a considerable increase in interest in popular pastimes, most of it indulgent in tone.

This is not to suggest that the hostile voices did not exist, for they certainly did. It is, however, to suggest that we regard such hostile commentary in a different way. The customs and pastimes of the poor had always had the power to divide social elites, and a current of concern about the pernicious consequences of recreation ran right through the century. But such concerns formed just one corner of a more complex debate about the place of popular recreations in English society. More striking than the occasional complaint is the marked increase in the interest that elite commentators took in the customs and pastimes of their poorer neighbors, the great majority of whom thought that some measure of regulated diversion was to be encouraged.

Notes

[1] The fullest account of popular recreations in the seventeenth century is contained in Ronald Hutton's *The Rise and Fall of Merry England: The Ritual Year, 1400–1700* (Oxford: Oxford University Press, 1994). A wealth of relevant material from the West Country has also been analyzed by David Underdown in *Revel, Riot, and Rebellion: Popular Politics and Culture in England, 1603–1660* (Oxford: Oxford University Press, 1985).

[2] Robert W. Malcolmson, *Popular Recreations in English Society, 1700–1850* (Cambridge: Cambridge University Press, 1973).

[3] Dennis Brailsford, *A Taste for Diversions: Sport in Georgian England* (Cambridge: Lutterworth Press, 1999), 57–73; Anthony Delves, "Popular Recreation and Social Conflict in Derby, 1800–1850," in *Popular Culture and Class Conflict, 1590–1914: Explorations in The History Of Labour And Leisure*, ed. Eileen Yeo and Stephen Yeo (Brighton: Harvester Press, 1981), 89–127, esp. 106–7; R.D. Storch, ed., "Introduction," *Popular Culture and Custom in Nineteenth-Century England* (London: Croom Helm, 1982); John Hargreaves, *Sport, Power and Culture: A Social and Historical Analysis of Popular Sports in Britain* (Cambridge: Basil Blackwell, 1986), 20–26, 114–15; Richard Holt, *Sport and the British: A Modern History* (Oxford: Oxford University Press, 1989), 38–43; J.M. Golby and A.W. Purdue, *The Civilisation of the Crowd: Popular Culture in England, 1750–1900*, rev. ed. (Stroud: Sutton Publishing, 1999); E.P. Thompson, *Customs in Common* (London: Penguin, 1991), esp. 382–94.

[4] Neil Tranter, *Sport, Economy and Society in Britain, 1750–1914* (Cambridge: Cambridge University Press), 5. See also Peter Bailey, *Leisure and Class in Victorian England: Rational Recreation and the Contest for Control, 1830–1885*, 2nd ed. (London: Methuen, 1987).

[5] Hutton, *Rise and Fall*, 153–226; Underdown, *Revel, Riot, and Rebellion*, esp. 44–105, 239–70.

[6] Anthony Wood, *The Life and Times of Anthony Wood, Antiquary, of Oxford, 1632–1695, described by Himself*, ed. Andrew Clark, Oxford Historical Society, vol. 19 (Oxford, Clarendon Press: 1891), 314.

[7] White Kennett, *Parochial Antiquities attempted in the History of Ambrosden and Burcester in the Counties of Oxford and Bucks*, 2 vols. (Oxford, 1695), 309.

[8] William Stukeley, *Itinerarium Curiosum* (London. 1724), 91.

[9] Thomas Staveley, *The History of the Churches in England* (London, 1773), 124–5.

[10] William Borlase, *The Natural History of Cornwall* (Oxford: W. Jackson, 1758), 300.

[11] Kennett, *Parochial Antiquities*, 302.

[12] *Spectator*, 4 September 1711.

[13] Sir Thomas Parkyns, *The Inn-Play: or Cornish Hugg Wrestler* (London: J. Bailey, 1727), 20. For similar views see also John Godfrey, *A Treatise Upon the Useful Science of Defence Connecting the Small and Back-Sword* (London, 1747).

[14] Nottinghamshire County Record Office, "Will and 4 codicils of Sir Thos. Parkyns, Bart," PR313.

[15] *London Magazine*, March 1738, 139–40.

[16] *London Magazine*, October 1736, 561.

[17] Ofspring Blackall, *The Lawfulness and the Right Manner of Keeping Christmas, and Other Christian Festivals: A Sermon* (London, 1705), 9–10.

[18] *Gentleman's Magazine*, October 1738, 523.

[19] Henry Bourne, *Antiquitates Vulgares; or, the Antiquities of the Common People* (Newcastle, 1725), 142.

[20] Bourne, *Antiquitates Vulgares*, 142–7.

[21] Hutton, *Rise and Fall*, 238.

[22] Bourne, *Antiquitates Vulgares*, 215, 198.

[23] Bourne, *Antiquitates Vulgares*, 228, 153, 181.

[24] Richard Baxter, *A Christian Directory: Or, a Summ of Practical Theologie and Cases of Conscience* (London, 1673), part 1, 460–61. Elsewhere, he fulminated against "*needless, inordinate sports and games*, which are commonly stigmatised by the offenders themselves, with the infamous name of PASTIMES; and marked with the deceitful title of *Recreations*" (Baxter, 291).

[25] *Gentleman's Magazine*, October 1738, 523.

[26] *London Magazine*, May 1747, 221–2.

[27] *The Servants Calling: With Some Advice to the Apprentice* (London, 1725), 80.

[28] Quoted in John Hatcher, "Labour, leisure and economic thought before the nineteenth century," *Past and Present*, no. 160 (1998), 64–115, esp. 79–80.

[29] John Clayton, *Friendly Advice to the Poor* (Manchester, 1755), 13, 29.

[30] Joseph Stot, *A Sequel to the Friendly Advice to the Poor of Manchester* (Manchester, 1756), 19–20. It was in fact the work of the printer and bookseller, Robert Whitworth.

[31] *London Chronicle*, 4–6 October 1764.

[32] *Public Advertiser*, 2 September 1757.

[33] *Gentleman's Magazine*, September 1743, 486.
[34] Adam Smith, *An Inquiry into the Nature and Causes of the Wealth of Nations*, vol. 2, ed. Edwin Cannan (London: Methuen, 1961), 318.
[35] Hutton, *Rise and Fall*, 235. For more on the fascinating life and work of John Aubery, see Michael Hunter, *John Aubrey and the Realm of Learning* (London: Duckworth, 1975).
[36] *Collections Towards a Parochial History of Berkshire, Being the Answers Returned to Mr. More's Circular Letters and Queries* (London, [1783]), see esp. sections on East Hendred, 29; Sparsholt, 37; Speen, 41; Shaw, 80; East Garston, 85.
[37] *Collections Towards a Parochial History of Berkshire*, 11, 34.
[38] *Collections Towards a Parochial History of Berkshire*, 55–7. He admittedly wrote nearly two pages about local dialect.
[39] Peter Burke, *Popular Culture in Early Modern Europe* (London: Temple Smith, 1978).
[40] Christopher Clarkson, *The History and Antiquities of Richmond in the County of York* (Richmond, 1821), 288.
[41] John Throsby, *The History and Antiquities of the Ancient Town of Leicester* (London, 1791), 166.
[42] Stebbing Shaw, *The History and Antiquities of Staffordshire*, 2 vols. (London, 1798–1801), 318.
[43] John Dunkin, *The History and Antiquities of Bicester* (London, 1816), 267.
[44] George Ormerod, *The History of the County Palatine and City of Chester* (London, 1819), 44.
[45] John Fuller, *The History of Berwick-upon-Tweed* (Edinburgh, 1799), 445–6.
[46] Stephen Glover, *The History and Gazetteer of the County of Derby*, 2 vols. (Derby, 1831), 311, 306.
[47] Jehoshaphat Aspin, *Ancient Customs, Sports, and Pastimes of the English* (London, 1832), 164, 202.
[48] Anon, *Popular Pastimes, Being a Selection of Picturesque Representations of the Customs and Amusements of Great Britain* (London, 1816), 57.
[49] Edward Moor, *Suffolk Words and Phrases* (London, 1823), 239.
[50] John Bowstead, *The Village Wake, or the Feast of the Dedication, its Religious Observance a Bond of Union between the Higher and Lower Classes. A Sermon* (London, 1846), 11.
[51] J.S. Henslow, *Suggestions Towards an Enquiry into the Present Condition of the Labouring Population of Suffolk* (Hadleigh, 1844), 25.
[52] Rev. J.A. Giles, *History of the Town and Parish of Bampton* (Bampton, 1848), 55.
[53] Robert Southey, *Letters from England* (London, 1807), 413.
[54] The expression is Lord John Manners's. See Lord John Manners, *A Plea for National Holy Days* (London, [1843?]), 7.
[55] James Pilkington, *A View of the Present State of Derbyshire*, 2 vols. (London, 1789), 2:55; John Farey, *General View of the Agriculture of Derbyshire*, 3 vols. (London, 1811–1817), 3:628.
[56] Glover, *The History and Gazetteer of the County of Derby*, 309.
[57] *Leeds Mercury*, 3 July 1824.
[58] *Monthly Magazine*, July 1798, 10. The theme was taken up by a second correspondent later in the year recommending music as an innocent amusement suitable for the poor. See *Monthly Magazine*, November 1798, 339–40.

[59] Rev. Aulay Macaulay, *The History and Antiquities of Claybrook* (London, 1791), 128.

[60] Rev. John Whitaker, *The History of Manchester*, 2 vols. (London, 1771–1775), book 2, 444.

[61] Anon, *Observations on Some of the Popular Amusements of this Country, Addressed to the Higher Classes of Society* (London, 1827), 4.

[62] George Burder, *Lawful Amusements* (London, 1805); *A Letter to the Rev. George Burder, Occasioned by his Sermon on Lawful Amusements* (London, 1805).

[63] *Edinburgh Review*, vol. 54 (1831), 100.

[64] See, for example, Anon, *Popular Pastimes*; Aspin, *Ancient Customs*.

[65] See, for example, Robert Forby, *The Vocabulary of East Anglia*, 2 vols. (London, 1830).

Chapter 2
Olympism and Pastoralism in British Sporting Literature

Jean Williams

Introduction

The Olympic Games, as a topic, metaphor, and sporting theme, increasingly received attention in English literature as the eighteenth century progressed. The available classical texts relied more upon poetic license than historical accuracy, enabling authors to reimagine Pan-Hellenic traditions. At the same time, Christian perceptions of classical works celebrating pagan sport and athleticism remained against the spread of the specialist study of antiquity. The ancient Olympic or Olympian Games were the largest of four Pan-Hellenic celebrations for which records date back to 776 BC but were likely to have had much older traditions. The four-year cycle of the festivals, held annually in mid-summer, was termed an Olympiad.[1] In year one, this sequence involved the Pythian Games, dedicated to Apollo and staged at Delphi. The second year, the Nemean Games were devoted to Zeus, at Nemea. The Isthmian Games, pledged to Poseidon, followed at Corinth. The largest and most significant, the Olympic Games took place every four years, near the town of Elis, in the northwestern part of the Peloponnese, on a walled site about a kilometer square called Olympia, and were also devoted to Zeus.[2]

There remains some conjecture about what sports took place and how this changed over the duration of the Olympic Games: a period of at least 1200 years from approximately 776 BC until 393 AD. However, for many interested in these ancient rites, literature provided a problematic, but important, historical link with the distant past. Perhaps one of the reasons that sport appealed so strongly as a subject of literary treatment was that each text, the material volume itself, had both an external and an internal history. Parallels with the interior life, embodied experience, and public reputation of the athlete were therefore significant.

This chapter explores the legacy of ancient Olympism and its combination with the pastoralism of early modern British sport, evident in the first printed texts in English. These processes accelerated from 1612 onwards, as versions of "Olimpick," "Ho-Limpyc," "Olympian," and "Olympiad" festivals were part of a wider engagement between the British people and the philosophies and practices of the ancient Olympic Games.[3] Many of these British manifestations contained reinvented or redefined elements, the most significant of which was connection of bodily practices with spiritual and ethical values.[4] Much of this involved the celebration of human interaction with nature and, by extension, the divine principles that crafted a harmonious environment. However, this could be disrupted by man-made conflicts. A rich seam of primary material available to contemporary researchers remains because of the widespread debates about the rights of individuals to spend what little free time they had in the way that they chose. Ultimately, what bodily and spiritual purposes should sport serve?

Ancient Olympic competitors were far less interested in taking part than in the glory of winning, since this indicated the good favor of the Gods. This had both personal and civic elements in that victory honored both the individual and his backers.[5] Before the Romans conquered Greece in the second century BC, participation was relatively limited to those born as free citizens from across the Hellenic world. Women, the "impious," and slaves were excluded, although the extent to which they were successfully prohibited remains a point of dispute.[6] Over a period of five days, running, jumping, throwing, combat, wrestling (pankreation), and equestrian sports were contested by males from Greek city-states. There was a permanent stadium and a horse racing track plus an infrastructure to support recreation at Olympia. Competing naked signaled balance and harmony, the education of the body and the mind. Leisure, such as baths for the athletes, and culture, such as singing and music, accompanied sporting excellence. For tokens of victory, such as the olive wreath and the chance to dedicate a statue in their honor at the Sanctuary of Zeus, the Altis, athletes competed for status as well as sporting satisfaction. Although many Hellenic athletes had patrons who would sponsor their specialized training and preparation, the related aspects of wealth, professional sporting careers and gambling combined with spiritual elements. Fame could also bring benefits once an athlete returned home.

One of the important aspects of religious and political observance during the festival was the Olympic truce. For the duration of the celebrations, conflicts and wars were suspended and competitors granted safe passage to Olympia. But the Games were not immune to controversy. In later centuries, with Zeus known as Jupiter by the Romans, more athletes came from across the Empire. It is unclear when the final versions were staged, and other sports festivals continued in the region, but antipagan laws were crucial in their demise. Given the scale of the Hellenic world and the subsequent influence of the Roman Empire, significant Asian and African influences remind readers to resist Eurocentric interpretations of the Olympic heritage. Sport was, though, inherently political and sought to pacify and unify select groups across the region. Equally important, the site of Olympia suffered a series of misfortunes; the Temple of Zeus was razed by fire, looted, and a church built on the foundations. Subsequent earthquakes, flooding, and erosion buried what remained, and for almost 1,000 years the site of so many religious pilgrimages was neglected, other than by local people. Scholars disagree whether Greek, French, or Austro-Prussian or German archaeologists were primarily responsible for the excavations at Olympia, but there seems to be a consensus that British interest was stimulated by the classical education of Richard Chandler (1738–1810) at Oxford University.[7] Chandler was by no means alone in his fascination with Olympic mythology.

The long tradition of the ancient Olympic Games and the only slightly shorter period of discontinuity following their proscription enabled myths to be built up about them, particularly among British classical scholars and aesthetes. Henry VIII had endowed the first professors of Greek at Cambridge University in 1540 and at Oxford in 1541. Volumes of Greek and Roman writers appeared more widely in English from 1579 onwards, often as anglicized and embellished translations. Among the most significant were Homer (circa eighth century BC), Herodotus (484–425 BC), Virgil (70–19 BC), Plutarch (46–120 AD), and Epictetus (AD 55–135). Homer's *The Iliad* contained one of the first references to the Olympic Games in English in 1598. The epic text was supplemented by other works, sometimes inaccurately transcribed and mythologized, so that Olympism became part of an educated young gentleman's library. For instance, the poems of Pindar (ca. 522–433) were collected in 17 books, and from these survived four volumes of Epinician Odes (choral songs written in honor of victories and heroes).[8] Chandler was influenced by Pausanias's 10-volume *Description of Greece* in which the beauty of the everyday Greek countryside is as noted as the sporting excellence at Olympia.[9]

This chapter explores the shifting meanings applied to sport in literary treatments from the first printed texts in English literature to the end of the eighteenth century. There were important continuities, in that the perceived strength, purpose, and beauty of the ancient Greek civilization could be symbolized in new forms of athleticism. However, there were also significant changes as early writers of printed books in English had begun to interpret sport through an engagement with the British countryside which also encouraged divine, rather than pagan, reflection. The ancient Olympics were little documented across their considerable history, and the site of the games was subsequently hidden by a millennium of man-made and natural disaster. This enabled European scholars from the Renaissance onwards who used the term "Olympic" to reinscribe it anew. Although many were fascinated by the combination of religious practices and sporting rites that took place at Olympia, their primary sources of information were textual rather than archaeological or geographic. On the one hand, these classical texts provided insights into a lost and golden age of sport and athletic pursuits to contemporary readers. On the other, neither pagan Hellenic Olympic values nor the original form of the sporting contests was replicated.

The vagueness of antiquity allowed for sporting activities to be revised according to modern morals and sensibilities.[10] A kind of literary-sporting palimpsest developed over which the ancient Olympic Games were reinscribed; consequently, both real and imagined philosophies from the original Hellenic festivities were reinterpreted in line with contemporary taste. Thus, some of the earliest examples of what might be termed English "sporting literature" reflect deep, and celebratory, engagements with leisure, recreation, nature, and spirituality.

The Emergence of English Sporting Literature

A wide range of classical literature had previously used sport to explore important facets of how the individual behaved within society and interacted with nature. These early texts exhibit attitudes toward sport, self, nature, and society that played an important role in the reimagining of Olympic festivals in the seventeenth and eighteenth centuries. Among the earliest exploration of sporting experience in a text printed in English was an excerpt, *Treatyse of Fysshynge wyth an Angle*, attributed to Dame Juliana Berners and first ascribed to *The Book of St Albans* printed at Westminster by Wynkyn the Worde in 1486.[11] In the colophon of the second edition of 1496, a rhymed treatise refers to a book of hunting by the same author, although the identity of the writer may never be categorically confirmed.[12] Similar passages on hunting, hawking, and fishing in other pamphlets and excerpts may have been more widely circulated than we currently understand. Fishing could be part of an easily sustained regimen for good health and a pious life. This literature has been explored in terms of popular arcadianism and sport in the oldest sense of the word as a struggle with nature, either for food or a trophy, which rarely involved risk for the human participant.[13] As feudal relationships in England began to decline and an individual's leisure became contested as a right, literally a chance to recreate the body and spirit worn down by work, increased scrutiny of organized games followed. This was especially the case regarding a calendar by which sporting character could be interpreted as communications and travel technology allowed for the gradual development of countrywide tastes.[14] As such, narratives of leisure began to link the responsibility of the individual for maintaining his or her own well-being (physical, spiritual, and moral) with the health of the nation. This was to be significant for later narratives about Olympism in the eighteenth century.

Dame Juliana Berners' *Treatyse of Fysshynge wyth an Angle* bridged the religious and secular divide by highlighting fishing as a solitary and diverting pastime. *Treatyse* was among the first English sporting texts, attributed to the Lady Prioress of Sopwell Nunnery near St Albans and printed commercially by Caxton's former apprentice. Julyans or Juliana Berners (otherwise spelt Barnes or Barners) was most likely born at Roding, Berners in Dunmow, Essex. Although the records of the Priory were lost and we know little accurate information about her life, she is thought to have been the daughter of Sir James Berners, a knight whose son, Sir Richard, was created Baron Berners under Henry IV.[15] Dame Juliana Berners, an illustrious and educated woman who also promoted heraldry, hawking, and hunting, in her *Treatyse of Fysshynge* advocated angling primarily to cultivate a good spirit: a benign and optimistic way of thinking about the world. Just as the Christian Church venerated its scriptures in order to provide a sense of tradition and signified the boundaries of permissible ways of writing about religion, sport became defined by its own set of textual references. In *Treatyse*, sport combined pleasant reflection, gentle exercise, and the possible reward of healthy nourishment. The sublime and spiritual benefits were therefore as much emphasized as the physical:

> The first of them is a mery thought. The seconde is a labour not outragious. The third is diet mesurable. The first if a man will euer more be in mery thought and haue a glad spyrite, he must eschew all contrarious company and all places of debate where he myght haue any occasions of melancholy & if he wyll haue a labour not outragious: he must then ordeyne hym to his hartes ease, and plesaunce without study, pensyfnes of trauayle, a mery occupacion whiche may reioyce his harte, and in which his spirites may haue a mery delyte. And if he will be dieted measurably he must eschewe all places of ryot, whiche is cause of surfet and of syckenesse, and he must drawe hym to places of swete ayre and hungry, and eate nouryshable meates and disyrable als.[16]

In what is presented as a healthy alternative to urban physical culture, the comparative democracy of fishing is symbolized by its simplicity. Hawks were the pride of royalty, the insignia of nobility, the ambassador's present, the priest's indulgence, companions of the knight, and the nurslings of gentlewomen. In comparison, the totemic objects of *Treatyse of Fysshynge* were the line, hook, and rod made by the angler from materials that were to be found at hand. Illustrated with extensive diagrams of each component and a strong sense of color, the images of the rod and tackle were extremely clear, as perhaps befits one of the first "how-to" coaching manuals of sport.

On the other hand, the meaning of *Treatyse*, like the rather poetic atmosphere of piety and placidity in fishing itself, is polyvalent. Meditation on simple rod and line, fashioned from nature in an activity that prioritizes patience, can be read as a practical form of solitary observance, with a tranquil and reassuring certainty that existence has a purpose beyond immediate function. The *Treatyse* concludes that fishing is a solace for the heart, a healthy activity for the body, and richly rewarding for the soul.[17] In this apparently simple celebration of angling, the authorial voice employs sport with a social and moral purpose. The didactic elements outline not just how angling *might* be pursued but the manner and spirit in which it *ought* to be done. Not least, it removed the individual from the profane curiosity of the ale house and the vulgar crowds of the town, unlike boxing and other more combative pursuits.[18] The angler did not obviously compete against others. These were narrative elements to which future writers would return in assigning moral values to sporting activity. Therefore, although *Treatyse* does not directly refer to Olympic and Olympian values, the work is nevertheless an important link between rural "real England" in its contemplation of arcadian sensibilities and later sporting literature. In many respects the fisherman replaces the shepherd of conventional pastoral Golden Age literature; he is a figure both employed and at leisure.

The *Treatyse* itself had a long legacy and may have given Izaac Walton the idea for the more popular *The Compleat Angler*, first published in 1653.[19] Walton borrowed the most important stylistic features of the earlier book, such as preferring the contemplative life over the athletic pursuit of glory. The particular aesthetics of fishing, its landscapes and bodily movements, were intimately tied up with the ongoing reproduction of Englishness. Published in the middle of the turmoil of the seventeenth century, Walton's text also celebrated the removal of the individual from conflict with guidelines that fishing was an art with an elaborate etiquette for conduct towards both other humans and nature.[20] However, the work is less solitary than *Treatyse*; Walton's anglers might sing together if they have been rained off. This gentle dogma was so conspicuously successful that it tended to overshadow the *Treatyse*. Walton was 60 years old when his angling book was published, and as a critically acclaimed biographer, he had written five books that had nothing to do with fishing. *The Compleat Angler* was, by intention, a piscatorial encyclopedia about fish, hydrography, and fish culture. Having arrived at a very philosophical approach to life and sport, Walton was a dedicated Royalist and devout churchman who regularly hiked 20 miles from London to the river Lea, focused on the joy of the waterside. The book is an example of early pastoral drama in the Georgic tradition, celebrating nature, harmony, security, and beauty. The blessings of angling are peace, happiness, and an escape from everyday worries and chores related to the court and the town. *The Compleat Angler* was popular in Walton's lifetime: there were five editions published between 1653 and 1676. It was not printed again until 1750 but has been in continuous publication since that date. Walton died in 1683 at age of 90 and is buried in the cathedral. *The Compleat Angler* remains one of the most published books in the world. An original edition would cost more than $12,000 on the present market, and it has appeared in at least 460 different editions or reissues.

Between Dame Juliana Berners and Izaac Walton, the English civil war and religious divides were to redefine British attitudes to Olympic festivals as provocative and divisive.[21] This political context has been explored at some length.[22] Processes that had accompanied the dissolution of the monasteries by Henry VIII had begun to make Puritanism a growing force in English life in the reign of Mary Queen of Scots and Elizabeth I. Originally published in 1617 by King James I, the *Book of Sports*, however, politicized leisure to an unprecedented degree, although there had been previous bans and edicts on particular pastimes. The strictness of the Puritans regarding the keeping of the Sabbath as the Lord's Day by avoiding "worldly activity" was rejected in favor of the pursuit of honest mirth and merriment.[23] Republished by Charles I in 1633, the *Book of Sports* sanctioned participation in "lawful recreations," such as archery and dancing, after church attendance on Sundays. Defense of the principle of a right to leisure after Sunday worship or on annual feast days, such as existing Whitsuntide festivals, was effectively a profanation of the Puritan Sabbath, especially after Oliver Cromwell became a Member of Parliament in 1628. After the execution of King Charles I in 1642, Commonwealth England under Cromwell enforced pious pursuits to the extent of making the regime unpopular. With the death of Cromwell in 1658 and the Restoration of the monarchy in 1660, Charles II sanctioned many pastimes, mainly because he enjoyed them himself. These included the theater, cards, and sports such as horse racing. However, this could have greater symbolic than practical resonance, and communal festivity could incorporate behavior which was not tolerated by local people, so the term "The Merry Monarch" is a stereotype requiring caution.[24]

Most accounts of this period acknowledge that William Shakespeare (1564–1616) was the most prominent writer combining older interpretations of sport, including forms of hunting and animal baiting, with newer forms such as fencing and tennis. Shakespeare interpreted sport variously across his output as sexual activity, from the French *desport*, a means of deceiving others, and a way of filling in idle time. Among the discursive slippage, specific activities are often referenced, from equestrianism and blood sports to wrestling, bowls, and camp-ball or football. As this letter from Theodore Cook, the editor of *The Field*, to leading Shakespeare scholar Sir Sidney Lee suggests, relatively little was written about early modern sport and its literary representations:

> Would it be possible to write ... of the magnificent passages he has about sport of various kinds and the bearing which those passages have upon his life and character? There is a splendid bit about deer hounds. There is the bit about tennis balls in Henry V and so on. I mean that he so thoroughly realised that sporting instinct in the English people which gave us our best voluntary army at this crisis; and, in another direction, it is curious that a man who was not a knight and who very likely had not travelled abroad, should have so just a knowledge of fencing as he shows both in Hamlet and in Romeo and Juliet. No better definition of fencing has ever been made than his 'time, distance and proportion. He rests me his minim rest, one two and the third in your bosom.' This is the more curious because in his time Englishmen nearly always used the edge.... I can include in this paper something about the poet whom every paper would wish to commemorate.[25]

Though too extensive to summarize here, Shakespeare's work subsequently produced prodigious quantities of sporting commentary as yet comparatively underdeveloped by academics.[26] If tennis players were usually courtiers, football was more of a lower-class game. Among the first Olympic references are lines from *Henry VI, Part 3*, with the Octavo written in 1595: "And, if we thrive, promise them such rewards / As victors wear at the Olympian games / This may plant courage in their quailing breasts; For yet is hope of life and victory. / Forslow no longer, make we hence amain" (II.iii.55–9).[27] However, these are the last lines of the scene, giving an ominous, fateful use of the term, with the prospect victory not so much uncertain as unlikely. The less well-known allusion in *Troilus and Cressida* has similar overtones: "I have seen thee ... / When that a ring of Greeks have hemmed thee in, / Like an Olympian wrestling" (IV.iv.215).[28] While athleticism combines with the godlike warrior qualities of Hector, the character to whom the description is directed, again the context is of preparation for impending conflict of which the outcome was uncertain.

However, though Shakespeare might have briefly mentioned the Olympic Games, the more important, and often overlooked, figure was Catholic Royalist

Robert Dover (1582–1652), who between 1612 and 1642 staged the Cotswold Olimpick Games as annual celebrations of community sport from the highest classes to the lowest.[29] There may have been a local precedent dating back to 1602, but Dover, who had trained as a lawyer at Gray's Inn before moving to Saintbury near Chipping Campden with his wife and children, developed the Whitsun ales to an Olimpick quasi-sporting festival. The site became known as "Dover's Hill," although the setting was a natural amphitheatre called Kingscombe Plain in Gloucestershire. Dover presided over the Games on horseback, dressed ceremonially in a coat, hat, feather, and ruff, donated by King James, possibly through Endymion Porter, a member of the court. Porter had an estate in the village of Aston-sub-Edge, close to Dover's home, and the latter acted as his legal agent between 1622 and 1640.[30] Although horses and men were decorated with Dover's yellow ribbons as favors and a wooden castle also erected each year in his name, the festivities lacked a permanent stadium, religious building, or gymnasium. Nevertheless, tenuous links were made with a much more ancient Hellenic celebration that seemed to symbolize the open and unrestricted right to compete in the great outdoors in peace. For instance, a wandering harp player dressed as Homer entertained the crowds, and there was also a maze, known as a Troy Town, constructed from piled up turf with walls about one foot (0.30 m) high, through which villagers would dance. The games had already happened in 1642 by the time of the Civil War, and the theaters were closed. The games were stopped in 1643, but the fortunes of Robert Dover did not seem to suffer too much. He held three courts at Wickhamford in 1647, 1648, and 1650 and died in July 1652.

While it is agreed that the games were revived after the Restoration in 1660, it is unclear exactly when. The advertisement in the *Gloucester Journal* for the games on 10 May 1725 suggests a continuous tradition, but it is unclear whether this is accurate. Though Juel-Jensen has them continuing until 1832, there are posters for games after this, although they increasingly lacked respectability.[31] Whether because of or in spite of the reputation for debauchery, 30,000 plus people were recorded from 1846 onwards when "the games … became the trysting place of all the lowest scum of the population which lived in the districts lying between Birmingham and Oxford" before they were stopped by act of Parliament in 1851.[32] It would appear that the land was unenclosed until 1853, when the 500 acres known as Dover's Hill became a considerably smaller area. At the same time that the games were terminated, focus on civic centers for commerce and pleasure meant that the text became an important "space" for the re-creation of the games as "authentic" almost a hundred years later. The events that were revived from 1951, moreover, fit models of Festival of Britain respectability in contrast to these later vulgar forms of the Cotswold Olympick Games.

Though it is possible to oversimplify the degree of regulation sought by each side (Catholic versus Protestant, Royalist or Parliamentarian, pleasure-seeking as opposed to the pious), Dover's reimagined Olimpick Games took the title both to secularize and gentrify proceedings. They also drew on much older traditions of the British sportscape, including traditional ales and rural festivities.

"Dover's Games" were a cross-class annual event incorporating leisure, games, and play. The tents for drinking and for chess and dice games contained little recreation that was healthy or rational in intent. Through the *Annalia Dubrensia* (the annals of Dover), a modest book of celebratory poems by Michael Drayton, Ben Jonson, Thomas Heywood, and others published in 1636 by Matthew Walbancke of the Gray's Inn gateway, we have some sense of what Dover himself was like, and the form of his festivities.[33]

There is enough warmth beyond the perfunctory praise of Dover to infer that he was in some respects noble, jovial, generous, and witty. The atmosphere of the verses, like the games themselves perhaps, in the defense of "honest mirth and recreation" are more about convivial spectacle and less about competition or winners. Michael Drayton, Ben Jonson, Thomas Heywood, Thomas Randolph, Owen Feltham, William Basse, and Shakerley Marmion were recognized poets. Jonson was obviously uninspired and wrote only 13 lines, in two of which he declared "I cannot bring my muse to drop vies, Twixt Cotswold and the Olimpicke [*sic*] exercise."[34] Other local or legal associates and relatives contributed, including "A Sirinx" (thought to be Dover's wife Sibella), who wrote a poem in the shape of a panpipe.

The poems collected in the *Annalia Dubrensia* seem to have been gathered over a number of years and are perhaps published in the order they were received rather than in terms of poetic "seniority."[35] Dover's single biggest innovation was that the aristocracy and the common folk were both present at the games. Among other evidence, this is supported by the Grenville copy of the *Annalia* in the British Library printed for Sir Thomas Trevor, one of the barons of the exchequer, and bearing a Dover signature, dated 1640. A reference to the games also appeared in the "green world comedy," Richard Brome's *Jovial Crew or The Merry Beggars*. It was acted in 1641 at the Cockpit Theatre, Drury Lane (and published in 1652), and in it two young men, Vincent and Hilliard, invite sisters Rachel and Meriel: "Will you go up the hilltop of Sports then, and Merriments, Dover's Olimpicks or Cotswold Games?" The story of "merry beggars" and their protection of the sisters does indicate a degree of wider awareness beyond the *Annalia Dubrensia* itself. Though the Barton entry of Robert Dover's burial is given as 14 July 1652, his will has yet to be found.

A grandson of Robert Dover, Thomas, reissued the *Annalia* on its centenary in 1736.[36] Another grandson, John, also entered Gray's Inn as a lawyer and also wrote a drama called *The Roman Generals, or the Distressed Ladies*, the quality of which I have not been able to discover. However, it was Thomas who would become the more celebrated as the Quicksilver Doctor, after inventing Dover's Powders, as well as publishing the *Annalia* in 1736 with the inscription "Dr Dover thought it his Duty to perpetuate the memory of that Good Man his Grandfather." In an original copy held by the British Library, a note has been posted into the front cover which perhaps was to inspire Whitfield and others. It begins with the reference to the *Merry Wives of Windsor* and is followed by this note:

Upon this passage Mr Wharton [sic] hath the following note. It is also in the editions published by Dr Johnson and Mr Steevens "Cotswold is a village in Worcestershire, or Warwickshire, and was famous for rural exercises and sports of all sorts.... Shakespeare makes Shallow talk of a stout fellow, a Cotswold man, that is, one who was a native of this very place, so famous for men of strength and activity. Mr Wharton [sic] has seen a collection of poems, called Cotswold Muse, containing a description of the games exhibited there."[37]

The spine title and running heading for each page containing the poems is "Cotswold Games" and is signed merely "D," so reinterpreting and reinscribing the games can be evident from the earliest editions. The addition of a poem "In celebration of the yearley Preserver of the Games at Cotswald," first published in Madagascar in 1638 by Davenant (also spelt D'Avenant), means that this centennial edition had contributions from two poet laureates, as he had succeeded Ben Jonson to the post the same year.

The first Shakespearean scholars to mention Dover in any sustained way were Samuel Johnson, George Steevens and Thomas Warton: "After Wharton's [sic] Note: 'The Cotswold Hills in Gloucestershire are large tracts of downs, famous for their fine turf, and therefore excellent for coursing. I believe there is no village of that name.'"[38] The *Annalia* and Dover's Games had at least two principal references in the seventeenth century after Dover's death in 1652, 15 in the eighteenth century, 20-plus in the nineteenth, and at least 25 by the time of Whitfield's edition in 1962 (followed by mass media and attendant multiplication of cross-referencing by the Internet), from which it is safe to conclude it has become an increasing and accelerating interest on behalf of academics, local historians, and fans of Olympic and Shakespearean trivia.[39] These overlapping sets of literature are significant in the subsequent publishing history of *Annalia Dubrensia* and related Cotswold Games writing. The confluence of British fascination with Olympic ideals therefore has a long literary tradition, linking media, sport, and festivals well before later Victorian revisions and reinventions.

Although the history of the ancient Olympic Games was as enmeshed in the economic, social and political context of its times just as much as the revised British versions which later borrowed versions of the name, in both, athleticism could be imagined both as a spiritual quest and bodily celebration of God-given abilities. The Reverend Alexander B. Grosart printed a copy of the *Annalia Dubrensia* in 1877 in his series *Occasional Issues of Unique or Very Rare Books*, printed in Manchester. This edition is now a rarity itself, having been issued in only 52 subscribers' copies, of which only six remain in the United Kingdom and Ireland.[40] Though sport was never as innocent as the ideal, Olympism became synonymous with the pursuit of personal excellence, civilized harmony, and natural simplicity and, as such, deserved to be made an exception, even during times of war or imminent conflict.[41] The symbolism of Dover's Hill as domestic Olympic arcadia became an enduring idea. As more of the population moved into urban centers during the increasingly connected world of eighteenth-century England, the village green and other free spaces for sporting and social interaction became strong ideological motifs.

While regular events of national and international importance became more frequent, the evocation of rural pastoralism in modern sport became integral to the imagined resonances with ancient, and less commercial, practices.

British Olympism from the Eighteenth Century

By the restoration of King Charles II in 1660, sports incorporated so many flourishing activities that any interest could be blamed for indolent and disorderly behavior or cultural and scientific rational behavior.[42] As restrictions on printing were lifted in England towards the end of the seventeenth century, early newspapers, though mainly concerning themselves with political and commercial intelligence, sometimes found space for sport. Derek Birley's *Social History of English Cricket* cites both advertisements for fixtures and match reports from 1700 onwards.[43] Features that have come to characterize the relationship between sport and the press were evident. Coverage helped to publicize particular disciplines and generate public interest in sporting events. Therefore, the press helped to attract spectators and interpreted the course of events for those who could not attend. Sport was also a source of advertising revenue and broadened the appeal of editorials to a wider readership. Blood sports, boxing, and other forms of violence were both ubiquitous and popular. Against this brutal and corrupting sporting influence, a neoclassical-influenced tradition promoted more rational interpretations of sport as cultivating manners, a strong body, and mind.

While highly gendered, the development of English character through sport could be applied to the domestic and public life. Eighteenth-century parenting guides advocated guided exploration, or what we might call "learning-through-play," as a vital part of good education.[44] Although it has been difficult to obtain more details as to who Kate Coventry Surtee was, the female voice is clearly evident in advising maternal pedagogical leadership. An upper class mother was "a mistress of the revels among her little people," teaching through guided play as an element of good childcare: "The sports of children, should afford exercise, either to body or mind and should contribute to their improvement, either in health or knowledge."[45]

Sport also had far less innocent etymological applications and became increasingly implicated in the blurring of the private and public sphere in Georgian England.[46] As Dennis Brailsford has shown, "Definitions of sport are never easy and seldom stable," and from 1715 sports reportage could encompass bat-fowling, bell ringing, and adultery.[47] The older word "disport" denoted a diversion from serious duties, relaxation, recreation, entertainment, and amusement. The sensual and sexual had long been implied as part of "taking ones pleasure," and prostitutes would "sport blubber," or bare a breast, to attract potential clients. The term "sporting girl" became slang for a sexually promiscuous woman; whereas a "sporting man" (as opposed to a sportsman) was also a mercenary but more inclined to gamble as a regular occupation.[48]

In terms of Olympic and arcadian motifs, the rural could be at risk of the cynicism of urban values. A popular ballad called *The Swimming Lady or a Wanton Discovery* printed in 1701 was accompanied by a woodcut in which a clothed voyeur observed a naked young woman in the river.[49] Whether we see this as evidence of the erotic fascination of the time or of swimming as a leisure activity, the motif repeatedly appeared in subsequent popular rhymes. The roles were reversed in an altogether more sinister way in John Cleland's erotic novel *Memoirs of a Woman of Pleasure* (popularly known as *Fanny Hill*) in which a 15-year-old orphan, Harriet, faints as she observes the son of the local nobility bathing on a hot day. This later allows him to take advantage of her unconscious body.[50] Given the description of the swimmer as "wantoning" with the water, the reader of *Fanny Hill* is invited to question the moral reliability of Harriet in her own undoing, and she later becomes a notable prostitute. Whereas the countryside in Walton's *The Compleat Angler* had provided solitude and reflection, this could not be relied upon by the more crowded eighteenth century. However, while "sporting women" could lack respectability, this was not necessarily the case. The Amazon, a warrior figure who liked physical challenge, was shorthand for those women who preferred the outdoor life.[51]

The excerpt in the British Library is no more than a page of lyrics for a popular song, and so it would be good to know in what context it was rehearsed and performed:

The Amazon[52]

Swains I scorn, who nice and fair, shiver at the morning air;
Rough and hardy, bold and free be the Man that's made for me;
Rough and hardy, bold and free be the Man that's made for me
Slaves to Fashion, Slaves to Dress,
Fops themselves alone caress;
Let them without Rival be,
They are not the Men for me
He whose nervous Arm can dart,
The Jav'lin to the Tiger's heart;
From all sense of Danger free,
He's the Man that's made for me.
While his speed outstrips the wind,
Loosely wave his Locks behind,
From fantastick fopp'ry free,
He's the Man that's made for me.
Nor simpring smile, nor dimpled sleek,
Spoil his manly sunburnt cheek,
By weather let him painted be,
He's the Man that's made for me.
If false he proves my Jav'lin can,
Revenge the Perjury of Man,
And soon another, brave as he,
Shall be found the Man for me.

Sport developed an increasingly moral, as well as political and commercial, economy during the eighteenth century, then.[53] Brailsford suggests that sports writing expanded outside of London to the provinces, and horse racing, like many other events, linked the upper classes with the masses.[54]

In the midst of debates about morality, long-forgotten Olympic Games came to be reimagined nostalgically in a mythical Golden Age fusing, and perhaps confusing, both classical and British elements. Born in Elson, Hampshire in 1737, Richard Chandler was educated at Winchester College before attending both Queens and Magdalen colleges Oxford.[55] Having published on classical poetry and the Arundel marbles, Chandler also wrote a series on Abyssinia serialized in the *St James's Magazine*.[56] He was commissioned by a group of 54 "noblemen and gentlemen of distinguished taste" known as the Society of Dilettanti to lead an expedition to Asia Minor and Greece to map monuments of antiquity in May 1764.[57] His companions were the established architect Nicholas Revett, already a veteran at age 43 of tours to Italy and Athens, and the much younger artist William Pars.[58] In the first publication attributed to the three men, the ruins of temples are often a backdrop for peasants who tend their goats in the foreground, and none of Pars's illustrations referenced Olympia.[59] The archaeological element of the two-year journey was much more seriously pursued than any interest in sport or recreation, although experiences of eating and leisure were often referenced. Finding the temple at Olympia was a brief disappointment, intensified by the general sense of vandalism and neglect at the site, and it was one of many things for which Richard Chandler became known. In 1772 he became a rector of the university and received his Doctorate in Divinity in 1773. After becoming a vicar near Alston in Hampshire in 1779, Chandler married and continued to travel, research, and write, often accompanied by his growing family. His later projects included collating manuscripts on his favorite poet, Pindar, and a history of Troy.[60] Nicholas Revett lived, unmarried, to 83 without excelling as an architect. He did, however, create a lasting legacy through the dissemination of classical architectural references to the eighteenth-century British cultural elite and particularly stylists of the Greek revival.[61] William Pars became a widely exhibited artist, especially of neoclassical design, before his death in 1782 at the relatively young age of 40.

Although the rediscovery of the site of Olympia was therefore underwhelming, the excursion caught the popular imagination, and many eighteenth-century rural gatherings appropriated terminology and characteristics to meet contemporary demands. As a relatively condensed way of denoting both respectability and excellence, local celebrations and urban festivals began to use variants of "Olympic" descriptors to elevate activities against other demands on people's time and purses. Equestrian displays and races often used the term, but these were often combined with other foot races, cricket matches, and celebrations such as Whitsun Ales, as recorded by Fanny Burney in her journals.[62] Subsequent editions and related talks also amplified the impact of the original tour. Published separately as *Travels in Asia Minor: or, an Account of a tour made at the expense of the Society of Dilettanti* in 1775 and *Travels in Greece or, an Account of a tour made at the expense of the Society of Dilettanti* in 1776, the books give a sense of the daily difficulties antiquarians were prepared to endure to pay pilgrimage to the sites of classical civilization.[63] Although notoriously unreliable as a historian of sport, Joseph Strutt gave tantalizing details of eighteenth-century Olympic sport, and these local histories are, therefore, a basis on which to build future research on the issue.[64] There were Cornish Games as well as Cotswold versions, for example.

Conclusion

Though mainstream eighteenth-century newspapers were slow to develop an interest in events titled Olympic contests, a specialist sporting press and literature inflected with classical themes appealed to relatively well-off enthusiasts. This was especially the case for horse racing, prizefighting, and pedestrianism. However, this influential but elitist and highbrow literature has often been overlooked by historians of sport in favor of the expanding middle-class press. The serialized monthly *Life in London*, written by Pierce Egan (1772–1849), was the most extended parable of how sporting life could lead to friendship and ruin.[65] A novelist and sports journalist, Egan was the author of four volumes of *Boxiana* between 1812 and 1829 that sought to parody the classical allusion of antiquaries and bring it to bear on everyday street life. In reprints that ran to many subsequent shilling reeditions, Egan's urbanite creation Corinthian Tom guided his country cousin Jerry through London. Their walks through the capital provided the reader with vicarious insights into dubious sporting events, exclusive clubs and high society, as French *flaneurs* would later in Paris. Tom's partner Corinthian Kate rose to live in the fashionable St James area of London and then fell to more modest lodgings, continuing the descent to street prostitution, followed by an undignified death. The narrative trigger for this downward mobility was Kate's infidelity to Tom, after which he took up with a new companion for "games." Since Kate was described up to the point of her disloyalty as a fashionably glamorous "cyprian" (a woman who sought, and embodied, pleasure), Egan moralized the behavior of those who put themselves very publicly "on the market" through his manipulation of the Corinthian ideal. Parallels with those who entertained, or competed, for money and hence literally named their price, were obvious.[66] Moral panics about gambling, commercialism, and sporting morality were, however, nothing new as this survey of literature related to Olympic themes has shown.

There was a long-standing relationship between sport and the press, and much less use has been made of other forms of writing, particularly those deemed to be "literary." Sport history in particular has been criticized for an overreliance upon newspapers as "historical sources."[67] *The Field* (1853) appealed to an upper-class and educated audience, although it was undoubtedly read aloud to a wider group of listeners. Expensive magazines, such as the *Illustrated London News* (1842) and the *Illustrated Sporting and Theatrical News* (1862), often focused less on the sporting event itself than on the spectators, or on a general view of the ground.

However, by the 1850s and 1860s, rival weekly publications priced at only a penny seem to suggest a growing cross-class market for sporting intelligence; *Sporting Life* (1859), *Sporting Telegraph* (1860), *Sporting Gazette* (1862), *Sporting Opinion* (1864), and *The Sportsman* (1865) were soon all competing for attention within a very crowded marketplace.

This focus on newspaper sources has ignored the way that literature, especially literature aimed at the elite, has been deployed to raise active leisure and physical culture above the level of mere sport into the domain of the spiritual and aesthetic. Two other things must be borne in mind in relation to the use of sources. Firstly, no Cotswold Games were held between 1851 and 1951, though a town festival took place. As the codified and increasingly regulated forms of sport gained sway, a sense of nostalgia is evident in the reporting of *The Warwick and Warwickshire Advertiser & Leamington Gazette* referring to the Cotswold Games under the subtitle "Glimpses of Olden England" in 1882:

> The sports were resorted to by large numbers of persons of either sex ... figures of all the characters referred to, handsomely represented in basso-relievo, stand in the north wall of Cirencester Church, and gives us proof positive of the antiquity of the Cotswold custom.... In 1636 a volume, now very rare, was published composed of commendatory verses ... besides the rhythmical celebrity given by the volume, the famous sports have elsewhere had a niche in our national poesy. Shakespeare whose slightest allusion to any usage gives it an undying interest in every true son and daughter of England has immortalised the old Gloucestershire custom.[68]

Secondly, Olympic revivals of several kinds grew during the period, including places of entertainment with the word in the title, specific festivals, local feasts, and a wide range of entertainments.[69] Of these, those led by William Penny Brookes were to have the most lasting influence. The Wenlock Olympian Society was to grow out of the Wenlock Agricultural Reading Society established in 1841 as an "Olympian Class" of 25 February 1850, and took on a life of its own for the "re-institution of the games of their forefathers ... to maintain that good feeling between the high and low, rich and poor, which happily for us, is the national characteristic of Old England."[70] While Penny Brookes was to be rudely treated by the Amateur Athletic Club in his attempt to hold a national London-based Olympics at the Crystal Palace in 1866, he felt able to welcome the 1894 international congress called by de Coubertin. If anything, the Wenlock tradition cemented the reputation of the Olympics as having an arcadian past that could be expressed through the green spaces of the British countryside. Posters of the International Olympic Committee versions of the games would often symbolically encircle a green space of infield that could also be read as suggestive of a village green; the 1908 London Olympics were a relatively low-budget affair and typical of this design. The 1948 London games echoed the motif, and the 1951 Festival of Britain provided an opportunity to revive Dover's Games in a form also effectively incorporating Scuttlebrook Wake. Last, but by no means least, the 2012 London

Olympic opening ceremony had a mound which at the same time represented the British Isles, Dover's Hill, and any number of revered green spaces in the land and sportscape, small and large. This article has only begun to unpick those geographical links and the history of their sporting literature.

While later archaeological excavations focused on buildings and religious sites, Chandler's pilgrimage to Asia Minor and Greece captured the popular imagination, even if it lacked tangible evidence. In some sense, as this article has illustrated, the many gaps in Olympic sporting historiography have allowed the values collected under that banner to be amorphous and shifting. Perhaps part of the attraction lies in the original gigantism of the enterprise, with its long history and large scale, enabling it to mean many things to different people. The changeability and shifting circumstances of Olympic discourse have only recently been clarified, largely due to copyright and intellectual property legislation enacted to protect commercial rights. Steve Redhead's recent study *Post-Fandom and The Millennial Blues* describes "literaturisation" as the process by which prominent and commercially aware writers attempted from 1993 onwards to rescue football's image, damaged in Britain during the 1980s by factors such as hooliganism and the Bradford, Hillsborough, and Heysel Stadium disasters.[71] Redhead's concept is a postmodern interpenetration of football and an increasingly complex popular culture by which literary treatment of soccer increases the sport's marketability to middle-class consumers. However, as this overview has suggested, the process whereby the quotidian enthusiasms of ordinary people began to have an elevated status bestowed upon them by considered literary treatment has much older precedents. Just as the lexicon of sport has been multiple and involved associations with violence, gambling, and absenteeism, Olympism was frequently the object of both censure and approval in various forms of official discourse. However, as it entered an increasing number of texts in the canon of English literature, sport also underwent a process of transformation that afforded it a range of moral, religious, and aesthetic attributes. While the more unseemly elements endure to the present day in some Olympic practices, forms of writing endowed others with the necessary cultural validation to become a symbol of personal fulfillment and, subsequently, national character.

Notes

[1] E. Norman Gardiner, *Athletics in the Ancient World* (Oxford: Oxford University Press, 1930; Devon: Dover, 2002), 76–7.

[2] "The Olympic Games in Antiquity," *The Olympic Museum*, 2nd ed. (Lausanne: IOC Museum, 2007), 2, http://www.olympic.org/Documents/Reports/EN/en_report_658.pdf.

[3] Margaret Timmers, *A Century of Olympic Posters* (London: V&A Publishing, 2012), 10.

[4] Heather Reid and Christos Evangeliou, "Ancient Hellenic Ideals and the Modern Olympic Games," in *Olympic Studies Reader: Multidisciplinary and Multicultural Research Guide Vol. 1*, ed. Hai Ren et al. (Beijing: Beijing Sport University, 2009), 237–48.

5   John J. MacAloon, *This Great Symbol: Pierre De Coubertin and the Origins of the Modern Olympic Games* (Oxon: Routledge, 2008).
6   Wolf-Dieter Heilmeyer et al, eds., *Mythos Olympia-Kult und Spiele* (Munich: Prestel-Verlag, 2012), 292–4.
7   Andreas Amendt et al, *Olympics Past and Present* (Munich, London, New York: Verlag, 2013), 64–5.
8   See, for example, H.T. Wade-Gery and C.M. Bowra, *Pindar: The Pythian Odes* (London: The Nonesuch Press, 1928); *The Odes of Pindar*, trans. and ed. Maurice Bowra (Harmondsworth: Penguin Classics, 1969).
9   Maria Prestzler, *Pausanias: Travel Writing in Ancient Greece* (London: Duckworth, 2007).
10   Arnd Kruger and John Marshall Carter, *Ritual and Record: Sports Records and Quantification in Pre-Modern Societies* (Westport, CT: Greenwood Press, 1990).
11   William Pickering, ed., *The Treatyse of Fysshynge Wyth An Angle, Attributed to Dame Juliana Berners reprinted from The Book of St Albans 1496* (London: John Baskerville, 1827). This and subsequent editions are held at the National Sporting Library in Middleburg, Virginia.
12   Julia Boffey, "Berners [Bernes, Barnes], Juliana (*fl.* 1460), supposed author and prioress of Sopwell," *Oxford Dictionary of National Biography* (Oxford: Oxford Dictionary of National Biography, 2004), accessed 9 October 2013, http://www.oxforddnb.com/index/2/101002255.
13   John Lowerson, "Fishing" in *Sport in Britain: A Social History*, Tony Mason ed. (Cambridge: Cambridge University Press, 1989), 12.
14   Derek Birley, *Sport and the Making of Britain* (Manchester: Manchester University Press, 1993), 37–8.
15   Boffey, "Berners [Bernes, Barnes], Juliana (*fl.* 1460), supposed author and prioress of Sopwell."
16   Dame Juliana Berners, *The Book of St Albans*, ed. Joseph Haslewood (New York: Abercrombie and Fitch, 1966), 5.
17   Dame Juliana Berners, *Dame Juliana Berners The Treatyse of Fysshynge Wyth An Angle, reprinted from The Book of St Albans 1496*, ed. George Van Siclen (New York: James L. Black, 1875), 41.
18   Kasia Boddy, *Boxing: A Cultural History* (London: Reaktion Books, 2008).
19   Rodoplhe L. Coigney, *Izaak Walton: A New Bibliography 1653–1987* (New York: James Cummins, 1989).
20   Izaak Walton and Charles Cotton, *The Compleat Angler Part 1 and 2*, ed. John Buchan (Oxford: Oxford University Press, 1935).
21   Robert W. Malcolmson, *Popular Recreations in English Society 1700–1850* (Cambridge: Cambridge University Press, 1979), 5–9.
22   Malcolmson, *Popular Recreations*; Birley, *Sport and the Making of Britain*, 56–61.
23   Alistair Dougal, *Charles I, The Book of Sports and Puritanism in Tudor and Early Stuart England* (Liverpool: Liverpool University Press, 2011).
24   Emma Griffin, *England's Revelry: A History of Popular Sports and Pastimes, 1660–1830* (Oxford: Oxford University Press, 2005), 26.
25   Theodore Cook, *The Field, the Farm, the Garden, the Country Gentleman's Newspaper*, Letter to Sir Sidney Lee, Windsor House, Bream's Buildings, London, 24 February 1916.

26 Jean Williams, "The Curious Mystery of the Cotswold 'Olimpick' Games: Did Shakespeare Know Dover … and Does it Matter?" *Sport in History* 29, no. 2 (2009): 150–70.

27 William Shakespeare, *King Henry VI Part 3*, eds. John D. Cox and Eric Rasmussen (London: Bloomsbury Arden Shakespeare, 2001), 246.

28 Kenneth Muir, *The Oxford Shakespeare: Troilus and Cressida* (Oxford: Oxford University Press, 1982), 154.

29 Christopher Whitfield, *A History of Chipping Camden and Captain Robert Dover's Olympick Games* (Windsor: Shakespeare Head Press, 1958).

30 Francis Burns, *Heigh for Cotswold! A history of Robert Dover's Olimpick Games. A new and revised edition* (Chipping Camden: The Robert Dover Society, 2000).

31 Bent Juel-Jensen, ed., *Matthew Walbancke Annalia Dubrensia 1636* (Yorkshire: first edition facsimile reprint, 1973), unpaginated. This is a self-published work.

32 E.R. Vyvyan, ed., *Cotswold Games: Annalia Dubrensia* (London: Tabard Press, 1970).

33 Christopher Whitfield, *A new edition of Annalia Dubrensia* (London: Sotheran, 1962).

34 Ben Jonson, "An Epigram to my Jovial Good Friend" in Christopher Whitfield, *Annalia Dubrensia*, 134; to "draw vies" is to make comparisons.

35 Whitfield, *A New Edition of Annalia Dubrensia*, 5.

36 Robert Dover, *Annalia Dubrensia: Upon the yeerly celebration of Mr Robert Dovers Olimpick Games upon Cotswold Hills* (London: Robert Raworth for Matthew Walbancke, 1636), British Library marks B.630; C.34; G.11(1).

37 Dover, *Annalia Dubrensia*, British Library mark B.630.

38 Samuel Johnson and George Steevens, *Supplement to the edition of Shakespeare's plays published in 1778, vol. 1: Supplemental observations* (London: C. Bathurst, W. Strahan et al., 1778), 90.

39 Peter Heylin, "To Mr Rob. Dover on his Pastorall and Wandering Jewe Presented before SR J.W," in *Collected Verses* (London, 1925), Addit. BL MSS.46885.

40 Rev. Alexander B. Grosart, *Occassional Issues of Unique and Very Rare Books in Seventeen Volumes*, vol. 5 (Manchester: C.E. Simms, 1877).

41 Martin Polley, *The British Olympics: Britain's Olympic Heritage 1612–2012* (London: English Heritage, 2012).

42 Neil Tranter, *Sport, Economy and Society in Britain 1750–1914* (Cambridge: Cambridge University Press, 1998), 2.

43 Derek Birley, A *Social History of English Cricket* (London: Aurum, 2003), 17.

44 Whyte Melville, Kate Coventry Surtee, and the Honourable Crasher, *The Art of Teaching in Sport: Designed as a Prelude to a Set of Toys for Enabling Ladies to Instil the Rudiments of Spelling, Reading, Grammar, and Arithmetic under the idea of Amusements* (John Marshall: London, 1770), British Library London Shelfmark 12983.b33.

45 Melville, Surtee, and the Honourable Crasher, *The Art of Teaching in Sport*, 24.

46 "Sport," *Oxford English Dictionary Online*, accessed 1 October 2013, http://www.oed.com/viewdictionaryentry/Entry/187478.

47 Dennis Brailsford, *A Taste for Diversions: Sport in Georgian England* (London: Lutterworth Press, 1999), 7.

48 "Sporting Girl or Woman," *Oxford English Dictionary Online*, accessed 1 March 2012, http://www.oed.com/view/Entry/187490.

49 Susie Parr, *The Story of Swimming* (Stockport: Dewi Lewis Media, 2011), 20.

50 John Cleland, *Memoirs of a Woman of Pleasure*, ed. Peter Sabor (Oxford: Oxford University Press, 1999; originally published in two parts in 1748 and 1749), 99.

51 Anon., *Lords and Ladies who deal in the Sport: The Pleasures of 1722* (London: Songs: 1722), unpaginated, British Library London Shelfmark 425aa7.

52   Anon., *Lords and Ladies*.
53   Williams, "The Curious Mystery of the 'Olimpick Games,'" 150–71.
54   Brailsford, *A Taste for Diversions*, 29–30.
55   Richard Chandler, *Travels in Asia Minor and Greece*, ed. Nicholas Revett (Oxford: Clarendon Press, 1825).
56   Richard Chandler, *Abyssinia Mythical and Historical ... Reprinted from St. James's Magazine, Illustrated with map of the seventeenth century* (London: C.J. Skeet, 1870).
57   Jason M. Kelly, "Society of Dilettanti (*act.* 1732–2003)," *Oxford Dictionary of National Biography*, Oxford University Press, May 2006; online ed., May 2013, accessed 31 October 2013, http://www.oxforddnb.com/view/theme/92790.
58   Richard Chandler, *Inscriptiones antiquæ, pleræque nondum editæ: in Asia Minori et Græcia, præsertim Athenis, collectæ. Cum appendice* (Oxonii: E Typographeo Clarendoniano, 1774).
59   R. Chandler, N. Revett, W. Pars, *Ionian Antiquities published, with permission of the Society of Dilettanti* (London: Society of Dilettanti, 1769).
60   W.W. Wroth, "Chandler, Richard (*bap.* 1737, *d.* 1810)," rev. R.D.E. Eagles, *Oxford Dictionary of National Biography*, Oxford University Press, 2004; online ed., May 2006, accessed 31 October 2013, http://www.oxforddnb.com/view/article/5108.
61   Anne Purchas, "Revett, Nicholas (1721–1804)," *Oxford Dictionary of National Biography*, Oxford University Press, 2004; online ed., May 2006, accessed 31 October 2013, http://www.oxforddnb.com/view/article/23395.
62   Pat Rogers, "Burney, Frances (1752–1840)," *Oxford Dictionary of National Biography*, Oxford University Press, 2004; online ed., September 2013, accessed 31 October 2013, http://www.oxforddnb.com/view/article/603.
63   Richard Chandler with Nicholas Revett, *Travels in Asia Minor: or, an Account of a tour made at the expense of the Society of Dilettanti* (Clarendon Press: Oxford, 1775) and Richard Chandler, *Travels in Greece: or, an Account of a tour made at the expense of the Society of Dilettanti* (Dublin: Price, 1776).
64   Joseph Strutt, *The sports and pastimes of the people of England; including the rural and domestic recreations, may games, mummeries, shows, processions, pageants and pompous spectacles from the earliest period to the present time* (London: Tegg, 1810); William Hone, *The sports and pastimes of the people of England; including the rural and domestic recreations, may games, mummeries, shows, processions, pageants and pompous spectacles from the earliest period to the present time*, ed. Joseph Strutt (London: Tegg, 1845).
65   Pierce Egan, *Tom & Jerry: Life in London, or, The Day and Night Scenes of Jerry Hawthorn, esq. and His Elegant Friend Corinthian Tom, in Their Rambles and Sprees through the Metropolis* (London: 1821).
66   Jane Rendell, *The Pursuit of Pleasure: Gender, Space, and Architecture in Regency London* (London: Continuum, 2002), 138–9.
67   Douglas Booth, *The Field: Truth and Fiction in Sports History* (Abingdon, Oxford: Routledge, 2005), 88–94.
68   T. Broadbent Trowsdale, "Glimpses of olden England," in *The Warwick and Warwickshire Advertiser & Leamington Gazette*, 29 July 1882, 3.
69   Polley, *The British Olympics*, 18–20.
70   Dr. William Penny Brookes, *The Salopian Journal*, 19 September 1852, 5.
71   Steve Redhead, *Post-Fandom and the Millennial Blues: The Transformation of Soccer Culture* (London: Routledge, 1997), 88–92.

Chapter 3
Sporting with Clothes: John Collet's Prints in the 1770s[1]

Patricia Crown

In the 1770s, John Collet (1725–1780),[2] often called "the second Hogarth," produced a number of mildly humorous paintings and prints of fashionably dressed women, but of indeterminate class, engaged in active sports of the kind usually thought to be properly masculine enthusiasms. Collet and other artists of the period made prints of women driving, riding, and shooting, but only Collet showed them also at skittles, cricket, ice-skating, rowing, and hunting. That he should be the only artist to devote so many prints to women and sport is worth trying to explain beyond their erotic connotations. In some of his images, women wear adaptations of male dress, symbolizing and facilitating their appropriation of masculine gender roles; in others, women in ordinary female garb engage in male activities. Collet's pictures suggest that in the politically and socially turbulent late 1760s and 1770s some English women and men experimented with conventions of dress and behavior—especially in sport—and explored the boundaries of social and moral arbitration concerned with keeping the sexes distinct.

In the later part of the century, sport was a large, loose category. It encompassed not only outdoor, primarily rural activities such as hunting, shooting, riding, walking, skating, and boating, but also gambling, brawling, pilfering, drinking—and amorous pursuit. The subtitle of *The Sporting Magazine* cast a wide net in defining sport as "Every Diversion Interesting to the Man of Pleasure and Enterprize and Spirit," and hunting women and hunting game were often equated, as by one of the magazine's correspondents: "It is not the quadruped and winged fowl that are my objects ... I dare to pursue the most exalted animal of the chase—woman is my mark!"[3] The sex chase did not require a literal hunt, however, and especially in the more feminized interior space, the male was not necessarily the hunter but the hunted. Although in *The Rival Milleners* [sic] (1772) a military gentleman hopes to snare one or both of the shop women—who were regarded as fair game in the amorous hunt—they set the hunt in motion, as the title suggests, and have circled back in pursuit of him. Below one of the boxes of goods for sale, appropriately labelled "Love," all three smile complicitly as the length and circumference of his metonymic parts are measured (Figure 3.1).

The roles played by both genders and both classes in *The Rival Milleners* are cultural stereotypes, but Collet's images often deal with an overlapping or reversal of stereotyped roles. A number of his prints show women playing masculine parts: in *The Discovery* (1774), a rich fat woman makes overt sexual advances

Figure 3.1   Robert Laurie after John Collet. *The Rival Milliners* (1772). Mezzotint. Courtesy, Colonial Williamsburg Foundation.

to a shy footman; in *The Refusal* (1767), a woman openly offers herself to a normally receptive taker—a military man—but is turned down; in *The Female Orators* (1768), two market women debate noisily and with aggressive gestures; in *Troops Fording a Brook* (1772), a slight, timid officer is carried across a stream by a strong rural woman; and in an untitled winter scene (1770), three women throw snowballs at a youth. In other of Collet's prints, women assume the character of the sporting man, that is of the thrill seeker as well as the pleasure seeker. In the *Shop-Lifter Detected* (1778), the woman has hidden expensive laces and ribbons under her clothes (Figure 3.2). As the trifles are being removed by men who search under her petticoat and down her corsage, the exchange of smiles and glances prompts us to regard her pilfering as initiating a game of skill, in which chances are taken and sometimes lost, with no very heavy punishment for losing. In fact, the statue of Mercury—god of thieves, businessmen, and artists—seems to protect Collet's pretty thief. In contrast to this situation, Defoe's Moll Flanders was deported for stealing ribbons and silk damask, as were many real-life thieves.

That a woman might outdo a man at a sport is shown in *The Female Fox Hunter* (ca. 1780) (Figure 3.3). Here a woman vigorously urges her horse to jump a five-barred gate, as a man who has failed the jump falls from his mount; and the subtitle of a painting similar to this—*The Joys of the Chase, or The Rising Woman and Falling Man*, which was exhibited at the Free Society in 1780—also indicates a spirit of competition between the sexes.[4] In both works, the female hunter in the

Sporting with Clothes: John Collet's Prints in the 1770s 57

Figure 3.2   John Collet, after. *Shop-Lifter Detected* (1778). Mezzotint. Courtesy, The Lewis Walpole Library, Yale University.

foreground wears a version of riding habit (in the painting, a red, cuffed jacket and matching skirt, a waistcoat with a stock or cravat, and a man's hat) that was an adaptation of male attire.

Late in the century, this costume became standard informal wear for such outdoor activities as riding, walking, and traveling: the Duchess of Devonshire wore it when strolling in Vauxhall Gardens and occasionally while campaigning for Charles James Fox in 1784. It had become established earlier in the century even for dancing, at least in rural towns, as seen in Hogarth's *Country Dance* (1745, Tate Gallery), and for fishing, as seen in Edward Haytley's *The Brockman*

Figure 3.3 John Collet, after. *The Female Fox Hunter* (ca. 1780). Mezzotint. Courtesy, The Lewis Walpole Library, Yale University.

Sporting with Clothes: John Collet's Prints in the 1770s 59

Figure 3.4   Joshua Reynolds. *Lady Worsley* (ca. 1776). Oil on canvas (Harewood House, Yorkshire). Courtesy, Lord Harewood. Photo: courtesy, Bridgeman Art Library.

Family (1744, National Gallery of Victoria, Melbourne). By the late 1770s, some riding habits had taken on a military air, partly because the large military encampments in Kent and Sussex attracted sightseers. The wives of commanding officers—for instance, the Duchesses of Grafton, Gordon, and Devonshire—had habits made in the colors of their husbands' regiments, and with their distinguishing accoutrements. Sir Joshua Reynolds's portrait of Lady Worsley (ca. 1776, Harewood House) shows her in such an adaptation, with red jacket, gold lace epaulets, buttoned cuffs, black revers, and ostrich-feather-crowned hat (Figure 3.4). Although the hat might be taken to be a bit of extravagant feminine garnishment, it is a copy of an officer's hat, such as that worn by Colonel Tarleton in Reynolds's 1782 portrait (National Gallery, London).

The adapted riding habit permitted women to assume the poses and gestures of men, to swagger, stride, swing the arms, and put hands on hips. These mannerisms were much criticized, for instance by Samuel Richardson, who wrote a public letter against a young lady's "affecting manly airs, also censuring modern riding habits."[5] To wear these clothes was to suggest that women might be as fond of sport as men were, fond of exciting, even dangerous, pleasures and of strenuous exertion. When women assumed masculine riding habit, however, they feminized it: Lady Worsley, and other women, wore dainty-heeled, ribboned, pointed-toed shoes, which were in piquant contrast to the masculine elements of the rest of their attire. The adapted habit did anything but suppress women's sexuality. In fact, it drew attention to the breasts and hips, which were prominently defined, even emphasized. To complicate matters, cross-gender behavior may accompany cross-gender sartorial borrowings:[6] Lady Worsley, for example, was fond of sport and risk, as was proved in the legal proceedings brought by her husband against one of her many lovers.

In the last decades of the century, driving carriages was a favorite sport of courtesans and other women given to flamboyance and brazen display. Impossible to ignore, it provoked attention and admiration. M. Dorothy George discusses caricatures of courtesans and other women riding and driving and quotes the prologue to Colman's *The Suicide*: "A female Phaeton all danger scorns, / Half coat, half petticoat, she mounts the box."[7] Earlier, in *An Officer in the Light Infantry driven by his Lady to Cox Heath* (1778) a bold woman appropriates the role of the man whose torpor has left it vacant (Figure 3.5). Collet has copied two women among the surprised onlookers from the first plate of Hogarth's *A Harlot's Progress*. The driver wears the colors, epaulets, waistcoat and revers of military uniform.

Many other instances of the convergence of appropriated physical self-presentation and role-playing may be cited. For example, the skittle players in *Miss Tipapin Going for All Nine* (ca. 1779) bend, crouch, and bowl uninhibited by traditional petticoats, tight bodices, lace kerchiefs, bows, and ribbons (Figure 3.6). Nor are their activities restricted by the stays worn by all classes under close-fitting bodices. Dress historians have tested the comfort and flexibility of eighteenth-century stays and have found that, if well made, they provided not only support but a sense of well-being. Colleen Gau reports that women who wore stays felt both comfortable and flexible wearing stays while weeding, picking, and canning tomatoes, cooking over an open fire, churning butter, and carrying buckets of slop for pigs.[8] In addition, it has been convincingly argued by David Kunzle and Anne Hollander that body molding was a form of sexual assertion that could confer inner and outer power. It was patriarchal males who complained most forcefully about stays, exposed breasts, face painting, and elaborate hairstyles, not the women who wore them, or the needleworkers who made and displayed the fashions.[9] Miss Tipapin and her companions, however, are more vehement than

Sporting with Clothes: John Collet's Prints in the 1770s   61

Figure 3.5   John Collet, after. *An Officer in the Light Infantry driven by his Lady to Cox Heath* (ca. 1770). Mezzotint. Courtesy, The Lewis Walpole Library, Yale University.

Figure 3.6　John Collet, after. *Miss Tipapin Going for All Nine* (ca. 1778). Mezzotint. Courtesy, Yale Center for British Art, Paul Mellon Fund.

normal and, as the title of the print tells us, are ungenteely determined to bowl the modern equivalent of a strike. Reinforcing the masculinity of their movements and goal, the women share a bowl of punch and crudely blow froth off their ale. And they have been smoking, as can be seen from the broken pipe in the foreground.

Cricket provided another opportunity for Collet's expression of mixed-gender behavior and clothing that allowed it. At least since the 1740s, women of all classes played cricket, and in clothing that freed them to do so well. A newspaper account of 1745 declared that young women dressed in white jackets, skirts, and *bergère* hats "bowled, batted, ran and caught as well as any men could do," and the account made no complaint that either the garb or the exertion was unfeminine.[10] At some point, however, cricket playing by women acquired unsavory associations, at least in some circles, so that Lady Sarah Bunbury's playing exacerbated her already notorious reputation for such things as eating beefsteaks "on the Steyne

Figure 3.7   John Collet, after. *Miss Wicket and Miss Trigger* (1778). Mezzotint. Courtesy, The Lewis Walpole Library, Yale University.

at Brighton" and, like Lady Worsley, committing adultery. Widespread must have been the opinion expressed by Hester Thrale that she was far less delicate and ethereal than when sacrificing to the graces in pseudoantique raiment in Reynolds's portrait of her (1762, Art Institute of Chicago).[11] In Collet's *Miss Wicket and Miss Trigger* (ca. 1779) the transgressive behavior of female cricketing is taken much further (Figure 3.7). Miss Wicket stands cross-legged and leans on her bat, a pose often seen in portraits of men but improper for a woman. Powder horn hanging from her shoulder, Miss Trigger wears a "shooter" (a long coat with deep pockets and buttoned cuffs) and laced boots, steps on a piece of paper inscribed "Effeminacy," and displays her gaming trophies—two partridges and a pheasant. Whether she only flaunts them or is offering them to Miss Wicket raises an issue of interpretation. As evidence that this is an image of a lesbian relationship, Stephen

Deuchar reproduces a drawing by Marcellus Laroon of a sportsman offering a pheasant to an attractive woman, where the intent is clearly amorous, and presents other instances in literature and art of the connection between sport and sexual conquest.[12] In many images, however, the male hunter-provider's proffering spoils of the chase to the female cannot bear such a meaning—in Arthur Devis's family portrait of *John, Anne and William Orde* (1755), for example, in which the son offers his mother the wild fowl he has shot. The appropriation of male clothing, bodily deportment, and sporting role in Collet's print is conspicuous, however, and suggests a relationship between the misses that confuses gender roles.

Although such a reading of *Miss Wicket and Miss Trigger* cannot be eliminated, Collet's attitude towards them is not readily identifiable. In fact, here and in most of his prints and paintings, he reveals little or no moral judgment. There were exceptions, most notably in the narrative series of four paintings called *Modern Love* (*Courtship, Elopement, Honeymoon, Discordant Matrimony*, exhibited as a group called "A Love Match" at the Free Society in 1763) (Figures 3.8–3.11). The theme of this group is similar to Hogarth's *Marriage-a-la-Mode*, and Collet employed many of Hogarth's visual and narrative devices, such as labels and captions, incongruous juxtapositions and contrast of types.

Collet's story, however, reverses the terms of Hogarth's narrative. Where Hogarth's couple are indifferent to each other and are forced into marriage by their parents, Collet's couple marry for love against their elders' wishes. Both marriages end badly: *Marriage-a-la-Mode* in disaster and death; *Modern Love*, less dramatically, in dissatisfaction and disillusion. Edward Edwards was the first to comment on a relative lack of moral purpose in Collet's humor, a judgment repeated by, among others, Richard Redgrave in *A Dictionary of Artists of the English School* ...,[13] who goes on to say that Collet was "a shy man, of grave habits and conversation, yet his pictures were sometimes displeasingly vulgar. His *Female Bruisers* is one of this class."

Collet presents his characters and situations with the relaxed jocularity of a man of the world, partly, perhaps, because he was of higher social class than Hogarth.[14] He was a "gentleman" with an independent income, about whom a pleasant comment was made by the author of the art column, "Junius on the Arts"[15]: "He was a man of genius, generosity and benevolence. He possessed an estate that made him independent of the world, and his tenants, knowing his disposition, often kept from paying much of their rents." Appropriate to his gentlemanly status, he was occasionally referred to as an amateur, as in this passage by G. Steevens:

> My ingenious friend, the late J. Collet, Esq ..., whose Pictures abounded with true, though what may be deemed broad humour, died at Chelsea, about twenty years since. He was a man of learning, of considerable fortune, and of the most amiable manners and benevolent turn of mind. He was, like his friend Dawes, who was also independent, languid in the pursuit of his art; and though he painted many Pictures, ... from which there are prints by Goldar, he is perhaps better known by *The Taylor Riding to Brentford* [1768] than any other of his works.[16]

The reference to William Dawes is the only indication of a friendship with a fellow artist. Dawes, like Collet, was an assistant of George Lambert, Hogarth's friend and sometime collaborator. Dawes exhibited at the Free Society 1764–1774. Sauer notes that his work is sometimes ascribed to Collet. Dawes produced humorous prints very like Collet's in subject and style, such as *The Hen Peckt Husband* (1768), published by Robert Sayer. Joseph Strutt's *Biographical Dictionary [of] Engravers* ... (London, 1785) seems to be the origin of the notion that Collet etched or engraved his own works. Strutt claims to have got his information from "Mr. Grosse" (Francis Grose, the amateur artist and writer on caricature). No example of any work engraved by Collet appears to exist.

A greater weight of evidence suggests that Collet actively sought to get his works published, exhibited, and collected. He did considerable early work as a landscape artist.[17] In the *William Nelson Letter Book, 1766–1775*, Nelson, who spent some time in England when a youth, refers to his "very old Friend & Acqaintance Mr Collet" and says that he has "a piece of Landscape of his son's work, that is much admired. I hear he hath fallen into old Hogarths Tract, & not without success; & that he hath lately entertaind the publick with a new piece. I forget the Title, but something like, the *Lamentations of Liberty* pray send it me & if necessary an Explanation of the Design of the piece."[18] This was written in 1770. The next year Nelson ordered two of Collet's landscapes: "As I think Mr. Collett shines most in Landscape painting (tho there was great Humour & Merit in the Prints you sent Me) I shall be glad if you will send me something of that Kind from him."[19] He had a grave and reserved manner in public, which was particularly commented upon because it contrasted with the often buffoonish, often bawdy, subjects of his prints. He had three residences: in Holburn, Chelsea, and Covent Garden. The first two belonged to his father until his death in 1771. The last was probably his studio and professional address in the 1760s; and it was there that he was in the center of London's artistic activity, sexual commerce, and luxury trade. Collet(t) was a Huguenot name, and many Collets who were artists or skilled artisans in France are listed in U. Thieme and E. Becker, *Allgemeines Lexikon der bildenden Künstler von der Antike bis zur Gegenwart* (Leipzig, 1907–1950). In the eighteenth century, Huguenots settled in Covent Garden and Chelsea, where Collet and his father lived and owned property. Collet exhibited a *View of Calais; taken from the side of the canal leading from thence to St. Omer's* in 1775; the topographical precision of the title indicates that he had actually worked on the site, implying at least one visit to France. Collet's several addresses suggest free movement among the diverse worlds of polite society, skilled artisans, city merchants, and demireps and help account for his observations of several social classes and diverse kinds of relations between the sexes.

Collet was by no means an obscure artist. Both his prints and paintings were well known. *The Female Bruisers*; *An Actress in her Dressing Room, or Miss Brazen Just Breecht*; *The Joys of the Chase*; and *An Officer in the Light Infantry Driven by his Lady*—all paintings—were exhibited to large and motley crowds at the Free Society of Artists; exhibition reviews in the May 1767

Figure 3.8 (*top*)   John Collet. *Modern Love: Courtship* (1763). Oil on canvas.
Figure 3.9 (*bottom*)   John Collet. *Modern Love: Elopement* (1763). Oil on canvas. Courtesy, Colonial Williamsburg Foundation.

Sporting with Clothes: John Collet's Prints in the 1770s 67

Figure 3.10 (*top*)   John Collet. *Modern Love: Honeymoon* (1763). Oil on canvas.
Figure 3.11 (*bottom*)   John Collet. *Modern Love: Discordant Matrimony* (1763). Oil on canvas. Courtesy, Colonial Williamsburg Foundation.

Gentleman's Magazine and the May 1775 *Public Advertiser* deemed him a worthy successor to Hogarth; and his publishers Robert Sayer and Carington Bowles were among the most prominent print sellers of the period. Sayer and John Smith together published a drawing book of *Designs by Jn. Collett, both Serious and Comic, Engraved on 36 Plates by Rooker, Grignion, Mason, Canot, Goldar, Byrne, Taylor, Pranker, Smith, &c, &c Intended for the Use of Artists as well as Gentlemen & Laydies* (1770). Sayer used six of Collet's works in 1777 in *The Draughtsman's Assistant; or, Drawing Made Easy ... Instructive Lessons.... Neatly Engraved on Seventy-Two Copper Plates*. The images, of men and women shown elegantly dressed indoors and out, in the country and in the city, are fashion plates and patterns of deportment. His paintings were collected by Thomas Bradford, one of the first art speculators, who bought contemporary paintings "with an eye to the wide audience needed for a profitable line-engraving."[20] In 1765 Collet and the engraver John Goldar, along with Thomas Bradford, advertised a subscription for a set of prints after the four paintings called *Modern Love*, then on exhibition at the Free Society.[21]

Collet's freedom of social movement across classes, occupations, and attitudes may help explain his tolerance and, at times, consequent ambivalence. What is difficult to measure is the degree to which his tolerance was shared by the viewers of his prints. Little is known about the nature and constituents of the market for this kind of print.[22] The print market usually has been assumed to have been mostly male, but women were certainly part of it; in fact, by investigating household inventories, Lorna Weatherill has concluded that women owned more prints—of all subjects—than did men.[23] Interesting and unusual visual evidence of this is provided by a print of 1772 titled *The Female Connoiseur* [sic] showing a well-dressed middle-aged woman holding a caricature print. Other anecdotal evidence is abundant: for example, William Bewick's aunt had a collection of prints that included landscapes and sheets from Boydell's Shakespeare Gallery, as well as risqué caricatures.[24] Although it was considered somewhat indecorous for women to be interested in political and social satire, which were often subversive of authority and disrespectful of religion, rank, and patriarchy, women not only collected such images but invented them. In their shop, Matthew and Mary Darly, for instance, held an exhibition of drawings, "106 by Gentlemen, 74 by Ladies, 27 by Artists, 26 unspecified."[25] Among the ladies, the Countess of Burlington, Lady Diana Beauclerk, and Anne Damer—all ladies of high rank—produced caricatures. In the *Public Advertiser* for 14 May 1774, the Darlys announced another exhibit of comic art: "This droll and amusing Collection is the Production of several Ladies and Gentlemen Artists.... N.B. By the kind assistance of the Ladies, there are near 200 new Subjects added to the Collection this year."[26] In addition, many women operated as print sellers in London and provincial capitals, the most successful and wealthy even owning large printing and bookselling businesses.[27] Women as collectors, artists, and dealers were an important part of Collet's public. Doubtless part of the pleasure of seeing and buying prints and paintings of this kind was knowing what clues to look for, and how to connect them; ambiguity may, in fact, have been a source of pleasure in itself, as Hogarth had intimated: "Wherein would consist the joys of hunting, shooting, fishing ... without the frequent turns and difficulties and disappointments, that are daily met with in the pursuit? ... How lively, and in spirits [the sportsman is], even when an old cunning [prey] has baffled, and out-run the dogs!"[28]

In the *St. James's Chronicle* for 14–17 May 1768, an exchange of letters, hitherto unnoticed, discusses and debates the topics, talents, and meanings of some of Collet's paintings, and they also demonstrate an ambivalent, bifocal reaction to them. Though not discussing Collet's sporting art, the letters are implicitly relevant to it. They also provide some idea of the range of reactions to humorous art in general, and in discussing the social issues raised by popular art they use tones varyingly sincere and cynical. The first letter (which begins by complimenting Collet as "in Humour, a second Hogarth with much better colouring") objects to *The Canonical Beau, or Mars in the Dumps*, a painting then on exhibit at the Free Society (Figure 3.12):

> [A] handsome smart Divine in his Canonicals sitting in a Bawdy House surrounded by Bawds and Whores.... At the other end of the room sits a disconsolate rejected Officer, with a wooden Leg, eyeing his happy Rival.... On the Table lies a Book, open, the Title of which is, The Church Triumphant, *Cedunt arma Togae*. A Picture over it represents a Martyr burning at the Stake. Allowing the Wit and Humour of all, will not every one, however, immediately discover by this Description a manifest Impropriety (not to say Indecency) in this Piece?[29]

Collet replied in the 19–21 May issue:

> The Canonical Beau is supposed to be in an Apartment in a private House, where the Lady of the Family is regaling a Clergyman, and other Visitors, with Chocolate, after the fatigue of the Morning's Devotion, and I am assured by my gay Friends, that the Nature of the Refreshment, the Dress, and the Manner of the Company, and every Circumstance in the Picture are too remote from what are met with in Bagnios and Brothels to excite the most distant Idea of Indecency in any Person at all acquainted with those Scenes of Riot and Debauchery ... [and] the intention of this little Piece is, gently to reprove those trim Divines who (in this luxurious and dissipated Age) too often trip into the Pulpit in a Manner and Dress apparently better calculated to attract the Regards of the Fair, than to inspire that Reverence, which the Dignity and the Importance of their sacred Office require.[30]

A few months later another writer agreed with the first: the "ingenious artist, our second Hogarth" exposes the church and its ministers to contempt in several of his works—*The Country Vicar going to Dine with the Squire* (1768), where "a rural Divine is made to seem ridiculous by his mean Appearance and bad Horsemanship," and *The Quiet Husband* (1768), which depicts a dozing clergyman whose wife is gladly receiving the advances of a gallant. "Let the Reader now judge whether

Figure 3.12 J. Goldar after John Collet. *The Canonical Beau, or Mars in the Dumps* (1768). Courtesy, The Lewis Walpole Library, Yale University.

such Representations deserve not Censure, as tending to destroy that Esteem and Regard which are due to all Professions, especially the clerical.... If the canonical Beau is also a Libertine, if the quiet Husband is also a contented Cuckold, common Practice cannot warrant such Representation, and therefore it must be condemned."[31] These may possibly be letters planted by Collet, his publishers, or friends to excite interest: the critics' tone of mild indignation (which could be construed as enticing an audience), combined with praise for the artist's skill and Collet's protestations of innocence, suggest fabrication. Whatever their origins and aims, the letters imply interpretative ambivalence.

One historical context that complicates interpretation of some of Collet's pictures—those of shooting—is the game laws, which restricted the right to shoot to a very few. For instance, only those who owned a substantial amount of property could legally shoot and hunt, and even with their permission it was illegal to shoot on someone else's property.[32] Not surprisingly, such restrictions were often ignored, yet Collet's shooting sportswomen must have been seen as defying some severe prohibitions, or—though it is improbable—they were taken to represent women landowners of substantial property. The game laws excited much argument, many perceiving them as a threat to English liberty, and Blackstone's *Commentaries on the Laws of England*, often quoted, asserted that "by the law of nature every man from the prince to the peasant has an equal right to take game."[33] Blackstone may or may not have intended to include women in the term "man," but in Collet's images women assert the right to hunt, though they may not be authorized to do so by either natural or civil law. One is reminded of Wilkes's exaltation of English liberty, which endowed even women with love of liberty, vigor, and high spirits. In Collet's works, they seem to demonstrate such traits by hunting, shooting, and riding, as well as by playing cricket, that peculiarly English form of recreation.

However masculine their behavior, none of the sporting women in Collet wears breeches. Sightings of women wearing breeches were reported occasionally in journals; however, the reports have an air of facetiousness or wishful thinking, as if concocted for the sake of titillation or shock. Even at masquerades when women were described as wearing male costume, this usually meant short skirts and exposed legs; for example, the "Diana costume" was called masculine because the short hunting tunic revealed the wearer's legs, not because the goddess was supposed to wear pants. When the *Town and Country Magazine* for May 1772 reported that at masquerades "many of the ladies of rank and beauty chose to adapt the male dress in domino,"[34] the meaning is that women wore a long voluminous cloak (domino) along with male accessories such as wig, cravat, and hat; even if breeches were worn, they would not have been seen. (Men, however, often wore full female dress with skirts to masquerades.) Terry Castle interprets references to women dressed in "men's clothes" at masquerades as women wearing breeches or complete masculine dress.[35] I think this may be a misunderstanding or overstatement of the actual practice. Cross-dressers who wished to be taken for males did, of course, wear breeches and boots in ordinary life. Angelica Kauffman painted portraits of women in Turkish costume wearing the very full ankle-length Turkish trousers.[36]

An example of what seems to me a fabricated description of women in male dress is in "Remarks on the Rage of the Ladies for the Military Dress" in which the anonymous writer speaks of women in riding habits, large hats, and tied-back hair, and of one of them "pulling her watch out of (I believe) a pair of tight leathern breeches."[37] The writer seems uncertain whence comes the watch. The woman may be wearing breeches under her skirt in accordance with Continental custom and English practice until the twentieth century. He next begins to discuss the sexually provocative quality of details of military dress worn by women, as does a writer in the June issue of the same magazine, who pretends to be morally disapproving of ladies in riding dress, while hinting that the "assurance, boldness, effrontery" that went with the dress might very well excite and captivate youthful males.[38] Compare "What the Fair Sex are, and what they will be,"[39] in which the writer predicts that women will soon throw away their caps and tippets, that petticoats already at the ankle will soon be midcalf, and declares that the freedom of women's fashions advertises their undisguised lasciviousness and causes the recent increase in divorce. A case of exaggeration and possibly willful misunderstanding is the representation of the costume worn by Elizabeth Chudleigh, maid of honor to the Princess of Wales, at a masquerade in 1749. As contemporary illustrations show, she was dressed as Iphigenia in a short opaque skirt and stays, her breasts barely veiled with some transparent fabric. Horace Walpole and Elizabeth Montagu, referring to her breasts and lower legs, say that she was "so naked." The result of such exaggerated verbal descriptions was a fanciful picture of 1788 showing her actually naked except for a narrow girdle of leaves and a transparent skirt.[40]

Before 1790 or so, only actresses and cross-dressers were reliably recorded to have worn breeches—for instance, the actress about to play the role of Macheath in *The Beggar's Opera* in *An Actress at her Toilet, or Miss Brazen just Breecht* (1779), a print that alludes to a contemporary production that had starred Mrs. Farrell as Macheath but has ramifications beyond the topical (Figure 3.13). A partially obscured playbill promises, "to be seen, a most surprising Hermaphrodite," and two pets identify the actress as a prostitute. "Squirrel" was eighteenth-century slang for prostitute, which explains why that animal sits on the dressing table. Because in allegories of the five senses the sharp-beaked bird, such as the parrot, was the emblem of Touch, it appeared often in seventeenth- and eighteenth-century images of prostitutes, and here perches on the edge of a wash basin.

Collet's career began and matured during the period of Wilkite agitation and its immediate aftermath, a period when calls for liberty, in its many manifestations, were everywhere. Nothing is directly known of Collet's political sympathies, but they were probably at least Wilkes-ish if not Wilkite. Robert Sayer, a major publisher of Collet's work, was a Wilkes supporter,[41] and Collet's few political prints favor the causes of liberty. *The City Chanters* (1771), in fact, is clearly pro-Wilkes. In the center of several aggressive female ballad-sellers, a buxom, smiling woman holds up a ballad titled "An irregular Ode to Wilkes and Liberty," and on her bodice is a tag inscribed "Squire Wilkes again and again." These references to Wilkes's politics also mark his popularity with women and his notorious libertinage. Wilkes always claimed, using himself and his lovers as an example, that his predatory sexuality honored women's charms, that women enjoyed the pleasures of the flesh as much as men did, and that women loved rakes.[42] In 1766 Collet exhibited a painting, now lost but probably irreverent and bawdy, titled *Essay on Women*, an allusion to the obscene poem attributed to Wilkes. The Collet that can be deduced from his prints was something of a libertine according to James G. Turner's "maximalist" definition: "a broad movement of sensibility, evolving towards cultured hedonism and incorporating the ideas of rakish vitality, psychological honesty, and a fair-minded assumption of combative equality between the sexes."[43] Combative equality is represented in most of Collet's pictures of sport, equality of hedonistic pursuits in nearly all of them. Once again, circumstantial evidence suggests that Collet possessed what we would call a "liberal" attitude towards various behavioral phenomena that transgressed both class and gender boundaries.

Sporting with Clothes: John Collet's Prints in the 1770s 73

Figure 3.13 John Collet, after. *An Actress at her Toilet, or Miss Brazen just Breecht* (1779). Mezzotint. Courtesy, The Lewis Walpole Library, Yale University.

Perhaps it is predictable, therefore, that the women Collet tends to depict correspond to descriptions of the social mutations of numerous working women around Covent Garden at that time. Like the artist himself they were not firmly placed within a distinct class or occupation and might move between being seamstress, actress, occasional prostitute, full-time mistress, business partner, or a combination of these. Women like these might be seen riding to hounds and shooting, with all that implied of property and privilege, but a few months earlier or later, their sports might be ice-skating and skittles, common diversions of the middling and lower classes. It became, in this period, difficult to determine rank by the traditional clues of clothing, and prostitutes were notorious for dressing above their station to attract clients. Whereas female shooters, hunters, and riders were specially dressed for their activities, in *The Female Bruisers* (1770) Collet depicts London prostitutes (who, incidentally, are embroiled in the men's sport of fisticuffs in order to see who wins the young rustic client) dressed in what would have been common street wear for a superior class of woman (Figure 3.14). The one who seems about to win is alluringly well dressed in fur muff, fur cloak, watch, and ribboned hat. Similarly, the women in *The Guards of the Night Defeated* (1774)[44] wear flounces, laces, aprons, and ever-astounding headdresses

Figure 3.14   John Collett, after. *The Female Bruisers* (1770). Mezzotint. Courtesy, The Lewis Walpole Library, Yale University.

while pummeling the confounded night watchmen in order to protect their evening pleasures and profits.

In Collet's time it was difficult to determine rank by the traditional clues of clothing. Frequently, the upper classes adopted the dress of the lower classes—rustics, courtesans, and coachmen. Verses appended to a typical Collet print of women wearing high ostrich-feather headdresses explains that the women are servants who have appropriated their mistress's finery. In a more easily legitimized variation of this trope of sartorial and social disruption, milliners (designer-seamstresses, later called dressmakers) had to be elegantly dressed to advertise their skill (as in *The Rival Milliners*, Figure 3.1 above), and outside a shop they could easily be taken for the fine ladies who were their clients. As needleworkers became successful, independent women, they generated speculation and complicated, ambivalent responses.[45] Anxious commentators saw them as having a disturbing amount of liberty to fashion themselves, as well as their superiors, and the 1770s produced many visual and verbal images of female clothiers and the innovative, specialized, and sometimes provocative fashions—sportswear, for instance—that they created, sold, and wore.

The most threatening kind of clothing for a woman to wear, of course, was breeches. As mentioned above, they were not worn in public except in very special circumstances, but Collet provides evidence that breeches might be worn in private for erotic sport. *A Morning Frolic, or the Transmutation of Sexes* (1780) shows the sexual game of exchanging articles of clothing, here played by a dominating woman and an effeminized man (Figure 3.15). In the background is a bed decorated with cupids and billing doves. The red great-coat is thrown over a screen; the woman's stays are lying on a chair. On the floor is a copy of *Ovid's Metamorphoses done into English*. Her legs apart, her arms akimbo, she wears the man's hat and sword. He is in uniform, yet he sits with his legs modestly together, his hands are folded, his glance and smile are demure, and he wears a woman's cap and holds a fan. The warrior is the submissive object of her commanding gaze in a mutually pleasing fantasy. None of Collet's prints suggests any condemnation of women's sports or sporting with clothes whether in the field or in the bedroom. Richard Newton's *Wearing the Breeches* (1794) (Figure 3.16), printed 14 years after *The Transmutation of Sexes*, implies something different. The male is not taking part in a mutually enjoyed game; the woman's usurpation is resented. The breeches are symbolic of power, and the woman wears them as a sign that she has won a battle. This is confirmed by Newton's companion print, *The Battle for the Breeches* (1794), which shows the struggle before the woman's triumph. What had been a frolic in 1780 was a threat in 1794; the indulgent, libertine attitudes of the 1760s and 1770s, of which Collet was a particularly involved recorder, had begun to seem dangerous in the 1780s, when even John Wilkes turned conservative, and after 1789 were coupled with political fears excited by the French Revolution. As Linda Colley observes,

Figure 3.15 John Collet, after. *A Morning Frolic, or the Transmutation of Sexes* (1780). Mezzotint. Courtesy, The Lewis Walpole Library, Yale University.

Figure 3.16   Richard Newton. *Wearing the Breeches* (1794). Etching. Courtesy, the Whitworth, The University of Manchester.

> Anxiety about women wearing pseudo-masculine dress was particularly prominent … and seems in retrospect absurdly overdone.… As the dozens of satirical prints devoted to this topic make clear, the changing silhouette of some women was interpreted as a further demonstration that the world was shifting dangerously.[46]

The Universal Spectator in 1728 proclaimed a notion repeated at many times and in many places: "In every Country Decency requires that the Sexes should be differenc'd by Dress, in order to prevent Multitudes of Irregularities which otherwise would be continually occasion'd."[47] Proper clothing regulated for certain places and activities was regarded as an important manifestation of social and sexual order. There was much that was excitingly transgressive about sport for both men and women in the 1770s, including the clothes that defined or enhanced various sports. If sporting women aroused moral disapprobation in some, they excited libidinous appreciation in others. Collet's pictures suggest that for a while, certain groups—déclassé gentlemen, artists, marginal or aristocratic women—could experiment, be adventurous, and explore the boundaries of that moral arbitration which was concerned with keeping distinct the behavior and appearances of the genders as well as of the classes, on which distinctions so much of the social economy depended.

Notes

I would like to thank Christopher Lennox-Boyd, Guy Shaw, William Drummond, Anita Burdett, David Alexander, and Ellen D'Oench; Joan Sussler and Catherine Justin of the Lewis Walpole Library; and Joanna Miller Lewis, Laura Barry, and Catherine Grosfils of the Colonial Williamsburg Foundation for helping my research in various ways.

The dates on Collet's prints were often obliterated at some time in the eighteenth century. I have used the dates provided in David Alexander's inventory of Collet's prints.

[1] A slightly different version of this chapter was previously published under the same title. See *Eighteenth-Century Life* 26, no. 1 (2002): 119–35.

[2] Because there is virtually nothing of a sustained nature on Collet, I here summarize the bits and pieces of biographical information that are known about him. The best source for Collet's life is still the *Dictionary of National Biography*. A similar but expanded and illustrated account by "J.L.N." appeared in *Walker's Monthly* (March 1932), 1–2.

[3] Quoted in Stephen Deuchar, *Sporting Art in Eighteenth-Century England: A Social and Political History* (New Haven and London: Yale University Press, 1988), 131.

[4] Judy Egerton, *British Sporting and Animal Paintings 1655–1867* in the Paul Mellon Collection (London: The Tate Gallery for the Yale Center for British Art, 1978), 106–7.

[5] Samuel Richardson, *Letters Written to and for Particular Friends on the most important Occasions* (London, 1741), 124.

[6] Marcia Pointon, *Strategies of Showing: Women, Possessions and Representation in English Visual Culture 1665–1800* (Oxford: Clarendon, 1997), says that Worsley is cross-dressing in "an approximation of male attire" (202, 204).

[7] M. Dorothy George, *From Hogarth to Cruikshank: Social Change in Graphic Satire* (New York: Walker, 1967), 66–9. Also see Diana Donald, *The Age of Caricature: Satirical Prints in the Reign of George III* (New Haven and London: Yale University Press, 1996), 138, for the popularity of driving, and no. 5375, "Phaetona or Modern Female Taste," in F.G. Stephens and M.D. George, *Catalogue of Political and Personal Satires. Preserved in the British Museum*, 2 vols. (London: British Museum, 1870–1954).

[8] Colleen Gau, "Stella Blum Grant Report: Physiologic Effects of Wearing Corsets: Studies with Reenactors," *Dress: The Annual Journal of the Costume Society of America* 26 (1999): 63–70. For a similar report see Peter McTaggert, "Some Aspects and Use of Non-Fashionable Stays," *Strata of Society, The Annual Volume of the Costume Society* (1973), 20–28.

[9] David Kunzle first made the historically founded case for stays as an instrument of female sexual assertion (rather than oppression) in *Fashion and Fetishism: A Social History of Tight Lacing and Other Forms of Body Sculpture in the West* (Totowa: Rowman and Littlefield, 1982). Also see Anne Hollander's eloquent and elegant summary of the inner and outer power conferred by corsets (*Sex and Suits* [New York: Knopf, 1994], 138–42).

[10] Quoted in Mary Ann Wingfield, *Sport and the Artist* (London: Antique Collectors Club, 1988), 97–8.

[11] Quoted in Nicholas Penny, *Reynolds* (New York: Abrams, 1986), 224.

[12] Deuchar, *Sporting Art in Eighteenth-Century England*, 130. See also Ann Bermingham, "Old Masters of the Hunt," *Times Literary Supplement* (4–10 August 1989), 840.

[13] Richard Redgrave, *A Dictionary of the Artists of the English School: with critical notices of their works, and an account of the progress of art in England* (London: George Bell, 1878).

[14] K.C. Sauer, *Allgemeines Künstlerlexikon; Die Bildenden Künstler aller Zeiten und Völker* (Munich and Leipzig: Saue 1992–2000), points out that early sources confuse Collet with his father, also named John Collet. Some of those claim that his father was an amateur artist, for example, Ephraim Hardcastle (J.H. Pyne), in the *Somerset House Gazette* 2 (1828), 142. This source also asserts that Collet's works were sometimes sold as Hogarth's. Edward Edwards, *Anecdotes of Painters Who Have Resided or Been Born in England* (1808; rpt. London: Cornmarket, 1970), 67–88, mentions the confusion of father and son in Horace Walpole's *Anecdotes*, octavo edition (later corrected). Redgrave also includes a John Collet, "portrait painter.... Little is known of him.... He was distinguished as 'John Collet, senior.'"

[15] In the *Repository of Arts* 8 (1812): 131.

[16] J. Nichols and G. Steevens, *The Genuine Works of William Hogarth* (London, 1808–1817), 1:419.

[17] For these see Kim Sloan, "A Cozens Album in the National Library of Wales, Aberystwyth," *Walpole Society* 1, no. 7 (1993–1994): 101; Elizabeth Einberg, "Catalogue Raisonné of the Work of George Lambert," *Walpole Society* 63 (2001): 116; Iolo Williams, *Early English Watercolours* (Bath: Kingsmead Reps., 1970), 136–7; and M.H. Grant, *A Chronological History of the Old English Landscape Painters* (Leigh-on-Sea: F. Lewis, 1958), 2:163. Williams discusses Collet's stylistic characteristics, as does Adolf Paul Oppé, *English Drawings, Stuart and Georgian Periods, in the Collection of His Majesty the King at Windsor Castle* (London: Phaidon, 1950), nos. 128–32.

[18] *William Nelson Letter Book, 1766–1775* (Library of Virginia, M-60).

[19] I am indebted to Joanna Miller Lewis for informing me of this correspondence.

[20] Timothy Clayton, *The English Print 1688–1802* (New Haven and London: Yale University Press, 1997), 195.

[21] Clayton, *The English Print 1688–1802*, 197–8.

[22] See David Alexander, "Kauffman and the Print Market in Eighteenth-Century England," in *Angelica Kauffman: A Continental Artist in Georgian England*, ed. W.W. Roworth (London: Reaktion, 1992), 341–78.

[23] Lorna Weatherill, "A Possession of One's Own: Women and Consumer Behavior in England, 1600–1740," *Journal of British Studies* 15 (1986): 150–55.

[24] Donald, *The Age of Caricature*, 15–19.

[25] George, *From Hogarth*, 58.

[26] Donald, *The Age of Caricature*, 203 n. 125.

[27] Clayton, *The English Print 1688–1802*, 237, 246–56; Hannah Barker, "Women, Work and the Industrial Revolution: Female Involvement in the English Printing Trades, c. 1700–1784," in *Gender in Eighteenth-Century England: Roles, Representations and Responsibilities*, ed. Hannah Barker and Elaine Chalus (London: Longman, 1997), 81–100.

[28] Ronald Paulson, ed., *The Analysis of Beauty* (New Haven and London: Yale University Press, 1992), 32.

[29] *St James's Chronicle* (London, 1768), n.p.

[30] *St James's Chronicle* (London, 1768), n.p.

[31] *St James's Chronicle*, 24–7 December (London, 1768), n.p.

[32] Deuchar, *Sporting Art in Eighteenth-Century England*, 105–26.

[33] Quoted in Deuchar, *Sporting Art in Eighteenth-Century England*, 118.

[34] Quoted in Aileen Ribeiro, *The Dress Worn at Masquerades in England, 1730 to 1790 and Its Relation to Fancy Dress in Portraiture* (New York and London: Garland, 1984), 76.

[35] See Terry Castle, "The Culture of Travesty: Sexuality and Masquerade in Eighteenth-Century England," in *Sexual Underworlds of the Enlightenment*, ed. Roy Porter and George Rousseau (Chapel Hill: University of North Carolina Press, 1988), 363 n. 28, 29; and in Castle, *Masquerade and Civilization: The Carnivalesque in Eighteenth-Century Culture and Fiction* (Stanford: Stanford University Press, 1986).

[36] See Ribeiro, *The Dress Worn at Masquerades in England*, plates 44–6.

[37] *Gentleman's Magazine*, February (London, 1781), 57–8.

[38] *Gentleman's Magazine*, June (London, 1781), 259.

[39] *London Magazine*, September (London, 1772), 404.

[40] See Ribeiro, *The Dress Worn at Masquerades in England*, plates 20a–c.

[41] Donald, *The Age of Caricature*, 200, n. 26.

[42] See John Sainsbury, "Wilkes and Libertinism," *Studies in Eighteenth-Century Culture* 26 (1998): 158–9, 163. On cartoons showing various classes of women supporting "liberty," see Donald, *The Age of Caricature*, 117–18, 123–7; also John Mullan and Christopher Reid, eds., *Eighteenth-Century Popular Culture: A Selection* (Oxford and New York: Oxford University Press, 2000), 239, where Wilkes's popularity with women is considered.

[43] J.G. Turner, "The Properties of Libertinism," in *Unauthorized Sexual Behavior during the Enlightenment*, special issue of *Eighteenth Century Life*, n.s., 9, no. 3 (1985): 77. Turner does not entirely accept this definition, which he thinks is too broad.

[44] See James Caldwell after John Collet. *The Guards of the Night Defeated* (1774). Image available at the British Museum collection online.

[45] For a discussion of the needle trades and images of women needleworkers, see Patricia Crown, "William Hogarth's Images of Working Women and Commerce," in *The Other Hogarth: The Aesthetics of DiVerence*, ed. Bernadette Fort and Angela Rosenthal (Princeton: Princeton University Press, 2001), 224–39, and "Clothing the Modern Venus: Hogarth and Women's Dress," in *Studies in Eighteenth Century Art and Culture*, ed. Elise Goodman (Newark: University of Delaware Press, 2001), 90–105. Also see Beverly Lemire, *Dress, Culture and Commerce: The English Clothing Trade before the Factory, 1660–1800* (New York: St. Martin's, 1997).

[46] Linda Colley, *Britons: Forging the Nation 1707–1837* (New Haven and London: Yale University Press, 1992), 242. Colley describes a "renovated cult of female propriety and domesticity evident in Great Britain from at least the 1770s" (262). A similar argument is made by A.D. Harvey, *Sex in Georgian England: Attitudes and Prejudices from the 1720s to the 1820s* (New York: St. Martin's, 1994), 154–69. Also see Lynn Hunt and Margaret Jacob, "The Affective Revolution in 1790s Britain," *Eighteenth-Century Studies* 34 (2001): 499–500.

[47] Quoted in Castle, "The Culture of Travesty," 156.

PART II
Sports

Chapter 4
The Uses and Transformations of Early Modern Tennis

Alexis Tadié

"A man, she would reflect, who could be so feeble and miserable a failure at tennis, could not be good for much in any department of life."[1] When P.G. Wodehouse thus conveys his hero's anxiety, he is talking about a different game from the game of tennis that was played in the early modern period. Lawn tennis, itself a probable revival of the late eighteenth-century "field tennis," had by then replaced the royal game, also known as "jeu de paume" in France. But the humorous dimension of the sport, which combines the metaphors of love and life, builds on centuries of writings about tennis. Indeed, the uses of tennis as a suitable medium for reflections on life can already be found in medieval literature.

Although "real" tennis[2] is still played nowadays in a few places in England, France, and the United States, numbers are low and the game survives thanks to the passion of a number of individuals rather than through mass practice—even though initiatives such as the Dedanists' Foundation and the Dedanists' Society aim at encouraging young players to take up the game. In actual fact, the decline of the game probably started at the end of the seventeenth century, and although there was still a fair amount of activity in the eighteenth century, by the 1750s numbers of tennis courts, both in England and in France, were steadily diminishing. Whereas Paris boasted 259 tennis courts at the very end of the sixteenth century, barely a dozen were left in 1800.[3] Tennis in its "royal" form died sometime in the eighteenth century. Lawn tennis was later born, at the end of the nineteenth century, out of the inadequacies of real tennis, a game that had become difficult to organize in terms of buildings, and irrelevant to the culture of the day. Beyond the name, though, the continuities between real tennis and tennis were activated in the late nineteenth century. This is apparent in the uses and celebrations of the game, in its potential for visual and literary disquisitions, in the attitudes generated by its place and growing importance in the culture of the time.

The fate of the game was similar in France and in England, suggesting a common history rather than separate traditions. Tennis was originally a royal and princely game, also played by the clergy, and possibly imported from France into England (as well as into a number of other European countries, not to mention India). It then spread to wider circles, before retreating in the eighteenth century. Tennis was conceivably the victim of a number of factors, ranging from the waning of physical exercise to the competition of other games that were being played within the precincts of the tennis courts, such as billiards or bowls. In both countries, tennis courts were increasingly used for theater performances, because their dimensions were suitable to such activities. There was a certain amount of mutual penetration of French and English tennis—French players were often reported to be playing in England, in particular in the early years of the nineteenth century, while French treatises were aware of English players and *maîtres paumiers*.[4] Joseph Barcellon, whose brother wrote an important contribution to the rules of tennis, settled in England and was commonly referred to as the "English Barcellon."[5] Most writings about tennis are French, but this reflects a different level of publishing activity rather than differing conceptions of the game. French and English treatises of tennis often refer to each other and provide a comprehensive picture of the game rather than competing perspectives.

Literary writings about tennis echo the tennis interactions between France and England. In a famous instance from Shakespeare's *Henry V*, tennis was used as a metaphor for the antagonism between both kingdoms. More generally, writings about tennis evolved along similar lines in both countries, so that the English eighteenth-century culture of tennis can be seen as the recipient of thinking about the sport in the two languages. This is no doubt the consequence of the centrality of tennis as a form of entertainment in both countries for a few hundred years. But the literary text also elicits perceptions of historical transformations, an understanding of the ways in which an essential social, cultural, and political phenomenon such as sport is appropriated and transformed. The purpose of this chapter, therefore, is not so much to study the "representation" of tennis but to understand the interactions between evolving perceptions of tennis in literature and the rise and fall of tennis as a sport central to early-modern sociability. Between the sixteenth century and the eighteenth century, a few treatises on tennis were published; they enable us to understand evolving and varying conceptions of the nature of the game. This picture can be usefully supplemented by literary references which construct the importance of the tennis court as an emblem of life but also as a place of enactment of conflicts. Finally, we will be concerned with the mutability of tennis, with the uses and transformations of tennis courts for different forms of entertainment.

The Nature of Tennis

What was tennis, though? In claiming origins in antiquity, writers described different ball games. The Greeks had several such games, including *harpastè* which became the *harpastum* of the Romans, and which was prescribed by Galen to patients who were overweight. Other sources suggest Middle Eastern origins. The word *tennis* itself is generally thought to originate from the French *tenez!* used by players before serving.[6] Until the Middle Ages, the game was played with a ball but with neither racket nor bat. Originally, it took place on an open court before moving to an enclosed court probably at the end of the thirteenth century.[7] Scaino, in the first treatise on tennis, described a game with several variants. An English version of the game existed under the name of "fives" or "hand-tennis," in which the ball was struck by the hand, and is still played in a number of public schools as well as in some sports clubs. In fifteenth-century France, tennis was first played outdoors (*longue paume*) and later came to be played indoors (*courte paume*). It is the latter version that became extremely popular in the sixteenth century and beyond, thanks to the patronage of the kings of France. The game spread, as did the number of tennis courts, and was no longer the privilege of the aristocracy or of the clergy but could also be played by students and artisans—although it was quite expensive. It was of course an urban game, and one that proved most popular in Early Modern France.[8] Its rules were set some time in the fifteenth century and first printed in the sixteenth century.

Tennis was imported from France into England, and most writers recognized its aristocratic nature:

> The Game at Tennis is a most Princely Exercise; having its first Original (as I have been informed) or brought over to us from the *French* Court; it is a Gentile, Cleanly, Active, and most ingenious Recreation, exercising all the parts of the Body; therefore for its Excellency is much approved of, and Played by most Nations in *Europe*, especially by our great Gallants of *England*, where such Tennis Courts are Built.[9]

Henry VIII, who complained about the decay of archery, blamed it on a number of games, including tennis:

> And it is thought by the King's highness and his most honorable council that the archery and shooting in longbows is like for evermore to be decayed and destroyed by the using hereof; and of divers and many other unlawful games as playing at tennis, bowls, closh, tables, dice, cards, and other unlawful games, contrary to the King's laws and honorable statutes made in that behalf.[10]

Only the aristocracy were authorized to play tennis—although gambling and disorder were major concerns, Henry VIII's main objective was of course to make sure that able men were available for war. James I, in his 1618 *Declaration of Sports*, opposed Puritans who wanted to ban all sports on the Sabbath; the only activities he banned were such sports as bear- and bullbaiting, thereby authorizing tennis. Charles I was said to have been a keen tennis player and was even allowed to play while in captivity at Hampton Court.[11] Charles II, himself a proficient tennis player, as recounted by Samuel Pepys, commissioned a renovation of the Hampton Court tennis court, which took about a year. And although the court was used for the storage of timber during the rebuilding of the palace under William III's reign, the King ordered its restoration in 1699. It is doubtful that he ever played on the refurbished court, but he enjoyed watching and had indeed practiced the game in his youth.[12] The first Hanoverian kings were not particularly interested in the sport, George I using the tennis court at Hampton Court for other purposes, but other members of the Royal Family remained faithful exponents of tennis, either at Hampton Court or on other courts, such as Windsor Castle. Thereby, tennis was supported, both in England and in France,[13] by the king's court—they built its aura and were possibly responsible for its inevitable decline.

Treatises on the game of tennis were published at two crucial moments, first at the beginning of the sixteenth century, when it was beginning to gain in popularity, and then at the end of the eighteenth century, when it was on the wane. They thus constitute interesting landmarks in the history of the sport. The necessity to lay down principles and rules first appeared as the game began to take hold of princely courts. The aristocratic dimension is clear from the first full treatise, Antonio Scaino da Salo's *Trattato del Giuco della Palla*, which was published in Venice in 1555 and is dedicated to the prince of Ferrara.[14] Scaino saw in Galen the first writer about the game, and he traced to the Roman physician and philosopher the idea that no other game was ever as beneficial to health as tennis—an idea still present, for instance, in the entry for "Paume" in the *Encyclopédie*.[15] In the third part, he further expanded the medical benefits suggested by Galen.

Although he claimed that the game was ancient, Scaino chose not to discuss its ancient principles, for lack of sources and information, but above all because, as a true modern, he insisted on recent achievements:

> But who can doubt that the Ball-Game to-day has reached a greater perfection than in past times? That this is so, we may be persuaded by the many ways of playing, by the many instruments and devices invented in our time for the amplification of the game and by the very great esteem in which it is held, above all other games in almost all provinces of the world and especially by noble people of high estate.[16]

He recommended tennis for the education of princes and sons of noble lineage and saw it as having been organized for a purpose, "to keep our bodies healthy, to make our young men stronger and more robust, chasing idleness, virtue's most mortal enemy, far from them and thus making them of a stronger and more excellent nature."[17] Its superiority over games of fortune, such as dice and cards, or over hunting, where the hunter is assisted by horse, dog, etc., was emphasized by Scaino, who was keen to show that tennis brought together all the qualities required of a man: "[O]ne sees just how strong, courageous, dexterous and well-mannered a man is, and at the same time how quick in making decisions in the very act of fighting."[18] The treatise offered not so much rules of tennis as principles of play, dealing with a range of issues from the structure and variety of the game to the chases and their numbers, or again to appropriate manners on the court. It aimed to be comprehensive, analyzing technicalities as much as physical requirements, through a reflection on movement. Tennis could thus be one of the organizing principles of an education.

The first treatise to print extensive rules for tennis was published in French a few years after Scaino's, in 1599, by the *maître paumier* Forbet l'Aisné, under the title *L'Utilité qui provient du Jeu de Paume au corps et à l'esprit*.[19] Allegedly a translation of Galen, Forbet's rules were reproduced until well into the nineteenth century. So that, paradoxically enough, until the second half of the eighteenth century, there were no other written sources for the rules of tennis in the playing world apart from Forbet's.

The middle of the eighteenth century marked a change in the publishing activity about tennis. In 1767, François de Garsault penned an important *Art du Paumier-Raquetier, et de la Paume*,[20] followed in 1783 by Manevieux's *Traité sur la connaissance du royal Jeu de la Paume et des principes qui sont relatifs aux différentes parties qu'on y joue*. In 1800, Pierre Barcellon published *Règles et principes de la Paume*. In 1822, the first treatise on tennis in English came out in London, written by Robert Lukin. The first comprehensive history of the game, which took in the development of the game both "abroad" and in England, was Julian Marshall's *Annals of Tennis* of 1878.

The paradoxical nature of these publications is obvious. It was at a time when the game was dying or had all but disappeared that authors printed rules and recommendations for better practice. This may have been due to the necessity precisely of rescuing a dying art—the books were possibly written in the hope that the publication might revive interest in the game—or perhaps of recording its definitive achievements—as if these treatises were lengthy obituaries of the sport. Robert Lukin, like Barcellon, was aware that understanding his book required some prior knowledge of the game:

> Few games can be taught by rule alone, and Tennis is, perhaps, less capable than any other of being so acquired,—it does not, however follow, that all written instruction must therefore be useless and unavailing. System and practice lead to perfection in all games; and it requires no great depth of reasoning to show, that practice may be so directed by theory, as to attain its object in much less time, than if left unassisted, uninstructed and uncontrolled.[21]

Lukin claimed further not to have had any access to works that might provide assistance on the subject. It was therefore from the point of view of the practitioner that he attempted to describe the game.[22]

Garsault's treatise is the more precisely technical of the writings of the period. It gives great details on the appearance of the courts (in particular depending on the type of tennis that is being played), on the fabrication of rackets, and on the nature of the sport. The description of the tennis court, for instance, contains dimensions and general principles so precise that they belong to a work of architecture rather than to the simple description of a tennis court:

> Every tennis-court is a long rectangle, enclosed by four walls; two complete walls form the long sides and gables at each end extend for the breadth of the court. The ground-space enclosed should be 96 feet long and 36 feet wide, so that when all the internal construction is complete the space to play on will be found to be 90 feet long and 30 feet wide. The two side walls should be 14 to 15 feet higher for a length of 6 or 7 feet, after which they slope down to the lower level. These four raised corners are called the *joues d'en haut*.[23]

The description of the racket is equally precise about its fabrication, the types of wood that are needed, the different stages in the construction of the object, as well as the instruments required in the process. The third part of the treatise investigates the language of tennis and provides a more comprehensive list of technical terms than other treatises. A supplement is composed of three vignettes and five plates which complement the descriptions and give visual support to the reader (Figure 4.1).

The author, who was a member of the French Académie des Sciences, obviously regarded his treatise as a scientific contribution—the style of the plates recalls the *Encyclopédie*, and the title page refers to the arts and techniques investigated by the members of the Académie des sciences. Garsault himself wrote several descriptions of mechanical arts, such as an art of the wig maker or an art of the cobbler. He considered tennis as the only game belonging to this family, both because it was in itself an art and because it was executed by means of another art—the fabrication of rackets and balls.[24] Considered as one of the mechanical arts, tennis was therefore much more than a game—a profitable exercise for the youth, beneficial to their health. In turn, this conception justified the plan of the work and the technical, detailed description of tennis—the description of the court, as well as of the manufacture of rackets and balls, made of tennis an object worthy of the endeavors of the Académie.

The complexities of tennis, as exemplified in the treatises, lay not only in the intricacies of the rules and the different types of games that were played but also in the very nature of the sport. It was of course a sport enduringly associated with the nobility and with the aura of royal abodes, such as Hampton Court or Versailles. Its medical importance was beyond doubt, as demonstrated by the venerable references to Galen as much as by an eighteenth century doctorate in medicine, quoted at the end of Garsault's treatise, which analyzed the benefits of tennis against rheumatisms. Its educational and recreational values were supplemented by its strategic dimension, perhaps superior to chess according to some authors. If properly analyzed, in terms of technical process, it could be construed as one of the mechanical arts.

The Celebrations of Tennis

These treatises were as much instructions on how to play the game and understand its rules as celebrations of the sport. They extolled its merits and general superiority over a number of other sports. Scaino thought tennis more rewarding than all the other pastimes of the nobility, including hunting. In 1822, Robert Lukin maintained that

> The Game peculiar to this country, and which comes in any sort in competition with Tennis, is Cricket; but without entering into a view of the comparative skill required to excel in each, the latter game must be allowed to be open to the following great objections:—That it can only be played during a small part of the year;—that a match cannot be readily made, on account of the number required

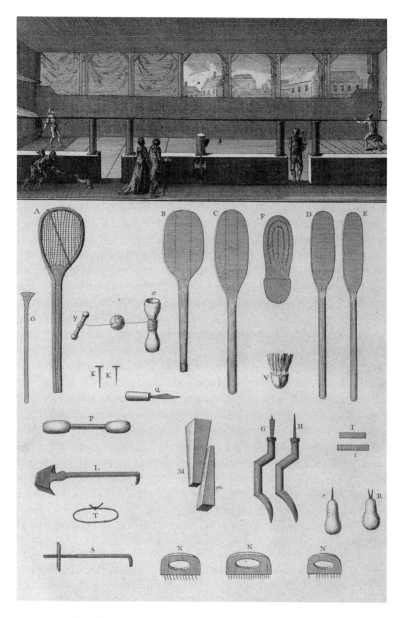

Figure 4.1   M. de Garsault. *Art du Paumier-Raquetier, et de la Paume* (Paris: chez Saillant and Nyon, chez Desaint, 1767). Pl. 3. Shelfmark: (Vet) 1773 b.19. Courtesy, the Bodleian Library, University of Oxford.

to form it, and of the inconvenient length of time that it frequently engages the players;—that it is open to much jealousy and dispute in the distribution of its several parts; and that the *innings* of the best players are too precarious; inasmuch as the slightest accident may defeat the Hero of the piece.[25]

James Love, in his poem about cricket, had suggested otherwise: "Not *Tennis* self, thy sister sport, can charm, / Or with thy fierce delights our bosoms warm."[26] It is in the nature of sport for exponents of a particular game to stress the superiority of their own art.[27] In 1891, the poet J.K. Stephen concluded a long poem about the beauties of tennis and its superiority over other sports, such as cricket or football, with a well-worn *cliché*: "The *king of games* is still the *game of kings*."[28]

Literature celebrated tennis as a pastime fit for the kings but which could also resonate in a pastoral context. In the sixteenth century, we find the son of Alexis, the main character of Francis Sabie's "Second Eclogue" (1595), testifying to the inscription of tennis in a pastoral literary landscape: "At this time the top, the tennis ball was a pastime: / At this time no smal delight he toke in a foteball."[29] The excellence of the game was constructed in such terms both in English and French writings. In the early nineteenth century, a French poem still finds tennis to belong to the pastoral. In *Eloge de la paume*, published in 1824,[30] the poet reflects on the pleasures of the game whose sounds are in harmony with the noises of the forest. It moves on to describe a match in epic terms. The poet examines the various aptitudes displayed by different players, insists on the importance of judgment in playing the game, on caution rather than on ambition, before praising the medical benefits of a day's match ("The racket is to you the sceptre of Asclepios"). Perhaps because the game was in danger of disappearing, the poet praised not only the happiness that it could bring but also its universally accessible character. He ends the poem with a reflection on old age—having enjoyed the game for 30 years, he contemplates the youth that play before his eyes, admires their innocence, remembers that tennis is responsible for his fondest memories, and suggests to the ladies that in order to secure their lovers they should send them off to play tennis. Such mock-heroic celebrations were not isolated, and sport poems of the eighteenth century sometimes resorted to this mode.

In an ironical variation on the mode of comparison and superiority, Hazlitt himself thought the game of tennis of more worth than writing:

> I am so sick of this trade of authorship, that I have a much greater ambition to be the best racket-player, than the best prose-writer of the age. The critics look askance at one's best-meant efforts, but the face of a racket-player is the face of a friend. There is no juggling here. If the stroke is a good one, the hit tells. They do not keep two scores to mark the game, with Whig and Tory notches. The thing is settled at once, and the applause of the *dedans* follows the marker's voice, and seconds the prowess of the hand, and the quickness of the eye. The accomplishments of the body are obvious and clear to all: those of the mind are recondite and doubtful, and therefore grudgingly acknowledged, or held up as the sport of prejudice, spite, and folly.[31]

The comparison between physical and intellectual achievements, the sincerity of tennis compared to the grumpiness of critics, together with the lack of political prejudice in the sport, fuel Hazlitt's stance towards writing and the "trade of authorship." Hazlitt's conceit reworks the relationship between sport and literature, making sense of a comparison which turns ironically to the advantage of sport. Sport is neither a metaphor nor the object of the reflection but a powerful way of putting in perspective the failings of writing and the shortcomings of the writer's social and political position.

Tennis provided writers with an occasion for literary games and meditations. On the opening page of Tobias Smollett's first novel, the hero, Roderick Random, recounts his mother's dream:

> She dreamed she was delivered of a tennis-ball, which the devil (who, to her great surprise, acted the part of a midwife) struck so forcibly with a racket that it disappeared in an instant; and she was for some time inconsolable for the loss of her offspring; when, all of a sudden, she beheld it return with equal violence, and enter the earth, beneath her feet, whence immediately sprang up a goodly tree covered with blossoms, the scent of which operated so strongly on her nerves that she awoke.[32]

The text subsequently provides an interpretation of the dream: "The attentive sage, after some deliberation, assured my parents, that their firstborn would be a great traveller; that he would undergo many dangers and difficulties, and at last return to his native land, where he would flourish in happiness and reputation."[33] This parable serves to announce the picaresque dimension of the narrator's peregrinations, the hazards of his travels, and of his possible return home at the end of his journey. It encapsulates the narrative destiny of the hero.

The presence of the parable at the outset of this eighteenth-century novel testifies both to the enduring presence of tennis in literary language and to a rhetorical tradition acknowledged by Smollett—and by Richardson before him, who described Pamela as a "mere Tennis-ball of Fortune."[34] This tradition goes back to the Middle Ages, when the allegorical potential of tennis was explored by writers for musings on life, and could surface in emblems. The French poet Charles d'Orléans famously composed an allegorical ballad that reflected on the passage of time, using ambiguously both the scoring method of tennis to refer to his score as well as to his age (45) and the technical language of the sport to define the quest of life (the chase). In the poem, the persona fears his opponents, Old Age, Fortune, and Worry, against whom he remains defiant, with the help of Hope and Good Fortune. For the humanists, such as Juan-Luis Vivès, who published some rules of the game in 1539, tennis served to illustrate the rules of sociability.

Scaino himself thought that tennis was a metaphor for life, where the tennis court, closed in on all sides by walls and barriers, as nothing more nor less than this troublesome world in which we who are all players are placed and across which is the cord, the brake or boundary of moderation or, better said, of justice, the source of every good. Looking fixedly at the cord, we must be careful not to throw the Ball too high so that it overtops the walls nor set our aimes too high and above our strength, nor again too low, under the cord, basely and terrestrially, nor exceed the boundaries; for in all these ways fault would be committed and the game lost.[35]

This conceit resurfaced time and again in literature. It may be linked to the need to justify the pastimes of kings. It springs more probably from the complexities of the game as well as from the meditative potential of the tennis ball, with which man is identified. The hazards of life often find a suitable metaphor in sports, but the links of tennis with a courtly tradition and with sociability allow for deeper exploration of the fate of man. In Sir Philip Sidney's *Arcadia*, mankind "are but like tenisbals, tossed by the racket of the higher powers."[36] In Webster's *The Duchesss of Malfi*, "We are meerely the Starres tennys-balls (strooke, and banded / Which way please them)."[37] The title of Middleton's courtly masque, *The World Tossed at Tennis* (1620), carries the same connotations. And a number of writings of the eighteenth century still use the metaphor of man as the tennis-ball of Fortune, referring to great men such as Charles I,[38] Walter Raleigh,[39] or simply to common man as the object of Fortune, as exemplified in the pseudo-Bunyan's *Meditations*: "[W]hat a Tennis Ball of Fortune that Man is, who places his Felicity in outward things."[40] From Sidney to Smollett, tennis balls lead a life of their own, bouncing about in a serious mode, the toys of higher powers that hit them at will. For a number of writers, they were the emblems of our helpless humanity.[41]

The game of tennis could thus be used and summoned by writers and poets to explore the hazards of life and destiny. But the dramatic dimension of a tennis match could also tempt writers away from its moral teachings towards the game of love. An early eighteenth-century treatise on fishing, hunting, and various other games such as cockfighting, bowls, and tennis, takes up the parallels offered by the structure of the tennis-court: "When as the hand at Tennis plays, / And Men to gaming fall, / Love is the Court, Hope is the House, / And favour serves the Ball."[42] But one of the more exciting instances is given by the French Renaissance poet Theophile de Viau, who circulated in his *Parnasse satyrique* a fifteenth-century erotic poem: "If you kiss her, count fifteen, / If you touch the buds, thirty, / If you capture the hill, / Forty-five comes up. / But if you enter the breach / With what the lady needs, / Remember well what I sing to you, / You will win the game outright."[43]

The political uses of tennis further show how literature can celebrate the game, turn it around for its own purposes, and use its dramatic and open-ended contests. In *Henry V*, on the eve of battle, the French Dauphin sends King Henry a gift of tennis balls.[44] The French envoys use the tennis balls as a disparaging statement about the king's military ability, suggesting that he might best pass his time in frivolous activities. To which Henry replies:

His present and your pains we thank you for.
When we have matched our rackets to these balls
We will, in France, by God's grace, play a set
Shall strike his father's crown into the hazard.
....
And tell the pleasant Prince this mock of his
Hath turned his balls to gun stones.[45]

Although, as has been argued by Winfried Schleiner,[46] this may point to a difference in the status of the game in France and in England, the reference partakes of the literary construction of tennis. Henry's retort elaborates on the metaphor of the tennis match, suggesting a superiority of the English at the game, before the final metamorphosis of the tennis balls into gun stones. The tennis balls had become weapons in a political game before turning, perhaps, into genuine projectiles.

The tennis court itself could be both the emblem of life, as developed by Scaino or Lathum, and a place of enactment of conflict and politics. One of the celebrated quarrels of the late Renaissance pitted Sir Philip Sidney against Edward de Vere, Earl of Oxford, when the latter stormed onto the tennis court where the former was playing; a quarrel ensued which led to insults being traded and to Sidney giving Oxford the lie. The difficulty lay in the fact that Oxford, who was of a higher rank than Sidney, could fight a duel only with someone of the same rank. This episode, which was recounted a number of times, reminds us that the tennis court was a place where, within the aristocracy, issues of rank and precedence could be argued and fought.[47] But the most famous use of a tennis court for politics took place during the French Revolution when the Third Estate swore not to dissolve until a constitution had been approved. Known as the "serment du jeu de paume," this famous incident took place on the tennis court at Versailles, on the edge of the castle, to which they had not been admitted. It made of the tennis court an important symbolic place in French political history and one forever associated with the will of the people against the power of privileged rulers. The tennis court would no longer be the preserve of the aristocracy.

The Transformations of Tennis

It would be wrong to see tennis as a pure game of aristocratic refinement. Since its origins, tennis had been associated with rowdy behavior, as well as with gambling and cheating.[48] In the same way that literary celebrations could turn from the nobility of the game to more pleasurable activities, the game itself was rarely played in a purely disinterested context. While the Earl of Oxford and Sir Philip Sidney were having their quarrel on a tennis court, a shady character was using the tennis court in Lesage's *Gil Blas* to assert his power. Don Rodrigo de Mondragon "had made himself tyrant of the tennis-court, where he judged all the disputes that happened among those who played," exerting such control that he "captivated the mistress of the tennis-court,"[49] a 40-year-old widow.

That the tennis court could be used for more activities than simply playing an elegant game is also apparent in financial dealings. Betting was an activity closely connected with tennis, as indeed with most games and sports. Henry VIII was a heavy gambler, on tennis as on other games.[50] As the game grew, more betting was involved, and it is possible that some changes, such as the introduction of handicaps or the alteration of certain rules, were made to enhance the excitement of the betting public.[51] Certainly, betting brought about cheating, then as now. As early as the sixteenth century, an example of cheating is recounted of a player who "was rid of six hundred pounds at the tennis in a week by the fraud of his stopper."[52]

In the eighteenth century, although the sport was on the wane, betting on tennis was as intense as it had ever been. In Thomas Holcroft's *The Road to Ruin*, a play which went through 37 performances in 1792, several characters are engaged in betting on a tennis match that opposes an English player and the best player in the world, who is French:

Milford.	The great match! The famous Frenchman and Will the marker! A thousand guineas a side!
Goldfinch.	What, tennis?
Milford.	Yes, the Frenchman gives fifteen and a bisque.
Goldfinch.	To Will the marker?
Milford.	Yes.
Goldfinch.	Will for a hundred!
Milford.	Done!
Goldfinch.	Done, done![53]

And drama unfolds because Milford is wanted by the Sheriff's officer. *Hoyle's Games Improved* gives a sketch of the complexity of the rules, before describing in some detail the odds.[54] The author of the *Annals of Gaming*, probably published in 1775, devotes a full chapter to tennis, in order to warn the gullible. He finds that of late "it has been greatly degraded through those pests of society called Sharpers, who have made it in some measure answer their iniquitous purposes, in being admitted by their superiors to play and bett at discretion, whereby they find opportunities of deceiving them with their eyes open."[55] The author proceeds to review the complexities of the game, including a description of the court, in order to explain the "methods of defrauding." He shows how the whole betting operation was controlled by a few individuals who were keen to prey upon lords and gentlemen: "[T]hese are always dupes to the knowing ones, who lay in wait for them, and generally entrap them by making sham betts one with another, and thereby lead them on to lay their money, as the sharping judge seems to bett."[56] Writing at about the same time, the anonymous compiler of *Interesting Anecdotes* warned likewise of the dangers of gaming, mentioning tennis in connection with Henry VIII's proclamation.[57] In France, Manevieux devoted a chapter of his treatise to those players who pretended that they could not play, usually lost the first few games in which they were involved, so as to increase the stakes and fleece their opponents. Manevieux recorded the French slang to designate such activities ("enfiler son homme," to skewer one's opponent). He further described a number of schemes developed by these characters. In the first years of the nineteenth century, Robert Lukin still found it convenient to include at the end of his *Treatise on Tennis* a table of "The odds, as usually betted."[58] Although he did not broach the topic of crooks and scams, Lukin seemed to regard betting as a perfectly ordinary practice, integral to the game.

Tennis was always associated with other games. The frontispiece to a seventeenth-century edition of the *Maison académique*, a publication which brought together descriptions and rules of a number of games, shows an enclosed space where tennis, at the top, is only one of a series of games that are played in the several parts of the building (Figure 4.2).[59]

More specifically, tennis was not unrelated to billiards in its development and was often associated with it in the seventeenth and eighteenth centuries, the marker from the tennis court also keeping the score at billiards.[60] In the eighteenth century, both in France and in England, and with different regulations, billiard tables and tennis courts could coexist—in fact, the French statute of *paumiers-raquetiers* required those that wished to add a billiard table to a tennis court to install it in the court.[61] In France, as Albert de Luze tells us, this may have been a consequence of Louis XIV's increasing taste for billiards as his interest for tennis waned, which meant that billiards sometimes came to replace tennis in the tennis courts. In his survey of tennis courts of the seventeenth and eighteenth centuries, Luze mentions a number of courts which boasted billiard rooms.

The plasticity of tennis courts appears further in the eighteenth century as the popularity of the game began to decline, and courts were gradually converted. They were frequently used as playhouses, both in France and in England, as early as the seventeenth century. Even though the courts would be in frequent use, they were available in the evenings, when a makeshift stage could be set up. Molière, for instance, performed at various tennis courts in Paris and in the provinces during his career, and indeed the first opera to be staged in Paris was shown at the Bequet tennis court in 1670.[62] With the decline of the sport, the managers of tennis courts found that the conversion of the courts into theaters was a convenient way of increasing their revenues, leading them, in the eighteenth century, to turn some of the courts permanently into theaters. The famous royal court at the Louvre, for instance, was used until the end of the Revolution and was later handed over to a company of actors—it survived as a theater until it was demolished in 1921.[63] Later in the century, theaters came in this spirit to be built in the shape of tennis courts.

In England, the same story as in France prevails, of decline of tennis gradually replaced by the theater. What was first a metaphor became a reality. The stage was likened to a tennis court in *Lust's Dominion*, a play generally ascribed to Thomas Dekker ("Me thinks this stage shews like a Tennis Court"[64]), but when theaters reopened at the Restoration, actors were in need of playhouses, so they came to use tennis courts because their dimensions—about 75 by 30 feet—were convenient for such purposes. In the early 1660s, the Duke's Men, Davenant's

Figure 4.2   Denis de la Marinière. *La Maison academique, contenant les jeux du picquet, du hoc, du tric-trac, du hoca, de la guerre, de la paulme, du billard, du palle-mail, divers jeux de cartes, qui se joüent en differentes facons ... & autres jeux facetieux & divertissans* (Paris: chez Etienne Loison, 1659). Frontispiece. Shelfmark: Jessel F.760. Courtesy, the Bodleian Library, University of Oxford.

theater company, used Lisle's Tennis Court in Portugal Row, in Lincoln's Inn Fields, while Killigrew's King's Men performed in Gibbon's Tennis court in Vere Street, in the same area.[65] Later, Thomas Betterton, who had been one of the leading actors in Davenant's company, restored (by subscription) the Tennis Court in Lincoln's Inn Fields. This "New Theatre" opened with Congreve's *Love for Love* in 1695—the epilogue views this state of affairs with a touch of irony and reactivates the metaphor of men likened to tennis balls: "And this our audience, which did once resort / To shining theaters to see our Sport, / Now find us toss'd into a Tennis-Court."[66] In Scotland, the tennis court at Holyrood House was also used as a theater after the Restoration and again in the eighteenth century.

The example of the James Street Theatre is illuminating.[67] In the early eighteenth century, James Street (now Orange Street) boasted two tennis courts. The original tennis court was built in the 1630s. In the early eighteenth century, the old court was used for various entertainments such as rope dancers or concerts. David Jenkins, who has reconstructed the history of this theater, tells us that from the middle of the 1720s, "the Old Tennis Court seems to be used for exhibits of puppets, conjuring, and automata."[68] It became known as Fawkes's Theatre, after the actor Isaac Fawkes who performed there, and was also associated with the name of Pinchbeck, who exhibited his "Musical Clock" in 1732. The theater itself, which was reconstructed within the walls of the old Tennis Court, was active as late as 1770, whereas the tennis court continued to be in use until the middle of the nineteenth century. It was dismantled in 1866, and its benches survive in the current tennis court of Merton Street, Oxford.

Similar stories may be told about other tennis courts. Higginson's tennis court was erected in the mid-1740s, in Windmill Street, and was attached to Piccadilly Hall, a gaming-house.[69] Higginson himself occupied the court until 1761. In the early nineteenth century, this particular tennis court became a place for entertainments such as circus and theater but also conjuring and ventriloquy. The fate of these tennis courts shows that even if the game was associated with royalty and the aristocracy, a number of them became used, in the eighteenth century, as theaters and places for entertainment. Other games and sports, such as bowls and billiards could be encountered in the tennis courts, along the lines of the "Royal Cockpit," a building situated behind the palace of Whitehall, which had a tennis court as well as a bowling alley and an area for cockfights. Thus tennis and its immediate environment could vary greatly from the royal courts at Hampton Court or at Versailles, to the tennis courts that were converted into theaters, either in the evenings or on a more permanent basis, as the game started to decline. The presence of other games as well as the betting activities around the matches suggests another dimension to the sport, which complements the "game of kings" with which it is often associated. Such a dimension is captured by an episode from Scarron's *Roman comique* wherein a play is performed at a tennis court. It later degenerates into a brawl, involving the tennis players who were still playing within the limits of the court; an engraving by Oudry captures nicely the tennis player using his racket as a powerful weapon (Figure 4.3).

Figure 4.3   Jean-Baptiste Oudry. *Bataille Arrivée Dans le Tripot* (1649–1657), illustration for *Le Roman Comique* de Scarron. Courtesy, Paris, Musée du Louvre, D.A.G. Photo (C) RMN-Grand Palais (Musée du Louvre) / Thierry Le Mage.

Conclusion

In 1876 and 1877, Julian Marshall, a music and print collector, and as such a major contributor to the first edition of Grove's *Dictionary of Music*, published in *The Field* a series of columns on the ancient game of real tennis, or *jeu de paume*, which he republished in 1878 under the title *The Annals of Tennis*.[70] It is an interesting document since it is arguably the most comprehensive treatise on tennis ever published, and this not only at a time when real tennis had all but disappeared but also when the new game of lawn tennis was emerging. Similarly, the most important treatise on the game of racquets was published in 1872, at a time when racquets was beginning to evolve into squash racquets, before being superseded in the early part of the twentieth century.[71] These treatises take on the form of last rites being paid to disappearing games.

A number of theories have been offered to explain the decline of a once famous sport, which all but died in the eighteenth century. They range from its aristocratic associations which, in France at least, became irrelevant with the French revolution, to more sport-centered explanations suggesting that the rules of tennis were written too late to ensure the preservation of the sport. On the other hand, it may well be argued that the writing down of the rules was helpless in the face of a decline that started perhaps at the end of the seventeenth century and carried on throughout the eighteenth century. It may also have been caused by the general waning of physical activity in the eighteenth century, at least in France.[72]

For centuries though, tennis mattered because it was at the heart of people's conceptions of the world. Montaigne could think of tennis when describing the art of conversation or mention the game of tennis together with hunting and shooting when reflecting on the paradoxes of blindness.[73] Poets were able to draw on the language of tennis for allegories and variations on well-known poetic genres. Smollett could still use the example of tennis balls to introduce the defining parable of his first novel. And even the revolutionaries in France, who could not gain access to the palace of Versailles, were happy to occupy the adjoining tennis court. The echoes of tennis resonated down to the end of the eighteenth century when the tennis court ceased to be a metaphor for life and its hazards and became the symbol of the steadfast resolution of the people. Tennis had ceased to be linked to the privileges of the aristocracy and with elegant pastoral musings on life but had become a place of enactment of politics.

The metamorphosis of the game became apparent in the gradual transformations of the buildings that housed the sport. Although there had always been a certain amount of flexibility in the uses of tennis courts that could also contain a bowling alley, tennis was slowly edged out of the tennis courts by billiards, and above all by the theater. The coexistence of tennis and theater in the seventeenth century became, in the eighteenth century, more or less a takeover. The ambiguities apparent in the references to the James Street tennis court, which, in actual fact, housed two tennis courts, only one of which became the James Street Theatre, reveal a physical and intellectual phasing out of the sport. Even though a number of writers at the turn of the eighteenth century thought it important to recount its history or to analyze its theory, one of them, Robert Lukin, could sign his *Treatise on Tennis*, "a member of the tennis club," because, at the time of publication, only the James Street tennis court survived in London. What was once a remarkable and intricate sport had all but died.

Notes

[1] P.G. Wodehouse, *Love Among the Chickens* [1906–1921] (London: Everyman, 2011), 103.

[2] It was renamed thus at the end of the nineteenth century to differentiate it from lawn tennis.

[3] See Albert de Luze, *A History of the Royal Game of Tennis*, trans. Richard Hamilton (Kineton: The Roundwood Press, 1979), 34; M. de Manevieux, *Traité sur la connaissance du royal jeu de paume* (Neuchâtel, 1783), vii; and Julian Marshall, *Annals of Tennis* (London: Horace Cox, 1878), 42.

[4] See for instance Mannevieux, 146–7 and 158.

[5] Marshall, *Annals of Tennis*, 99.

[6] The difficulty with this etymology lies in the fact that players were not required to warn their opponents before serving. The word *tennis* will be used hereafter in its common English usage, which is the equivalent of the *jeu de paume* in France.

[7] See Roger Morgan, "A Fifteenth-Century Tennis Court in London," *The International Journal of the History of Sport* 13, no. 3 (1996): 418–31.

[8] See Luze, *A History of the Royal Game of Tennis*, 1–70.

[9] Randle Holme, *The Academy of Armory*, book 3, chapter 5 (Chester: Printed for the author, 1688), 264.

[10] Proclamation "Enforcing Statues on Archery, Handguns, Unlawful Games, Reforming High Grain Prices" (4 December 1528). In Paul L. Hughes and James F. Larkin (ed.), *Tudor Royal Proclamations* (New Haven and London: Yale University Press, 1964), 1:176.

[11] See David Best, *The Royal Tennis Court: A History of Tennis at Hampton Court Palace* (Oxford: Ronaldson Publications, 2002), 47.

[12] Best, *The Royal Tennis Court*, 62–3.

[13] The king of France had a tennis court in each of his palaces—in Versailles, in Fontainebleau, in Saint-Germain, and in Compiegne—while other princes had tennis courts in their own castles, such as the Prince de Condé at Chantilly.

[14] Antonio Scaino, *Scaino on Tennis*, trans. W.W. Kershaw (London: Strangeways Press, 1951).

[15] "[S]i l'on on croit quelques auteurs, Galien l'ordonnoit à ceux qui étoient d'un tempérament fort replet, comme un remede pour dissiper la superfluité des humeurs qui les rend pesans & sujets à l'apoplexie: quelques—uns disent que c'etoit le jeu de la pelotte, mais comme cette pelotte n'étoit autre chose qu'une balle, on croit qu'ils se sont trompés." Translation: "If some authors are to be believed, Galien prescribed it to those who were of too plump a temperament, as a remedy to dissipate the superfluity of humors that left them heavy and prone to apoplexy; some said it was the game of 'pelotte,' but since that pelotte was nothing but a ball, it is believed that they are mistaken" (tr. Sharon Harrow).

[16] Scaino, *Scaino on Tennis*, 133.

[17] Scaino, *Scaino on Tennis*, 11.

[18] Scaino, *Scaino on Tennis*, 12.

[19] *L'Utilité qui provient du jeu de la paume au corps et à l'esprit. Traduict du grec de Galien en françois* (Paris: impr. de T. Sevestre, 1599).

[20] M. de Garsault, *Art du Paumier-Raquetier, et de la Paume* (Paris: chez Saillant and Nyon, chez Desaint, 1767). Translated as *The Art of the Tennis-Racket-Maker and of Tennis*. Privately printed, 1938.

[21] Robert Lukin, *A Treatise on Tennis* [1822] (Oxford: Ronaldson Publications, 1991), 10–11.

[22] Barcellon was likewise a distinguished member of a family of players. And, like Lukin, Manevieux also claimed to have been the first man ever to write a treatise on tennis.

[23] M. de Garsault, *The Art of the Tennis-Racket-Maker and of Tennis* (privately printed, 1938), 3.

[24] Garsault reminded the reader that these makers were indeed authorized to form a company in 1610 ("Communauté des Maîtres Paumiers-Raquetiers, Faiseurs d'Eteufs, Pelotes & Balles"), and were granted the privilege of running a tennis court as well as of making rackets and balls.

[25] Lukin, *A Treatise on Tennis*, 5–6.

[26] James Love, *Cricket. An Heroic Poem Illustrated with the Critical Observations of Scriblerus Maximus* (London, 1770), 5.

[27] Izaak Walton, likewise, had mentioned tennis in the "Angler's Song," only to discard it: "But these delights I neither wish, / Nor envy, while I freely fish." Izaak Walton, *The Art of Angling* [1676], ed. Marjorie Swann (Oxford: Oxford University Press, 2014), 66.

[28] James Kenneth Stephen, "Parker's Piece, May 19, 1891," *Cambridge Review* (May 1891).

[29] James W. Bright and Wilfred P. Mustard, "Pan's Pipe, Three Pastoral Eclogues, with Other Verses, by Francis Sabie (1595)," in *Modern Philology* 7, no. 4 (April 1910): 451.

[30] M. Bajot, *Eloge de la paume et de ses avantages sous le rapport de la santé et du développement des facultés physiques* (Paris: Bachelier, Nepveu, 1824).

[31] William Hazlitt, "On the Qualifications Necessary to Success in Life," in Duncan Wu (ed.), *The Plain Speaker*, vol. 8 of *The Selected Writings of William Hazlitt* (London: Pickering and Chatto, 1998), 193–4.

[32] Tobias Smollett, *The Adventures of Roderick Random* [1746], introduction and notes by James G. Basker, Paul-Gabriel Boucé, Nicole A. Seary, ed. O M Brack Jr. (Athens and London: the University of Georgia Press, 2012), 17.

[33] Smollett, *The Adventures of Roderick Random*, 17.

[34] Samuel Richardson, *Pamela*, ed. Thomas Keymer and Alice Wakely (Oxford: Oxford University Press, 2001), 145.

[35] Scaino, *Scaino on Tennis*, 4–5.

[36] *The Countess of Pembrokes Arcadia*, 1598, Lib. 5, 453. Quoted in Jeremy Potter, *Tennis and Oxford* (Oxford: Oxford Unicorn Press, 1994).

[37] John Webster, *The Duchess of Malfi* in *The Works of John Webster*, ed. David Gunby, David Carnegie, Antony Hammon, and Doreen DelVecchio (Cambridge: Cambridge University Press, 1995), V.iv.569.

[38] Alexander Fyffe, *The Tragedy of the Royal Martyr, K. Charles I*, 2nd ed. (Edinburgh, 1712), 43.

[39] William Oldys, *The Life of Sir Walter Ralegh* (London: printed for the booksellers in town and country, 1740), 148.

[40] Pseudo-Bunyan, *Meditations on the Several Ages of Man's Life: Representing, the Vanity of it, from his Cradle to his Grave* (London: printed for J. Blare, 1700–1701), 38.

[41] Heiner Gillmeister gives further examples of such use of the emblem of the tennis ball, quoting for instance from Henry Peacham's *Minerva Britanna* (1612) : "The *tennis-ball*, when strucken to the ground, / With Racket, or with gentle Schoole-boies hand, / With greater force, doth back againe rebound, / His fate, (though senceless) seeming to withstand." See Heiner Gillmeister, *Tennis: A Cultural History* (London: Leicester University Press, 1997), 137–40. See also Anthony W. Johnson, "Tennis in Early Modern Poetry," in Martin Gill et al, *Language, Learning, Literature. Studies Presented to Håkan Ringbom* (Turku: Åbo Akademi University Press, 2001), 215–45. The second meaning for "tennis-ball" in the *Oxford English Dictionary* is "a thing or person that is tossed or bandied about like a tennis-ball." The first occurrence recorded by the *OED* is a 1589 quotation from William Warner.

[42] *Fishing and hunting* (London: Thomas Bailey, n.d.), 29.

[43] Translation from Gillmeister, *Tennis: A Cultural History*, 132. The French text reads : "Si vous la baisés comptés quinze / Si vous touchés le tetin trente / Si vous auées la motte prinse / Quaranate cinq lors se presente / Mais si vous metés en la fente / Ce de quoy la dame a mestier / Notés bien ce que ie vous chnate / Vous gaignés le Jeu tout entier."

Gillmeister seems to ascribe authorship to Viau, but it was an older poem. There are many other instances of such games with tennis, both in French and in English; see for instance Henry Porter's lines taken from his comedy *The Pleasant Historie of the Two Angrie Women of Abington* (1599): "And by my troth my sisters maiden head / Stands like a game at tennis, if the ball / Hit into the hole or hazard, fare well all" (Gillmeister, 145). Pantagruel, going through Orléans, adopts the motto of the students of Orléans: "So you have in your hand a racket, / A tennis-ball in your cod-placket." François Rabelais, *Pantagruel*, book 2, chapter 6, "*Un esteuf en la braguette, En la main une raquette.*"

[44] "In answer of which claim the Prince our master / Says that you savour too much of your youth / And bids you be advised. There's naught in France / That can be with a nimble galliard won; / You cannot revel into dukedoms there. / He therefore sends you, meeter for your spirit, / This tun of treasure, and in lieu of this / Desires you let the dukedoms that you claim / Hear no more of you. This the Dauphin speaks. / KING What treasure, uncle? / EXETER Tennis-balls, my liege." William Shakespeare, *Henry V*, ed. T.W. Craik (London: Routledge, 1995), I.ii.250–59, pp. 147–8.

[45] Shakespeare, *Henry V*, I.ii.261–83, pp. 148–50.

[46] Winfried Schleiner, "'We Who Are All Players:' Constructing Early Modern Tennis," *Aethlon* 22, no. 1 (Fall 2004): 15–31.

[47] See Marshall, *Annals of Tennis*, 76–8, for similar instances of duels and brawls on the tennis court.

[48] This is apparent in the use of the French word *tripot* to refer to the tennis-court, although it came to be more widely used to describe shady establishments where gambling took place.

[49] Alain René Le Sage, *The Adventures of Gil Blas of Santillane. A new translation, by the author of Roderick Random* (London: J. Osborn, 1750), 149.

[50] Roger Morgan, *Tennis: The Development of the European Ball Game* (Oxford: Oxford University Press, 1995), 161.

[51] See for instance, Robert J. Lake, "Real Tennis and the Civilising Process," *Sport in History* 29, no. 4 (2009): 566. More generally on the construction of the Early Modern spectator and the importance of betting in the process, see Allen Guttmann, "English Sports Spectators: The Restoration to the Early Nineteenth Century," *Journal of Sport History* 12, no. 2 (Summer 1985): 103–25.

[52] Quoted in Morgan, *Tennis*, 163.

[53] Thomas Holcroft, *The Road to Ruin. A comedy. As it is acted at the Theatre Royal, Covent-Garden* (London: printed for J. Debrett, 1792), 32.

[54] *Hoyle's Games Improved*. Revised and corrected by Charles Jones, Esq. (London: printed for J. Rivington and J. Wilki St. Paul's Church-Yard, 1775), 204–8.

[55] *Annals of gaming; or complete directions for whist, quadrille, piquet, billiards, ... in which is contained, the method of playing ... Including the laws of the several games* (London: printed for William Lane, et al., n.d.), 46.

[56] *Annals of gaming*, 55.

[57] See for instance *Interesting Anecdotes, Memoirs, Allegories, Essays, and Poetical Fragments, Tending to Amuse the Fancy, and Inculcate Morality. By Mr. Addison*, vol. 3 (London: printed for the author, 1794), 54–6. The piece was reprinted from the *Weekly Miscellany* 11, no. 275 (4 January 1770): 318–20; as identified by Edward W.R. Pitcher, *The Magazine Sources for Interesting Anecdotes, Memoirs, Allegories, Essays, and Poetical Fragments ... By Mr. Addison* (Lewiston: The Edwin Mellen Press, 2004).

[58] Lukin, *A Treatise on Tennis*, 111–12.

[59] Denis de la Marinière, *La Maison academique, contenant les jeux du picquet, du hoc, du tric-trac, du hoca, de la guerre, de la paulme, du billard, du palle-mail, divers jeux de cartes, qui se joüent en differentes facons ... & autres jeux facetieux & divertissans* (Paris: chez Etienne Loison, 1659).

[60] Morgan, *Tennis*, 160.

[61] Morgan, *Tennis*, 176.

[62] For a detailed account in France, see Luze, *A History of the Royal Game of Tennis*, 75–95.

[63] Luze, *A History of the Royal Game of Tennis*, 24–5.

[64] See Ernest L. Rhodes, "Me thinks this stage shews like a Tennis Court," *Renaissance Papers* (1968): 21–8.

[65] J.L. Styan, *The English Stage. A History of Drama and Performance* (Cambridge: Cambridge University Press, 1996), 238.

[66] William Congreve, *Love for Love* (London, 1695), "Epilogue, Spoken at the Opening of the New House." This echoes Dryden's comment in the Prologue to Nathaniel Lee's *Sophonisba*: "Yet *Athens* never knew your learned Sport / Of tossing Poets in a *Tennis-Court*."

[67] On the James Street Theatre, see David Clay Jenkins, "The James Street Theatre at the Old Tennis-Court," *Theatre Notebook* 23 (1969): 143–50. See also "Great Windmill Street Area," *Survey of London: volumes 31 and 32: St James Westminster, Part 2* (1963), 41–56, accessed 22 July 2013, http://www.british-history.ac.uk/report.aspx?compid=41453.

[68] Jenkins, "The James Street Theatre," 144.

[69] "Great Windmill Street Area," *Survey of London: volumes 31 and 32: St James Westminster, Part 2* (1963): 41–56, accessed 7 August 2013, http://www.british-history.ac.uk/report.aspx?compid=41453.

[70] The first installment was published on 19 August 1876, p. 220. The essays were collected under Marshall, *Annals of Tennis*.

[71] J.R. Atkins, *The Book of Racquets. A Practical Guide to the Game and its History, and to the Different Courts in which it is Played* (London: Frederick Warne, 1872).

[72] This is the explanation favoured by Luze, *A History of the Royal Game of Tennis*, 70.

[73] Michel de Montaigne, *Essais*, ed. Jean Balsamo, Michel Magnien, and Catherine Magnien-Simonin (Paris: Gallimard, 2007), III.xiii.1136; II.xii.626.

Chapter 5
Archery in the Long Eighteenth Century
Linda V. Troost

Although well established in many cultures, the longbow has always been important to England as a national and cultural symbol. The longbow gave England victories over the French at Crécy (1346) and Agincourt (1415), and parliamentary statutes mandated archery practice for men and the establishment of shooting butts (earthen targets) in villages. England's medieval folk hero Robin Hood was a master archer. But after the battle of Flodden (1513), the bow lost ground to gunpowder. Once the musket became the weapon of choice at the end of the sixteenth century, archery became a recreational pursuit rather than a national imperative. After the restoration of the monarchy, the archaic sport became the preserve of the British upper classes; just as Robin Hood gentrified in early modern British literature, transforming from common outlaw into nobleman-turned-outlaw, archery's practitioners shifted from the yeomanry to the nobility and gentry.[1] By the end of the eighteenth century, the sport was deemed suitable exercise even for ladies, who participated in several mixed-sex archery clubs.

The shift started in the second half of the seventeenth century. The first revival of archery was initiated by the Finsbury Archers, founded in London in 1652. Its members practiced at the Artillery Grounds since several were also part of the Honourable Artillery Company.[2] They shot annually for prizes such as spoons and silver arrows, relying on fortune as much as skill: the top prize went not to the archer with the highest cumulative score but to the first archer to hit the center of the target. With the shooting distance starting at "eleven score yards," one can only assume that there were not many arrows hitting targets until the distances decreased with each round. Regulations, however, stipulated a still-impressive minimum distance of 160 yards.[3] (By comparison, Olympic archers today shoot at 70 meters.) William Wood was a major force in the Finsbury Archers, serving for many years as the society's marshal, participating in its five parades (the first in 1661 modeled on an Elizabethan precedent), and authoring a historical treatise in 1682, *The Bowman's Glory or Archery Revived*.

Other societies, largely in the north, formed soon thereafter. They maintained practice grounds, regulated competitions, and arranged accompanying festivities. In 1673, the Scorton Archers in Yorkshire formed and established an annual contest for a silver arrow, a competition still in existence (the Scorton Silver Arrow is regarded as the oldest existing sporting trophy in use).[4] To win the Arrow, one had to be the first archer to pierce the center of the target. The order of shooting was determined by lottery so that "not only skill but also fortune should play a part in the day's shooting."[5] This was probably a way to ensure that the competition gave genteel amateurs a chance. Other groups revived lapsed competitions. The Royal Company of Archers in Edinburgh, established in 1676 and "consisting of the prime nobility, gentry, and other persons of distinction," competed annually for various prizes, including the ancient Musselburgh Arrow. This competition is widely regarded as the oldest continuous, documented sporting event, with records of winners dating back to 1603.[6] Similarly, the gentlemen of Kilwinning, Scotland, revived the medieval papingo shoot in 1688, which required participants to knock a wooden bird (popinjay) off its perch atop a church tower by shooting blunted arrows vertically; in 1724, David Muir presented a prize silver arrow for the winner. As in other contests, "fortune" was as important as "skill."[7] The fashion for competitions reached schools, too. Harrow instituted an annual student competition for a silver arrow presented in 1684 by Sir Gilbert Talbot.[8] By the middle of the eighteenth century, Arrow Day was a highlight of the London social season, but it eventually became a disruptive nuisance and was abolished in 1771 by the new headmaster, Dr. Benjamin Heath.[9] The popularity of silver arrows as archery prizes goes back at least to the early modern period: Robin Hood wins one in *A Gest of Robyn Hode*, for instance.

The competitions were regional, and the sport often in danger of vanishing. After Wood's death in 1691, the Finsbury Archers in London, "deprived of his leadership and inspiration, declined again quite rapidly," ultimately dissolving in 1761.[10] Various rural archery societies rose and fell after a decade or two of activity. Two of the more robust groups, both in the north of England—the Richmond Archers (founded 1755) and the Darlington Archers (founded 1758)—were created to compete for the Scorton Silver Arrow, their local prize, but interest waxed and waned.[11] In 1769, instead of the usual 15 to 20 competitors that the Scorton shoot formerly attracted, only seven archers competed. Things got worse during the war with the America colonies: five times in the 1770s, "*the* ARROW *was not shot for, no Gentlemen appearing.*"[12] To survive, the archaic sport of archery needed to become less parochial and move from the rural to the urban landscape.

That meant London. Some 15 years after the official end of the Finsbury Archers, Sir Ashton Lever (1729–1788) started a new society in London. Lever was a wealthy magistrate, collector, and antiquarian who had brought his Holophusikon, a museum displaying his private natural history collection, from his home in Lancashire to London in 1774. He also brought to London his secretary, Thomas Waring (1730–1805), and the two of them are responsible for the second revival of the sport.

Because of Waring's quest for improved health, archery gained a wider currency. An oft-reprinted anecdote tells the tale:

> About the year 1776, Mr. Waring (who resided with Sir Ashton Lever, at Leicester House, and who may justly be stiled the *father* of *modern* archery) having, by continual application to business, contracted an oppression upon his chest, (arising principally from sitting too closely to his desk, and pressing his breast too much against it …), resolved to try the effect of the bow in affording

himself relief. He accordingly made it a regular exercise, and in a short time derived great benefit from the use of it; and ascribes his cure, which was perfect, solely to the use of archery. Sir Ashton Lever, perceiving the good effects, which so engaging an amusement had upon the constitution, followed Mr. Waring's example, and took up the bow; he was soon joined by several of his friends, who, in the year 1780, formed themselves into a society, under the title of *Toxophilites*, and met regularly at Leicester House, having butts erected in the gardens belonging to it. And this society was the parent stock of the numerous societies of Archers.[13]

This anecdote, however, glosses over some details. Archery did not spring out of nowhere: both Waring and Lever had already been connected with the sport. Before entering Lever's employ, Thomas Waring had studied bowyering (bow-making) with the Kelsals of Manchester, "the best bow and arrow makers in England."[14] Sir Ashton Lever was a member of the Broughton Archers, an exclusive group in the Manchester area, and had founded another society in the area, the Middleton Archers, in 1777.[15] But the important things are here: Lever and Waring were the major forces behind the successful revival of archery as a British sport, and it was this archery society that inspired the creation of numerous other groups in the south of England and in Wales.

The London archers evoked the past. They gave themselves an archaic name, the Toxophilite Society, after *Toxophilus*, Roger Ascham's 1545 archery manual dedicated to Henry VIII, the first such book to be published in English (*toxophilus*, a term coined by Ascham, means "lover of the bow"). They dressed in green and wore feathered hats that recalled medieval yeomen. The Society included Lever, Waring, and the few remaining Finsbury Archers, one of whom, Philip Constable, as custodian of the defunct society's archery trophies, transferred them to the new society.[16] The Toxophilites drew up a list of rules and orders in 1781 and, within a year, had a handful of members. Between them, Lever and Waring had what was needed to spur a revival in the metropolis: Lever had experience in running sporting events (he had been steward for the Manchester Races in 1761[17]), had already founded an archery society, had good social connections, and possessed a large back garden in London suitable for practice. Waring had a practical knowledge of equipment manufacture and the entrepreneurial drive to turn it into a thriving family business.

At first, members met twice a week in the summer for archery practice and, in winter on the first Monday of the month for a dinner. Three Targets (formal matches) were held, all around days of national importance: on St. George's Day (the Easter Target), the king's birthday (the Whitsun Target), and the birthday of the Prince of Wales in August (the Annual Target), with small cash prizes for hits.[18] The members shot at paired targets a hundred yards apart (walking repeatedly back and forth between them), and the member who struck the gold (the gilded center of the target), not first but most centrally, was designated Captain of the Target. The next-best shot gained one the title of Lieutenant of the Target.[19] A few years later, the society added medals and cups to the trophies to reward those with the most hits (Captain of Numbers and Lieutenant of Numbers), so for the first time, skill more than luck was rewarded. Because of the small size of the Leicester House garden, only practices took place there; the Targets were held at larger venues in London such as Canonbury House or Highbury Barn. In later years, the Toxophilite Society used the Artillery Grounds and Lord's Cricket Ground in Marylebone until they leased land near Bedford Square in 1791, at which time they added a fourth Target.

It is difficult to determine how good the archers were, but one suspects that, initially, the skill level was low. Frances Burney visited Sir Ashton's museum shortly after the Toxophilites were formed and was unimpressed by the archery practice taking place in the garden of Leicester House. Sir Ashton

> had Dressed not only 2 young men, but himself, in a Green Jacket, a round Hat with Green Feathers, a bundle of arrows under one arm, & a Bow in the other; & thus, accoutered as a *Forrester*, he pranced about, while the younger fools who were in the same Garb, kept running to & fro in the garden, carefully contriving to shoot at some mark just as any of the Company appeared at any of the Windows![20]

The uniformed archers were shooting not at targets but at "marks," small objects or pieces of paper on the ground at short distances (20 or 30 yards), a standard way for beginners to train, especially in a small space.[21] Clearly, Burney finds the entire venture silly and suspects the "prancing" archers of being more interested in personal display than in practicing their sport.

Personal display was an important part of the sport, as was exclusivity. The Toxophilite Society was an all-male private club, and membership was limited and expensive. In the first years of the Society, each member paid three guineas a year for the privilege of practicing at Leicester House and participating in the Targets, but they also had to contribute an additional five shillings toward a dinner to be held after the Annual Target.[22] Members had to be nominated by another member and voted on. Blackballing took place. Who were the members? The 1791 membership list for the Toxophilites includes, to choose at random, the publisher Francis Newberry, several members of Parliament, Charles Hoare of Hoare's Bank, the Duke of Norfolk, the Duke of Leeds, the artist George Romney, several members of the clergy, and many lawyers and barristers—in other words, eminent professionals, the gentry, and the aristocracy. The post-Target dinners could get fairly lively, hence the introduction of Bylaw 8, "every Person who shall break Glasses, or Decanters, or damage [other] Property of the Society, shall reinstate the same." And there were many opportunities for socializing: Bylaw 9 required that "every Member who shall happen to marry, shall treat the Society with a Marriage Feast."[23] Such a "mix of sport and conviviality" was ideal for an elite that "had considerable time and money on its hands."[24]

On top of expenses for shooting, eating, and drinking, equipment had to be purchased, conveniently available from Waring's archery manufacture and warehouse, established to cater to the new society and, eventually, to others in

Figure 5.1 Thomas Waring, *Senior, shooting on Blackheath with the Royal Toxophilites in spring 1789* (after Joseph Slater, engraved by James Heath). Published March 2, 1789, by Joseph Slater. Image courtesy, the Heath-Caldwell Family Archive.

the London area. Waring was also good with budgeting and finances, serving as perpetual secretary-treasurer of the Toxophilites from 1781 to 1804.[25] Archery required expensive tackle. A good longbow (usually close to six feet long) could cost up to two guineas, men's arrows were 18s a dozen (plain) or 20s for a dozen with fluted shafts.[26] In addition, one needed a few bowstrings at a shilling each, a bow case, a quiver to hold one's arrows, shooting gloves, and a leather brace to protect the forearm from bowstring abrasions. The arrows all needed to be painted with the archer's personal mark, an inch-wide band of colored stripes near the feathered end designed to forestall identification problems when it came time for scoring.[27] Waring kept track of every shooter's pattern in a book at the warehouse to simplify reordering and prevent duplication, and he stocked matching satin ribbons to be tied to an archer's bow or worn as a sash. He also sold archery-related paraphernalia such as books and prints (Figure 5.1).

Then there was the uniform to purchase. In 1784, the Toxophilite uniform was simple: a green coat with arrows marked on the buttons, white waistcoat and breeches, all to be worn on Target Days and at society dinners.[28] By 1791, when membership had risen to 168,[29] the designated uniform had become more elaborate and costly: "A Green Cloth Coat and White Waistcoat and Breeches of Cloth, or

Kerseymere, with Gilt Arrow Buttons, White Stockings and Black Hussar Half Boots; a Black Round Hat, with the Prince of Wales's Button, a double Gold Loop, and one Black Cock Feather." In addition, one needed accoutrements to complete the outfit: "A Black Leather Brace, a Buff coloured Leather Belt, with a Pouch and a Green Tassell."[30] Why the change? In June 1787, the Prince of Wales became patron of the Toxophilites, and one suspects his artistic hand behind the elaboration in costume. Archery-society uniforms, with their green coats and feathers, as Miss Burney recognized, evoke the forester. Archery in the eighteenth century had more than a whiff of the antiquarian about it, and the Toxophilite uniform pointedly paid homage to England's beloved outlaw and archer Robin Hood, not the red-coated British army. Details of the uniforms changed in small ways over the years. By 1794, for example, gaiters replaced the boots and the feather was dropped, probably a nod to military elements in fashion during the war with France.[31] Elaborate and expensive uniforms were a way to keep the price point of membership high enough to guarantee exclusivity, and conformity was expected. Members could be charged a stiff penalty of as much as one guinea for not being properly attired for Target Days.

Archery's popularity gained rapidly, with many societies modeled on the Toxophilites being formed mainly in the Home Counties but also farther afield. The founders tended to be Britain's statesmen. For example, James Cecil, 1st Marquess of Salisbury, and his wife, Emily, founded the Hertfordshire Archers at Hatfield House, and the Earl of Aylesbury supervised the Woodmen of Arden in Meriden, near Coventry. *The English Chronicle or Universal Evening Post* on 30 June 1789 wrote that "The rage for this noble art is astonishing; there are already near sixty societies in this kingdom." And that "noble art" attracted nobility, with the Prince of Wales's early adoption of archery assuring its future among people of fashion (Figure 5.2). The prince served as patron of three archery societies: the Toxophilites, the Royal British Bowmen, and the Royal Kentish Bowmen. For the last group, he again applied his design skills. As of January 1789, the uniform was "to consist of: A grass green coat, buff linings, and buff waistcoat and breeches: black collar to the coat, uncut velvet in winter, tabby silk in summer, with yellow buttons according to the pattern sent to Nutting's, No. 16, *King Street, Covent Garden*, by His Royal Highness's order."[32] The prince had his portrait painted in this uniform in 1791, and it was on display "at the top of the room" in the society's lodge on Dartford Heath, along with a "very good cast of the Apollo Belvedere."[33] Archery ran in the royal family: the prince's brother, the Duke of Clarence, served as patron of the Royal Surrey Bowmen, another extremely fashionable society.

One of the Prince's three groups, the Royal British Bowmen, established 1787, was distinctive. Founded by Sir Watkin Williams-Wynne and Sir Foster Cunliffe, the society included the leading families in North Wales.[34] Meetings were held at the "Houses of those members" living within "80 Bow-shots from the Town of *Wrexham*" (about five miles).[35] The members spent a great deal of money on their sport: for instance, the host for the next meeting was expected, "at his own

Figure 5.2   John Russell, The Prince of Wales (later George IV) in the uniform he designed for the Royal Kentish Bowmen (1791). Oil on canvas, 250.2 x 180.3 cm. Royal Collection Trust / © Her Majesty Queen Elizabeth II, 2015.

Expence," to transport the society's large refreshment tent from its present location to his own house, and those members with gardens were "expected to bring with them a Basket of Fruit to every Meeting, if convenient."[36] What was unusual about the Royal British Bowmen, though, was that it admitted women as equal members. The ladies competed for their own prizes, wore green and buff uniforms, and their archery victories were written up in the newspapers alongside those of their male colleagues.

Figure 5.3   The Fairlop Oak with a meeting of the Hainault Foresters (engraved by Cook). Frontispiece for the January 1794 issue of *The Sporting Magazine*. Image courtesy, HathiTrust Digital Library.

Women of the gentry and aristocracy quickly took up this "manly" amusement.[37] In addition to the Royal British Bowmen in Wales, the Hertfordshire Archers, the Hainault Foresters, and the Union Society of Harlow permitted women full membership. The regulations of the Hainault Foresters specified one of the more elaborate uniforms for its female members:

> Nankeen great coat, black silk collar, dark green silk cape; lappels, cuffs, and pockets, bound with black; full green sleeves down to the elbow, tied with black ribbon in the middle of the arm; a single row of uniform buttons, the front of the coat bound with green; black beaver hat, plain green band around the crown, buttoned up on the right side with uniform button [depicting the Fairlop Oak and an arrow] and gold twisted loop, with green cockade and feathers.[38]

With green coats and feathers in their hats, the archers standing under the ancient Fairlop Oak of Hainault Forest, the archers were clearly trying to look like Robin Hood's merry band under the giant oak of Sherwood Forest (Figure 5.3). The pillars of society who comprised its membership must have had fun playing at outlaws, and both men and women could participate. There were also more informal opportunities, such as the public breakfasts *cum* archery parties held in the early 1790s by the celebrated Mrs. Crespigny at her home in Camberwell (Wednesday mornings from May to July).[39] Men shot at 100 yards, and the ladies at 70. Tickets were widely sought after, and all proceeds went to charity.

The all-male societies had roles for women, too. Ladies were permitted to attend Targets as spectators, to serve as Lady Patronesses and present awards, and to dance at archery balls. Mrs. Crespigny, for example, became Lady Patroness for the Royal Toxophilites in 1801.[40] They often held a lottery for the "ladies' prize," normally a bracelet or a brooch, and the winner had her name published in the papers alongside those of the winning archers. Some societies even permitted wives and sisters to practice at their targets. Not only did the groups provide a moral environment for well-bred ladies (swearing and gambling were forbidden, or at least heavily fined), but a woman armed with a longbow in a carefully vetted group did not need to worry about inappropriate advances.

Most important, the meetings provided men and women a way to socialize with potential spouses guaranteed to be of the correct background. The membership roster of the all-male Woodmen of Arden of Meriden bears this out. An 1885 history of the society notes, in its comprehensive numbered list of members, who married a daughter or sister of a fellow Woodman. For example, among members who joined in 1786, two married within its ranks:

> 35. Mills, William, res. 1792, of Bisterne, Hants, married Elizabeth, daughter of Hon. Wriothesley Digby (sister of No. 2); Director of Hon. East India Company, d. 1820.

> 36. Bankes, William, of Winstanley Hall, High Sheriff of Lancashire 1784, married Mary Anne Bunney, sister of No. 16.[41]

Likewise, *The Morning Herald* of 26 July 1787 notes that, in the mixed-sex Royal British Bowmen, "several young ladies have added to their conquests the hearts of young gentlemen of honor and fortune; and of consequence, not a few happy couples have paid their vows at the altar of Hymen."[42] An archery match provided a lot of time for conversation, perhaps better than a ball did, and it allowed ample opportunity for self-display. Cupid, the most famous of archers, was also shooting arrows.

There were some single-sex archery opportunities for women in London. On 19 August 1792, the *Star* reported that Theresa Cornelys, the "once celebrated" masquerade entrepreneur, "has taken the house lately occupied by the dealer in *asses' milk*—and the grounds are now to be laid out in a very superior stile as a *female archery*." One all-female society existed, albeit briefly, to judge by its minute paper trail. On 28 December 1789, *The Oracle or Bell's New World* reported that the

> fair Archers of Blackheath, associated under the name of British Amazons, gave on Saturday the 19th instant, an elegant Supper and Ball to the Admirers of themselves and their amusement; at which a numerous train of Cupids attended as Quiver-bearers; nor was Apollo himself, the God of the Silver *Bow*, an absentee, as an admirable Ode recited on the occasion, sufficiently testified.

This description of a winter meeting seems to be the only reference to the group in the newspapers. Part of the appeal of archery was that it offered women healthy, outdoor exercise but also an opportunity to look elegant: "[T]he attitude of an archer drawing the bow ... cannot fail of displaying the graces of the female form, in a considerable degree"[43] (Figure 5.4). For that reason, a mixed society was more useful than a single-sex one since it provided a male audience for the elegant females. Archery was not just about getting exercise while competing with one's fellows for points; it was also part of a larger competition for husbands.

In the mixed societies, men and women may have competed against each other during informal events, but at the Targets, they vied only with their own sex because they shot at different distances and used different bows. Men's bows for target shooting typically required a draw weight of 50 pounds, and women's 24 to 34 pounds.[44] The discrepancy arises not just from muscle strength but also from height and arm length: a bow must match the shooter's body. The draw weight of a bow determines the distance it can shoot; a shorter, lighter bow cannot convey an arrow as far, no matter how accomplished the archer. However, women did not get special treatment. They may have used lighter bows and, therefore, shot at shorter distances (50 to 70 yards instead of the 90 or 100 men used), but their targets were smaller to compensate. In 1814, Waring describes women's targets as about 26 inches in diameter to the men's 48 inches.[45] Target sizes could vary, however. In 1803, for example, Sophia Banks ordered some for use at her home, Revesby Abbey, that had a 35-inch diameter.[46]

A sample Target will demonstrate how much stamina this sport required of its participants, how good the shooters were, and how much drama there could be. A united society comprised of the Woodmen of Arden, the Broughton Archers, and the Lancashire Bowmen held a joint Target on 6 July 1792 at Cannock Chase, Rudgley, Staffordshire, the results recorded in *Diary or Woodfall's Register* on 21 July. The gentlemen were competing for a silver bow, a prize given to the society by the Lady Patroness, Miss Curzon of Hagley, Worcestershire:

> The silver Bow was shot for by 25 archers, at three targets (each 100 yards) two hours before and two hours after dinner.—At the end of the morning shooting, Mr. Thackeray and Mr. Hobson (both Lancashire archers) were each 19 shot in the target; and at the conclusion, in the evening, were each 37; the dubious shot, had it been allowed, was Mr. Thackeray's, and would have made him 38; but being given against him, it was agreed each to shoot a pair of arrows at a strange target; when all the four arrows were in the circles, but Mr. Thackeray's being the more central, he obtained the prize.

Four hours of fine shooting, with eight or nine archers to a target, each shooting, in turn, two arrows and then walking to the opposite target to retrieve the arrows to do it again ... and again ... and again. This is considerable exercise. (Thomas Waring, Jr., calculated that a typical archer walked six miles in the course of a Target.[47]) The two leaders from the Lancashire Bowmen are well matched, yet, it comes down to the wire, and after four hours, the match is settled with a tiebreaker.

Figure 5.4 Archery at Hatfield, depicting the Marchioness of Salisbury and members of the Hertfordshire Archers (engraved by Cook, after Richard Corbould). Illustration for the November 1792 issue of *The Sporting Magazine*. Image courtesy, HathiTrust Digital Library.

Diary or Woodfall's Register also records a competition for ladies, which had been held two days earlier:

> The Ladies Prize, a Silver Medal, was warmly contested: it was shot for by eleven Ladies in a most elegant uniform, at a target the distance of 60 yards, on the Wednesday; and at the conclusion of three hours shooting, Miss Kinnersley and Miss Wedgewood, being each 15 shots in the target, the contest was obliged to be decided by each a pair of arrows; each had one arrow in the circles, but Miss Kinnersley's, being more central, obtained the prize.

They, too, decided the match on a tiebreaker. The ladies shot for only three hours and walked shorter distances, but they still needed considerable endurance and mental focus.

Several women took the sport to a higher level. Lady Salisbury of the Hertfordshire Archers, for example, was a fine archer and was illustrated at the targets in the *Ladies' Pocket-Book* for 1791 and *The Sporting Magazine* for November 1792. Among the archery ephemera collected by Sophia Banks are notes on sporting victories by women and her own assessment of the best female archers. One item is particularly interesting. A document "copied April 1798 by Mr. Jones from a writing in a frame in the Toxophilite Room" describes a private match between the sexes:

> October 1st, 1790. A match was shot at Mr. Wybergh's at Bramhope Hall in Yorkshire, at 100 yards, between Miss Littledale, Mr. Gilpin, and Mr. Wybergh, in which Miss Littledale was victorious. During the shooting, which lasted 3 Hours, Miss Littledale hit the Gold 4 times; and what evinces superior skill, the 3 last hits made by Miss Littledale were all in the Gold![48]

What makes Miss Littledale's accomplishment notable is the fact that her best hits were at the end of the match, when archers are most tired. She also must have been shooting with a 50-pound bow since the distance was 100 yards. The three competitors were well connected and accomplished archers. Thomas Wybergh, at whose home the match took place, was a barrister at law and had recently been appointed Clerk of the Peace for the West Riding of the County of York. He had joined the Toxophilite Society in 1788, but after his appointment, shot with the Yorkshire Archers, serving as steward in 1791 for the Grand Meeting and winning Lord Fitzwilliam's Silver Bugle in 1793.[49] William Gilpin was involved in the business of "military outfitting" and had been admitted to the Toxophilites on 18 May 1789.[50] Miss Littledale cannot be identified, but she might have been the sister or cousin of Joseph Littledale, who later became a judge on the Queen's Bench. He was a member of Lincoln's Inn, as was Wybergh, which provides a logical connection.[51] The fact that this match was written up to be posted in the Society lodge suggests that the men acknowledged Miss Littledale's excellent marksmanship even if the Royal Toxophilites could not admit her as a member.

Not all archers, however, were good. Banks also records a Target shot by the Woodmen of Arden on 27 August 1802, in which only one archer out of a field of

25 managed to hit the center gold. No single archer landed more than 13 arrows in the targets, and many never hit it at all, a pretty miserable showing.[52] One assumes that the men were out of practice, having just returned from fighting Bonaparte and resuming their former sporting activities during the Peace of Amiens.

The Targets offered diversion, but they also offered prizes, perhaps as compensation for the restrictions on wagers. While the grand trophies for the best shot or the greatest number of hits consisted of silver arrows or silver bugle horns (another nod to Robin Hood), competitors also won cash prizes for each hit, paid out of the annual dues. In the beginning, the amounts were small. At the Toxophilites' Annual Target on 3 August 1782, Lever and Waring each won 4s, and other competitors won between 1s and 6s. The total pool paid to the 14 competitors was £2, 2s, 6d.[53] After dues were tripled from one to three guineas and additional fees added, the payouts became more generous. At the Prince's or Autumn Target in 1793, for example, Robert Glen won 64s, 6d, and Peter Cazalet won 62s, 6d.[54] A typical reward system was as follows: each hit in the gold paid 2s, 6d; the red, 2s; inner white, 1s, 6d; black, 1s; outer white, 6d.[55] Since a typical afternoon involved nearly 100 arrows shot by each competitor, a nineteenth-century archery historian speculated, "No wonder they shot so many Arrows, when they were paid so well for shooting."[56]

Shooting arrows for prizes was not the only amusement the societies offered. The Targets invariably concluded with a supper at Willis's Rooms in King Street or the Thatched House Tavern in St. James Street, followed by the singing of catches and archery-themed songs (after all, Apollo was both musician and archer). The Banks Collection contains many examples of these songs, and they were often printed in the morning papers or published in anthologies. Some societies held "winter meetings" (actually, dinners or balls) when shooting was out of season. For example, the Robin Hood Society near Gloucester gave a ball on 31 December 1789 for "about one hundred of the genteelist part of the country round about Wotton Underedge."[57] Men came in their uniforms and the ladies wore dresses "of the like colour." Dancing and entertainment was on offer, including a new dance called "Cupid's Arrow" devised by a member for the occasion, the music by George Hickes. Again, we see the link between archery and courtship. A supper catered by "a person from Bath" was followed by songs and musical medleys until six in the morning. Clearly, no expense was spared. Sophia Banks received from a correspondent a description of a ball given by the Bowmen of the Wye, a small group of archers near Chepstow. All the ladies were asked to wear "a muslin dress trimmed with green sattin ribbon, a green or white ribbon sash, a small green sattin Hat with a white Feather tipt with green, with a motto on the Bandeau."[58] The men, of course, wore their society uniforms. Spectacle and uniformity of appearance was important at these private dinners and balls, just as they were at the more public summer Targets. Expensive costumes conveyed exclusivity, and the shared costumes, no doubt also provided a feeling of solidarity among the gentry.

The greatest spectacle came at the public events, the Grand Meetings held between 1789 and 1795. All the male British archery clubs were invited, although only a handful actually came to compete, and the events drew hundreds of spectators (at a guinea a head admission). Newspaper journalists gushed over the handsome uniforms of the ladies in the audience, who did not shoot, and the elegant uniforms of the male archers, who did. At first, the events were simple, as a description of the meeting in 1790 indicates:

> On Friday last there was a grand meeting of archers on Blackheath, at which all the Societies who pursue that manly amusement were present. ... The field was rendered a very beautiful spectacle by the shew of tents and the profusion of charming females who were attracted by the Knights of the Bow.[59]

The evening ended with the archers repairing to Willis's for the traditional supper and obligatory archery-themed songs. By 1792, the event was more elaborate, mimicking a military review. The Grand Meeting commenced on Blackheath with archers from 10 different societies and in full uniform marching to music from their societies' hospitality tents to the 10 pairs of targets. In front of a large audience, no more than 10 archers to a target, they shot from noon to three o'clock and then, after a break, from half-past three to six o'clock, a real test of stamina. At the conclusion of shooting, the archers formally marched back to their tents, again accompanied by music, and everyone was dismissed to dinner, "the societies to be seated according to seniority."[60] The four champions were announced later, after the target papers had been examined. Prizes were awarded to the Captain and Lieutenant of the Target and to the Captain and Lieutenant of Numbers. By 1794, the spectators had become so numerous and caused such "great Confusion" that the Grand Meeting, now moved to Dulwich, was not advertised in the papers.[61] There had to be balance between public spectacle—a proxy display by the higher classes of their abilities—and social exclusivity.

The spectacle of archers also appeared on the London stage.[62] In keeping with archery's historic associations, the first theatrical offerings were inspired by figures from England's past. Two years after the founding of the Toxophilite Society, Philip Astley produced Charles Dibdin's version of *Robin Hood* at the Royal Circus and Equestrian Philharmonic Academy. A year later, Leonard MacNally wrote a comic opera mainpiece, the music composed by William Shield, called *Robin Hood; or, Sherwood Forest*, which opened at Covent Garden in April 1784 and ran for several years. MacNally partners Robin Hood with Clorinda, a spunky female archer who appears in the Restoration-era ballad "Robin Hood's Birth, Breeding, Valor, and Marriage" (a ballad which appeared in the Robin Hood anthologies, called *garlands*, published throughout the eighteenth century). All the Merry Men (except Little John) have ladies: a reviewer explains that they all have "been obliged to yield to the superiority of the Cyprian archer," Venus.[63] Four months later, Thomas Holcroft used material in the English ballad about archers Adam Bell, Clym of the Clough, and William of Cloudesley for another comic opera, *The Noble Peasant*, music also by Shield, which played at the Haymarket in August of 1784. This opera features a scene in which Cloudesley shoots an apple off his son's head (a key plot detail shared with the medieval Swiss legend of William Tell, the ancient Scandinavian story of Egil the archer, and the twelfth-century story of Toko as retold by Saxo Grammaticus[64]).

Theater pieces placing archery in an historical context were successful, but so were works that commented directly on the current rage for archery. Henry Bate Dudley immortalized the Hainault Archers in *The Woodman*, a comic opera which opened at Covent Garden on 26 February 1791, music once again by William Shield. This work featured a chorus of female archers in uniform, an onstage archery contest under the famous oak, and a climax that included the heroine's hitting the center gold on stage (not that hard at a short distance, but the reviewers were impressed nonetheless). The opera was extremely successful. However, not every archery-themed play was suitable for performance. In 1792, during the French Revolution, Richard Brinsley Sheridan, manager at Drury Lane, turned down a comic opera on the subject of William Tell on the grounds that it was "too much in favour of the liberties of the people to obtain the Lord Chamberlain's license."[65] The work was shortly thereafter published anonymously as *Helvetic Liberty* in 1792 and dedicated to the archers of Britain.

Other forms of theater also capitalized on the vogue. Charles Dibdin performed songs about archery in his timely cabaret shows at the Sans Souci during the 1792 and 1793 seasons, and John O'Keeffe's *Merry Sherwood; or Harlequin Forester* served as Covent Garden's Christmas pantomime in 1795. It concluded with a procession representing the various stages of "The Triumph of Archery": mythical, ancient, British, and modern. One reviewer called it "the very worst pantomime which has been produced for years,"[66] but another thought it pleasant enough: "The men proved themselves to be *good shots*, and the ladies never failed to *hit the mark*."[67] The pantomime must have captured some of the spectacle of the Grand Meetings with its pageantry, music, and processions.

The presentation on stage of "ancient" archery highlights an important aspect of the sport: antiquarianism. The first historical study in the eighteenth century was by Daines Barrington, who, on 27 February 1783, delivered "Observations on the Practice of Archery in England" to the Society of Antiquaries, a talk subsequently published in the society journal and reprinted in both the *European Magazine* and the *Annual Register*. Barrington had been made an honorary member of the Toxophilite Society the previous year, on 27 April 1782.[68] A new edition of the archer's Bible, Ascham's *Toxophilus*, was published in 1788 in Wrexham, home base of the Royal British Bowmen. There was also interest, not just in ancient British toxophily but also in Greek, Persian, Chinese, Turkish, and American Indian archery.

England's prime archer, Robin Hood, attracted the antiquarian scholar and amateur archer alike. Histories of archery learnedly speculated on the life, times, and accomplishments of the famous outlaw of Sherwood Forest. For those of a less-learned bent, collections of Robin Hood ballads were widely available as inexpensive garlands and, after 1795, in a fine, two-volume scholarly edition prepared by Joseph Ritson and illustrated by Thomas Bewick (the fashion for archery must have been a factor in the preparation of this work). Toxophilites like Sophia Banks bought Robin-Hood-related prints from Mr. Waring's shop and solicited information from correspondents about the measurement of a thigh bone found in the purported grave of Little John in Hathersage churchyard.[69] Robin Hood was an appealing figure because he could be appropriated by everyone, aristocrat and commoner alike. Even his politics were flexible. Some saw him as a conservative—a staunch supporter of his king and English tradition—while others, like Joseph Ritson, identified with his radical, outlaw side.

As archery mania spread, three book-length studies of the history of archery were published within two years of each other: Henry Oldfield's *Anecdotes of Archery, Ancient and Modern* (London, 1791), dedicated to the Marchioness of Salisbury; Ely Hargrove's *Anecdotes of Archery, From the Earliest Ages to 1791* (York, 1792), dedicated to George Allan, founder of the Darlington Archers;[70] and Walter Moseley's *An Essay on Archery* (Worcester, 1792). A fourth, written around the same time by William Latham, F.S.A. and Royal Kentish Bowman, lies unpublished in the British Library's manuscript collection.[71] All of them focus on ancient history and mythology—Robin Hood, of course, but also Ulysses and the longbow men of medieval England. Some also examine archery in other countries (Turkey, Flanders, America) and other types of shooting in addition to target shooting (butts, rovers, flight). None pays attention to technique, and only Hargrove includes significant information on the current societies in Britain.

How-to books had to wait until the next century. Thomas Roberts published *The English Bowman; or Tracts on Archery* in 1801, a combination of antiquarian history with selections from and commentary on Ascham's *Toxophilus*. Ascham, apparently, had been serving as the standard handbook for eighteenth-century archers. Roberts's tome had to serve until 1814, when Thomas Waring, Jr., published *A Treatise on Archery; or The Art of Shooting with the English Bow*, a book that went through nine editions, the last in 1832. Sold only at Waring's archery warehouse and shop, *A Treatise* was the first practical guide, and it trained a new generation of British archers after the sport's 20-year hiatus caused by the war. Waring, however, knew that archery's attraction was bound up with its history: his treatise begins with several pages of antiquarian lore about the longbow.

The practice of archery was firmly connected in the minds of its practitioners with Britain's glorious past. In 1793, the radical John Thelwall, on seeing the Lodge of the Royal Kentish Bowmen on Dartford Heath, mentioned feeling the "glow of national vanity at the prospect, and the contemplation of the growing popularity of an amusement so connected with the study of antiquities and the history and manners of our ancestors."[72] Such a comment helps position archery as part of the revival of interest in cultural primitivism and medievalism that developed in the final decades of the eighteenth century.[73] One needs to place the sport of archery alongside Horace Walpole's Strawberry Hill, Gray's poetry, and Percy's *Reliques* as well as cricket and horse racing.

That antiquarianism, however, defined the British character. As France was throwing over its past, the aristocratic archers of Britain, in contrast, were drawing closer to it. The longbow symbolized the Good Old Days and Merrie England, when a mythological forester like Robin Hood could defend the English against oppression and when longbowmen could beat the French at Agincourt and Crécy. That is why many of the groups had names that linked them to the past, either genuine or mythological: Woodmen of Arden, Robin Hood's Foresters, John O' Gaunt's Bowmen. By taking up the "antient" bow and arrow at a time of war and revolution, the gentry and the aristocracy of Britain appropriated the cultural power of Robin Hood and the yeomen of England as symbols of their ability to defend "liberty."

The year 1795 was the last big year for the sport for decades. Once political matters turned serious, most of the archery societies disbanded, their male members "obeying the mandate of more immediate and more imperious avocations, arising from revolutions on the Continent."[74] The fashion for archery ignited by Lever and Waring had not waned, nor had a new sport displaced it. Instead, life intervened. The men of the archery societies gave up the "the bow for the musket,"[75] and war against French and Spanish soldiers displaced mock competition on the archery field. Archery may have been initially revived in the 1780s for health and fashion, but at the end of the century, during a time of national crisis, wielding the longbow must also have been an act of social cohesion and an expression of national identity for Britain's gentry and aristocracy, justifiably anxious after a revolution across the channel. A mere handful of archery societies continued throughout the war years, but their memberships plummeted. The third revival of archery would have to wait until after the Battle of Waterloo.[76]

Notes

[1] Stephen Knight, *Robin Hood: A Complete Study of the English Outlaw* (Oxford: Blackwell, 1994), 41–3, 88–97, 123.

[2] Most competition records for the Finsbury Archers survive for these years. See *Gentleman's Magazine* 151 (1832): 602; also George Alfred Raikes, *History of the Honourable Artillery Company*, 2 vols. (London: Bentley, 1878), 1:154–5.

[3] Thomas Roberts, *English Bowman* (London: for the author, 1801), 244; C.J. Longman and H. Walrond, *Archery*, Badminton Library of Sports and Pastimes (London: Longmans, Green, 1901), 169–70.

[4] It was called by two names in eighteenth-century newspaper accounts: gilded between 1750 and 1760, it became the Golden Arrow; when the gilding wore off some decades later, it reverted to its original name (Philip Rolls, "A Brief History of the Society of Archers," *The Society of Archers and the Antient Silver Arrow*, http://www.scortonarrow.com/history/history1.htm). Also see Ben Hird, *The Antient Scorton Silver Arrow*, ed. E.G. Heath (London: Society of Archer-Antiquaries, 1972; rpt. PDF e-book, 2002).

[5] Michael Leach, "The Scorton Shoot of 1948: A Recollection," *Journal of the Society of Archer-Antiquaries* 49 (2006): 20. The arrow is displayed in the Hunting Gallery of the Royal Armouries Museum, Leeds.

[6] Walter Moseley, *An Essay on Archery* (Worcester: Hall, 1792), 347. There were some gaps during periods of war, but unlike many other historic sporting competitions, it

did not lapse in the nineteenth century. The current trophy dates from 1713 and replaces an earlier arrow. It is kept in Archers' Hall, Edinburgh.

[7] W. Allan Jamieson, "Archery at Kilwinning and Irvine," *Archer's Register for 1895–96*, ed. Fred Follett (London: Horace Cox, 1895), 196, 198. The papingo shoot continued until the 1860s (200); the contest was resurrected in 1951 and continues today. The Silver Arrow, complete with medallions listing the names of winners, can be seen in the Kilwinning Library, Ayrshire.

[8] *Public Advertiser*, 30 July 1753.

[9] In addition to winning an arrow, the student-champion served as host at a ball in the evening (Christopher Tyerman, *A History of Harrow School, 1324–1991* [Oxford: Oxford University Press, 2000], 46, 62).

[10] Tony Kench, "Sir William Wood (1609–1691) and the Society of Finsbury Archers," *Worshipful Company of Bowyers*, http://www.bowyers.com/bowyery_finsburyArchers.php. Wood was buried in St. James, Clerkenwell, "with full archer's honours of three flights of whistling arrows shot over his grave."

[11] Arthur G. Credland, "Archery and its Art in Britain," *British Sporting Art Trust* 26 (January 1994): 6.

[12] Ely Hargrove, *Anecdotes of Archery from the Earliest Ages to the Year 1791* (York: for the author, 1792), 85.

[13] Roberts, *English Bowman*, 79.

[14] Hargrove, *Anecdotes of Archery*, 72.

[15] E.G. Heath, *History of Target Archery* (Newton Abbot: David and Charles, 1973), 62.

[16] *History of the Royal Toxophilite Society* (Taunton: for the society, 1867), 115–16. Their most notable trophy was the Catherine of Branganza Shield, a silver piece commissioned by the Finsbury Archers in 1676 and presented to its marshal, Sir William Wood. It is now in the Victoria and Albert Museum.

[17] "Manchester Races, 1761," *London Evening Post*, 6–8 August 1761.

[18] *Rules and Orders of the Toxophilite Society* (London: for the society, 1784), 12–13.

[19] *Laws of the Toxophilite Society ... Revised and altered in the year MDCCXCI* (London: for the society, 1791), 18, 20.

[20] Journal entry for 31 December 1782 (*Early Journals and Letters of Fanny Burney*, vol. 5: *1782–83*, ed. Lars E. Troide and Stewart J. Cooke [Montreal: McGill-Queens University Press, 2012], 237).

[21] Roberts, *English Bowman*, 198.

[22] *Rules and Orders of the Toxophilite Society*, 15.

[23] *Rules and Orders of the Toxophilite Society*, 18.

[24] Martin Johnes, "Archery, Romance and Elite Culture in England and Wales, c. 1780–1840," *History* 89 (2004): 194.

[25] Waring's seventeen-year-old son, also named Thomas, took over the business upon his father's death in 1805 (Hugh D.H. Soar, *Romance of Archery: A Social History of the Longbow* [Yardley, PA: Westholme, 2008], 93).

[26] Prices recorded by Sophia Banks, one of Waring's regular customers. Her extensive collection of archery memorabilia, now in the British Library, includes notes on conversations with Waring about prices and a receipt dated 17 July 1791, for a lady's bow (£2, 12s), two dozen arrows (£1, 6s), four bowstrings (4s), and arrow-pattern painting (5s) (Banks Collection, MS Add.6315, 30r–30v, 79r).

[27] The Banks Collection includes a book with arrow patterns (in the form of snippets of ribbon) used by all those who shot with the Bankses at Revesby Abbey in Lincolnshire. Pinks and greens dominate the colors (MS Add.6320).
[28] *Rules and Orders of the Toxophilite Society*, 7–8.
[29] *History of the Royal Toxophilite Society*, 17.
[30] *Laws of the Toxophilite Society*, 6.
[31] Banks's annotation, dated 17 April 1794, on a colored print of the Toxophilite uniform (Banks Collection, MS Add. 6315, 54r).
[32] *Rules of the Society of Royal Kentish Bowmen* (London: for the society, 1789), 17. Joseph Nutting was a maker of military and livery buttons; however, 15 is the street number given in London directories, not 16.
[33] James William Dodd, *Ballad of Archery* (London: Evans, 1818), 139, 126. Apollo, of course, was an archer. John Russell's portrait *George IV (1762–1830), when Prince of Wales* is now part of the Royal Collection.
[34] An oil portrait by John Hoppner of Sir Foster Cunliffe in his RBB uniform is in the University of Michigan Museum of Art.
[35] *Regulations of the Society of Royal British Bowmen* (Wrexham: for the society, 1787), 12.
[36] *Regulations of the Society of Royal British Bowmen*, 6, 11.
[37] Ascham often used the adjective *manly* to describe the sport in *Toxophilus*, and the term is widely used in the press.
[38] *Rules and Regulations of the Hainault Foresters* (London: for the society, 1789), 14–15.
[39] George Agar Hansard, *Book of Archery* (London: Henry G. Bohn, 1841), 153–5. See, for example, the announcement of the public breakfasts in the *Morning Chronicle* of 14 May 1793.
[40] *History of the Royal Toxophilite Society*, 21.
[41] *Records of the Woodmen of Arden from 1785 with Roll of Members of the Society*, ed. William Kirkpatrick Riland Bedford (Edinburgh: privately printed, 1885), 74.
[42] Johnes (199) brought this reference to my attention; I quote from the original newspaper source. The group was initially named the North British Archers.
[43] Roberts, *English Bowman*, 87.
[44] Thomas Waring, Jr., *Treatise on Archery; or The Art of Shooting with the English Bow* (1814), 4th ed. (London: for the author, "sold only by him at his Archery," 1822), 24. Similarly, Roberts notes bow weights for target shooting as 50–55 lbs for men and 27–32 lbs for women (220).
[45] As he calculates, 550 in^2 for a woman's target to a man's 1754 (Waring, *Treatise on Archery*, 34, 38, 41).
[46] Banks's instruction to James Keel on the painting of a target cloth (Banks Collection, MS Add. 6318, 20).
[47] Waring, *Treatise on Archery*, 8.
[48] Banks Collection, MS Add.6318, 4r–4v. Punctuation modernized.
[49] "Sporting Intelligence," *The Sporting Magazine* 3 (October 1794): 51–2.
[50] "Davenport and Gilpin, 432 Strand" is listed as an "army clothier" in several London directories, and the address matches the one given for Gilpin in *Names of the Members of the Toxophilite Society for the Year MDCCXCII* (London: for the society, 1792), 14–15.
[51] *Records of the Honourable Society of Lincoln's Inn: Volume One: Admissions from A.D. 1420 to 1799* (London: Lincoln's Inn, 1896), 482, 517.

[52] Banks Collection, MS Add.6318, 38r.
[53] *History of the Royal Toxophilite Society*, 42.
[54] *History of the Royal Toxophilite Society*, 18.
[55] Banks Collection, MS Add.6318, 38r.
[56] *History of the Royal Toxophilite Society*, 19.
[57] "Archer's Ball," newspaper cutting in Joseph Haslewood, "Anecdotes of Archery: A Thing of Shreds and Patches," MS Osborn d.20, Beinecke Library, Yale University.
[58] Banks notes that she heard this from Mrs. Tyndell, who got it in a letter from Mrs. Jones of Monmouth (Banks Collection, MS Add.6315, 55r).
[59] *London Chronicle*, 22–25 May 1790.
[60] Hansard, *Book of Archery*, 277.
[61] This information was conveyed by Mr. Waring (Banks Collection, MS Add.6315, 62v).
[62] Some of the material on women's archery and on theatrical productions appeared earlier in my "Diana's Votaries; or, The Fair Toxophilites," *East-Central Intelligencer* 10, no. 1 (1996): 9–15; and "Robin Hood Musicals in Eighteenth-Century London," *Robin Hood in Popular Culture: Violence, Transgression, and Justice*, ed. Thomas Hahn (Cambridge: Brewer, 2000), 251–64.
[63] *Universal Magazine* 74 (1784): 202.
[64] Geoffrey Gibson, "Origins of William Tell," *Journal of the Society of Archer-Antiquaries* 18 (1975): 6.
[65] *The Sporting Magazine* 1 (1792): 35. Spoken drama had to be licensed for performance; as times were politically strained, plays featuring themes or dialogue that seemed revolutionary needed significant revision before being granted a license. Some plays were denied outright.
[66] Newspaper clipping in Haslewood, "Anecdotes of Archery."
[67] *The Sporting Magazine* 7 (1795): 117.
[68] *Names of the Members of the Toxophilite Society*, 4.
[69] Thirty-three inches, according to measurements taken by James Shuttleworth (Banks Collection, MS Add.6318, 15r).
[70] Arthur G. Credland, "The Grand National Archery Meetings 1844–1944 and the Progress of Women in Archery," *Journal of the Society of Archer-Antiquaries* 43 (2000): 94.
[71] William Latham, Collection for a history of archery, toxographia, anecdotes of archery, MS Add.29788–29791, British Library.
[72] John Thelwall, "Dartford Brink: Memorials of Antiquity," *The Peripatetic*, ed. Judith Thompson (Detroit: Wayne State University Press, 2001), 92.
[73] Johnes, "Archery, Romance and Elite Culture," 204.
[74] Dodd, *Ballad of Archery*, xvi.
[75] Letter from Sir Foster Cunliffe to Philip Davies Cooke, quoted in Johnes, "Archery, Romance and Elite Culture," 204.
[76] The Toxophilites, for example, had 162 members in 1792, but 31 in 1798, and only 16 in 1816 (C.B. Edwards, *The "Tox" Story* [Canterbury: for the Royal Toxophilite Society, 1968], 22).

Chapter 6
Jockeying for Position:
Horse Culture in Poetry, Prose, and
*The New Foundling Hospital for Wit**

Donald W. Nichol

The eighteenth century witnessed the formalization of the sport of kings with the founding of the Jockey Club. Scholars and sports enthusiasts have long held that the Jockey Club was founded early in the 1750s. However, this essay offers evidence from contemporary newspapers and an engraving that a group calling itself the Jockey Club gathered on several occasions over the preceding 40 years. In addition to the importance to sporting history, this antedating emphasizes the fact that horse racing was more deeply rooted in the nation's identity and became an obsession with peers of the realm earlier than has been commonly assumed.

The Restoration has long been recognized as an important period in the organization of horse racing. Take, for instance, *Articles for the Newmarket Town Plate*, which were written in 1664.[1] According to Newmarket's official website, "the Newmarket Town Plate was the first race of its kind to be staged under written rules." An able and devoted horseman, Charles II "did more than any other monarch to advance the sport of horse racing in this country—he instituted by Act of Parliament in 1665 the first race to be run in Britain under written rules and exported the name of Newmarket and the sport of horseracing to America that same year."[2] While the Jockey Club eventually served as a governing body, the rules outlined in the *Articles for the Newmarket Town Plate* endured throughout the eighteenth century. Early members of the Jockey Club were caricatured as convivial tipplers who fell about brawling with dissipated gamblers. Satirical verse and engravings give the impression that racing and gambling became a national obsession that spread to the highest offices of parliament in the period leading up to the American Revolution. So, as horses had traditionally been used to symbolize war and sex, horse racing became analogous with politics in the eighteenth century. By midcentury, satirists mocked the Jockey Club and metaphorized horse racing as a way to critique politicians as venal and corrupt. The Jockey Club and horse racing were potent weapons for *The New Foundling Hospital for Wit*, a satirical miscellany published by John Almon of Piccadilly in six volumes between 1768 and 1773. Satirists used the sport to lampoon royalty, parliamentarians, and England's domestic and imperial power. As we shall see, by the end of the century, the sport of kings was used to make sport of those in power.

❦ ❦ ❦

Ever since Odysseus came up with the perfect prize that would trick the Trojans into opening their city gates after a 10-year siege, the horse has held sway in literary imagination, representing sex and status, writing and war. Alexander Pope's translation of Homer's *Odyssey* (1725–1726) captured the awe of the Trojan Horse as the hero descended into Hell and told Achilles of the victory he missed:

> When *Ilion* in the horse receiv'd her doom,
> And unseen armies ambush'd in its womb;
> *Greece* gave her latent warriors to my care,
> 'Twas mine on *Troy* to pour th' imprison'd war.[3]

Pope's Homer enthralled Byron's imagination a century later. In mock-epic simile, Jonathan Swift likened a passenger abandoned in a sedan chair during a London downpour to Odysseus's men hiding with nervous anticipation inside the wooden horse in his 1709 iambic "A Description of a City Shower":

> So when Troy chairmen bore the wooden steed,
> Pregnant with Greeks, impatient to be freed;
> (Those bully Greeks, who, as the moderns do,
> Instead of paying chairmen, run them through)
> Laocoon struck the outside with his spear,
> And each imprisoned hero quaked for fear.[4]

Pope's and Swift's references to "womb" and "pregnant" suggest that the Trojan horse might more precisely be called the Trojan *mare*. Apollo has often been depicted racing through the skies on a horse-drawn chariot. Dr. Thomas Sheridan applied the Apollonian trope in paying a compliment to Swift in 1718:

> … thinking two hours for a rhyme as you did last,
> When your Pegasus cantered in triple, and rid fast.
> As for my little nag which I keep at Parnassus,
> With Phoebus's leave, to run with his asses,
> He goes slow and sure, and he never is jaded,
> While your fiery steed is whipped, spurred, bastinaded.[5]

In a more dramatic fashion, William Hogarth, just a few weeks away from death, predicted the end of art symbolically with Apollo's steeds dead in the sky in his final engraving, *The Bathos* (1764).

Horses were vital in winning wars, even literary ones. In the Ancients *versus* Moderns in Swift's *Battle of the Books*, the Moderns' horses were "large, but extremely out of case and heart; however, some few, by trading among the Ancients, had furnish'd themselves tolerably enough."[6] One Ancient philosopher mocked some of the Moderns, boasting of their self-sufficiency, "'our horses are of our own breeding, our arms of our own forging, and our clothes of our own cutting out and sewing.' Plato was by chance upon the next shelf, and observing those that spoke to be in the ragged plight mentioned a while ago; their jades lean and foundered" (7). The battle commenced with Homer "at the head of the cavalry, mounted on a furious horse" (15). After overthrowing Gondibert ("horse and man, to the ground, there to be trampled and choked in the dirt"), "Homer slew Wesley with a kick of his horse's heel; he took Perrault by mighty force out of his saddle, then hurled him at Fontenelle, with the same blow dashing out both their brains" (15). The Romans then entered the fray:

> On the left wing of the horse, Virgil appeared, in shining armour, completely fitted to his body. He was mounted on a dapple grey steed, the slowness of whose pace was an effect of the highest mettle and vigour. He cast his eye on the adverse wing, with a desire to find an object worthy of his valour, when, behold, upon a sorrel gelding of a monstrous size appeared a foe issuing from among the thickest of the enemy's squadrons; but his speed was less than his noise, for his horse, old and lean, spent the dregs of his strength in a high trot, which, though it made slow advances, yet caused a loud clashing of his armour, terrible to hear. (15)

Virgil swapped armor with his modern translator Dryden: "Then they agreed to exchange horses; but, when it came to the trial, Dryden was afraid and utterly unable to mount" (16). The book-man-horse metaphor continues: "The difference was greatest among the horse, where every private trooper pretended to the chief command" (11). Even through Swift's satiric filter, readers will appreciate the necessary synchronization of cavalry, equipment, and mount.

It would be a serious understatement to observe that Swift had a soft spot for the equine genus. The very pronunciation of "Houyhnhnm" hangs on one's ability to whinny like a horse. Early on in Lilliput, Gulliver becomes something of a master of ceremonies and racecourse rolled into one:

> The Horses of the Army, and those of the Royal Stables, having been daily led before me, were no longer shy, but would come up to my very Feet, without starting. The Riders would leap them over my Hand as I held it on the Ground; and one of the Emperor's Huntsmen, upon a large Courser, took my Foot, Shoe and all; which was indeed a prodigious Leap.[7]

Gulliver, who is sometimes wont to get carried away, then makes a soft parade ground out of his handkerchief which is big enough to accommodate two dozen horses and riders until one pair trips on a hole in the fabric.

When Swift culled his imagination for a species Gulliver would rather have been a member of, he chose the Houyhnhnm. At the end of his *Travels*, Gulliver favors the stables to his wife's bed and family home, having been outed as a human and rejected by Houyhnhnm society when his equine hosts finally see him without the clothing that distinguished him from his fellow beasts and witness a female Yahoo attempting to copulate with him. Jeanette Winterson, in her introduction to the 1999 Oxford edition of *Gulliver's Travels*, goes so far as to say that by the end of it all, apart from loathing humans, retreating to the stables, and generally going off the deep end, Gulliver is also more in touch with his feminine side; after all, he now "swoons, he faints, he trembles, he weeps, he does not speak unless he is spoken to, he sits quietly at dinner enjoying the conversation of others."[8] In short, one of the side effects of his equine revelation is: he becomes more like Mrs. Gulliver.

One of the later ironies of *Gulliver's Travels*, which Swift added in 1735, was "A Letter from Capt. *Gulliver*, to His Cousin *Sympson*." A first time reader will come across a couple of mentions of "Master *Houyhnhnm*" long before discovering what this name means. A common sight in London has become abhorrent to our narrator: "Have not I the most Reason to complain, when I see these very *Yahoos* carried by *Houyhnhnms* in a Vehicle, as if these were Brutes, and those the rational Creatures?"[9] The world would be a better place if the situation were reversed: if beggars wore saddles and horses could ride. Swift wasn't the only one to value horses above humans. Horses have, in times of war and pestilence, been regarded as more valuable than humans. One of the earliest records we have of Geoffrey Chaucer's worth is a £16 ransom paid by the King while the young writer was captured during a campaign in France, which suggests that Edward III valued him almost as much as Robert de Clynton's horse, for which his majesty paid 13 shillings and sixpence more.

Horses measured worth on other levels as well. In his "Epistle to Miss Blount, on her Leaving the Town after the Coronation," Pope warned one of his most cherished female acquaintances against being courted by the kind of country squire

> Who visits with a gun, presents you birds,
> Then gives a smacking buss, and cries—No words!
> Or with his hound comes hallowing from the stable,
> Makes love with nods, and knees beneath a table;
> Whose laughs are hearty, though his jests are coarse,
> And loves you best of all things—but his horse. (*TE* 6:125; lines 25–30)

Pope's satirical warning to Martha about the choice of a horse-mad mate would have resonated more seriously with a woman like Anne Vaughan, daughter of the third Earl of Carbery, whose marriage to Charles Powlett or Paulet, third Duke of Bolton (1685–1754), ended shortly after her honeymoon because her groom spent more time with his horse than his bride.[10] Bolton later married his mistress, Lavinia Fenton, who had starred as Polly in John Gay's *Beggar's Opera*; she presumably had more tolerance of her husband's Gulliverian habit of spending so much time in the stable.

The preparation of a young horse for riding was likened to the loss of virginity. In John Cleland's *Memoirs of a Woman of Pleasure* (1748–1749), Fanny Hill is "broken in" by "the hackney'd, thorough-bred *Phoebe*, to whom all modes and devices of pleasure were known and familiar, found, it seems, in this exercise of her art to break young girls."[11] When Fanny is presented by Mrs. Brown to her first client, a short, elderly, unattractive man, she is paraded like a new-sprung filly:

accordingly, she made me stand up before him, turned me round, unpin'd my handkerchief, remark'd to him the rise and fall, the turn, and whiteness of a bosom just beginning to fill; then made me walk, and took even a handle from the rusticity of my gait, to inflame the inventory of my charms: in short, she omitted no point of jockey-ship. (16)

By "jockey-ship" Cleland connotes the sort of inspection—checking the teeth, examining the hooves, testing the flanks—that might take place at a horse auction where the sprightliest filly could fetch the highest bid. The old lecher offers 50 guineas in advance as if it were a wager against impotence—a bet he loses, much to the relief of Fanny. Shortly afterwards, Fanny peeks from a closet at Mrs. Brown being "handed in by a tall, brawny young Horse-grenadier, moulded in the Hercules style.... Her sturdy stallion had now unbutton'd, and produced naked, stiff, and erect, that wonderful machine" (25). Cleland extends the metaphor to the end of the sexual ride when the young man "dismounted." Outside the brothel, johns come and go by horse-drawn conveyances. The sight of someone holding the reins outside the establishment indicates a quickie in progress inside: "a single horse-chaise stopt at the door, out of which lightly leap'd two young gentlemen, for so they seem'd, who came in only as it were to bait and refresh a little, for they gave their horse to be held in a readiness against they came out" (156). Inside the brothel, sexual potency is singled out for praise in a boy who otherwise would be regarded as mentally challenged:

The boys, and servants in the neighbourhood, had given him the nick-name of *Good-natur'd Dick*, from the soft simpleton's doing every thing he was bid to do at the first word, and from his naturally having no turn to mischief; then, by the way, he was perfectly well made, stout, clean-limb'd, tall of his age, as strong as a horse. (160)

Such similes suggest virility; in the case of both male and female riders, the rhythm of horseback riding has been known to cause sexual arousal. Laurence Sterne, who declares Parson Yorick's "lean, sorry, jack-ass of a horse" to be "full brother to *Rosinante*,"[12] remarks upon "heated parts" caused by excessive riding on a hobby-horse:

A man and his HOBBY-HORSE, tho' I cannot say that they act and re-act exactly after the same manner in which the soul and body do upon each other: Yet doubtless there is a communication between them of some kind, and my opinion rather is, that there is something in it more of the manner of electrified bodies,— and that by means of the heated parts of the rider, which come immediately into contact with the back of the HOBBY-HORSE,—By long journeys and much friction, it so happens, that the body of the rider is at length fill'd as full of HOBBY-HORSICAL matter as it can hold;—so that if you are able to give but a clear description of the nature of the one, you may form a pretty exact notion of the genius and character of the other. (61)

A "hobby," as defined by Samuel Johnson, can mean (among other things) "A stick on which boys get astride and ride" or "An Irish or Scottish horse; a pacing horse; a garran [i.e. a gelding]." While the "man" in the above passage refers to Uncle Toby, Sterne (who uses "hobby-horse" and its variants three dozen times throughout *Tristram Shandy*) leaves the reader guessing as to the full extent of his war wound, which Widow Wadman fears may have left him "a garran." "Hobby-horse" might refer to an obsession, but also, as Ian Campbell Ross notes, a prostitute (543).

A more pronounced example of the relationship between rhythmic riding and copulation may be heard in Thomas D'Urfey's "When for Air I take my Mare" as performed by The City Waits on their album, *Pills to Purge Melancholy*. Here, D'Urfey's musical ride turns into a rhythmic romp in the hay.[13] The rider's mount "wriggles like a bride at night," with a motion that is "straight again, up and down, up and down, up and down, till she comes home with a trot, trot, trot, trot." The second verse extends the simile: "Just so Phyllis, fair as lilies, as her face is, as her pace is, and in bed to light my pad … flirting, spurting, artful are her ways." The mare is personified as mistress in an analogy that blurs the boundary between rough sex and bestiality: "'You devil,' she cries, 'I'll tear your eyes' / When mane's seized, bum squeezed / I gallop, I gallop, I gallop, I gallop." The ride, like the act of coition, starts slowly, builds up through numerous repeated grunts to a climax followed by a dénouement or detumescence: "so ends the love of chase."

Learning to ride brought with it a specialized vocabulary. Being presented with one's first horse and learning to ride were rites of passage for any young person of privilege. In *Tom Jones*, after our eponymous hero is (horse) whipped by Thwackum for refusing to name Black George as his accomplice in poaching, Squire Allworthy compensates his adopted son by giving him a little horse (III. ii). Love blossoms at the Westerns' manor during Tom's recuperation from a broken arm. When Squire Western learns of Sophia's feelings towards Tom (which jeopardizes plans for marriage to Blifil which would unite the Western and Allworthy estates), "He then bespattered the Youth with Abundance of that Language which passes between Country Gentlemen who embrace opposite Sides of the Question; with frequent Applications to him to salute that Part which is generally introduced into all Controversies that arise among the lower Orders of the *English* Gentry at Horse-races, Cock-matches, and other public Places."[14] Clearly, horse racing had developed its own special parlance and tonal colorings by 1749.[15] William Pulteney, Earl of Bath, devoted a column in the *World* on 26 April 1753 to "the Races at Newmarket and Elsewhere," in which he commented on the splendour, language, obsession with pedigree, the great reputation of British breeds throughout Europe, and the "many hundreds of thousands of pounds" that change hands.[16]

Jockeying for Position 131

☙ ☙ ☙

Tied ineluctably with the outcome at the finishing line is the wager won or lost. Gambling has been synonymous with racing as long as owners, trainers, and jockeys have argued over whose horse is faster. In his admirably erudite synopsis, Roy Porter notes:

> At the Restoration the turf had been exclusively aristocratic, the sport of kings; Ascot was Queen Anne's own estate. But under the Georges many towns got their races: Norwich held them regularly from 1710, Warwick from 1711, the sport becoming so popular that grandstands had to be built to corral the rich away from the crowds. The turf became big business. The Jockey Club was set up in 1752, the horse-dealers, Tattersalls, in the 1770s. Professional trainers and jockeys took the initiative. The successes of thoroughbreds such as Eclipse gave rise to blood-stock pedigrees and equine ancestor-worship. 'Classic' races such as the St Leger (from 1778), the Oaks (1779), and the Derby (1780) created the racing calendar. And once again, betting made the wheels go round.[17]

Early in *A Tour through the Whole Island of Great Britain*, Daniel Defoe spends a day at the races in Newmarket.[18] He is first struck by "a great concourse of the nobility and gentry, as well from London as from all parts of England," although the monstrous display of capitalism at its worst soon disgusts him:

> [T]hey were all so intent, so eager, so busy upon the sharping part of the sport, their wagers and bets, that to me they seemed just as so many horse-coursers in Smithfield, descending (the greatest of them) from their high dignity and quality, to picking one another's pockets, and biting one another as much as possible, and that with such eagerness, as that it might be said they acted without respect to faith, honour, or good manners. (32)

Defoe diverts himself by inspecting the horses. In spite of all the rampant chicanery, he manages to get caught up in the spell:

> Here I fancied myself in the Circus Maximus at Rome, seeing the ancient games, and the racings of the chariots and horsemen; and in this warmth of my imagination I pleased and diverted myself more and in a more noble manner, than I could possibly do in the crowds of gentlemen at the weighing and starting posts, and at their coming in; or at their meetings at the coffee-houses and gaming-tables after the races were over, where there was little or nothing to be seen, but what was the subject of just reproach to them, and reproof from every wise man that look'd upon them. (32)

Regrettably, Defoe doesn't tell us who raced that day, who won, and whether he came out ahead, but he does, however briefly, feel the excitement of it all.

The popularity of horse racing grew in the latter half of the eighteenth century with race-courses becoming established wherever sufficient areas of good, flat turf could be found. One fictional day at the races is recorded in Charles Johnstone's novel *Chrysal*. An inanimate but articulate guinea (worth 21 shillings, thereby trumping a pound in wagers), Chrysal travels the world from pocket to pocket. During one transition, Chrysal goes through several owners in quick succession, from a lady to her coach-man, to a farrier, then a tavern-owner, an attorney, a knight of the post, and a highwayman, "who lost me that evening to a nobleman at an horse-race."[19] From this knight's pocket, Chrysal has "an opportunity of seeing a noble jockey practise part of the mysterious science of the turf." By "mysterious science," Johnstone means race-fixing. Chrysal's owner takes him to the Jockey Club, where "my master pressed through the mob of pick-pockets, bubbles, lords, and jockies" and loses a £500 wager he cannot repay. The groom comes up with a plan:

> "Now Jack, what think you of my little *stun-orse* [i.e. stone-horse, stallion]?" (says his lordship). You must know that I have *measured the foot* of them all, in this heat, and find that I *have the heels* by a *distance* at least; but the weights are above my *trim*. However, we have a remedy for that; look at this cap" (taking one out of a chest, in which his running dress had been brought to the ground,) "this is a *leaden skull*, and weighs above two *stun*; put this on your head, the thickness of your own skull will prevent its giving you the head-ach: aye, it fits you very well. Now I will wear this to the post, and, just before we start, complain that my cap is too wide, and borrow yours to ride in, and when I alight at the *scales*, after the heat is over, I will pull off yours, as if to wipe my face, and give it to you to hold, who can return me this, to weigh in, and as I wear the same trusses, stuffed with handkerchiefs, in which I carried the weight last heat, they will never suspect us.—Ha, Jack, what say you to this! match me this, among all your *Hibernian* tricks, if you can. Go your way: double with his Grace, and *lay* all you can, I'll *go* with you; but be sure to meet me at the post before, and at the scales after the heat, and not to blow the business, by being in too great a hurry." (1:299–300)

The ruse works, and Chrysal's owner comes out ahead, although one of the grooms, perhaps wearing a heavily weighted cap, ends up breaking his neck. This scene might have been adapted from a deception Tregonwell Frampton (1641–1728) attempted to perpetrate on Sir William Strickland by making him think his own Old Merlin was the faster horse in a forthcoming race. Frampton's plan involved secretly increasing his jockey's weight to slow his horse down during a heat, but Sir William, who had also weighted his horse, proved even wilier than Frampton. The ruse backfired, resulting in Frampton's loss on a substantial bet. He was in Newmarket on the day Defoe visited:

> There was Mr Frampton, the oldest, and as some say, the cunningest jockey in England, one day he lost 1000 guineas, the next he won two thousand; and so alternately he made as light of throwing away five hundred or one thousand pounds at a time, as other men do of their pocket-money, and as perfectly calm, cheerful, and unconcerned, when he had lost one thousand pounds, as when he had won it. On the other side, there was Sir R—Fagg, of Sussex, of whom fame

says he has the most in him and the least to show for it, relating to jockeyship, of any man there; yet he often carried the prize; his horses, they said, were all cheats, how honest soever their master was; for he scarce ever produced a horse but he looked like what he was not, and was what no body could expect him to be. If he was as light as the wind, and could fly like a meteor, he was sure to look as clumsy, and as dirty, and as much like a cart-horse as all the cunning of his master and the grooms could make him; and just in this manner he bit some of the greatest gamesters in the field.[20]

Frampton, painted by John Wootton shortly before his death in 1728, managed the royal stable through five reigns, Charles II, James II, William III and Mary II, Anne, George I, and (for the first year) George II. Something of a Beau Nash, Frampton became the arbiter in any inquiries, fouls, and disputes at the finishing line—a duty once carried out by Charles II. Truly, Newmarket was the place where commoners could feel like kings. Ditch diggers and dukes alike had ample opportunity to make—and just as easily lose—a lifetime's earnings in a day.

Perhaps because of its association with gambling, horse races were especially popular at the time of electoral races. Peter Plain-Truth (whose pseudonym was further qualified by pointing out that he was "not Lord Puff") included some verses on a local horse race in a political lampoon, *The Litchfield Squabble* (Foxon L175; London: B. Dickinson, 1747). *The Tricks of the Town Laid Open* by a "Gentleman at London" (London: H. Slater and R. Adams, 1746) warned his country counterpart about *the Cheat of Horse-Races* among many other hazards of coming to town. A year after his death in 1794, Charles Pigott's name was joined with that of the arbiter of card games in *Pigott's New Hoyle.*[21] It is worth noting that 21 out of 27 "betting" titles on the *English Short Title Catalogue* [*ESTC*] come from Edmond Hoyle (1672–1769), suggesting that gambling addiction was associated more with whist and other card games than horse races. The *ESTC* throws up a mere three results for the word "gambling" in a title, none ostensibly linked to horse racing. Of the 162 hits for "gaming," only 19 intersect with "horse," including *The Gamester's Law* (1708, 1710, 1711). Parliamentary concern is implicit in *An Act to Restrain and Prevent the Excessive Increase of Horse Races*, passed in 1740, and its amendment in 1745. The Act seems to have had limited effect in curbing the nation's growing obsession with the turf.

Some early animals' rights activists considered the poor creature's point of view. Empathy for the horse's burden is offered as a brief it-narrative in "*The* PETITION *of Justice* Boden's *Horse to the Duke of* Newcastle":

> Quite worn to the Stump, in a piteous Condition,
> I present to your Grace this my humble Petition.
> Full twenty-five Stone, as well the World says,

(To me it seems more) my plump Master weighs,
A Load for a Team this, yet I all alone
To *Claremont* must draw him, for Help I have none.
O'er *Esher*'s hot Sands, in a dry Summer's Day,
How I sweat, and I pant, and curse all the Way.
But when I return, the Draft is increas'd
By what he has cram'd, a Stone at the least,
No single Horse can be in Conscience thought able
To draw both the Justice, and eke half your Table.
Thus my Case, gracious Duke, to your tender Compassion,
I submit, and O take it into Consideration.
To drive with a Pair put the 'Squires in the Way,
Your Petitioner then, bound in Duty, shall Neigh.[22]

One of Robbie Burns's best-known poems, *Tam O'Shanter*, pays due heed to the importance of his trusty mare Meg. Tam decides to have a few more drinks than he should on market day in Ayr. Riding home late and drunk, he passes the Kirk of Alloway where he sees warlocks and witches dancing to the bagpipes played by Old Nick. When he drunkenly reveals himself to the "bogillis" or spirits, the chase is on. He narrowly makes the Bridge of Doon which his hot pursuers cannot cross, but not in time to save Meg's tail from a witch's clutch. It's arguably one of the greatest literary chase scenes of the eighteenth century. A fast horse is also needed in order for Sir Walter Scott's Young Lochinvar to complete the kidnapping of his beloved.

Injury and death caused by falling from a horse or in coach accidents were not uncommon. One of the earliest recorded rider fatalities occurred in 800 A.D. when a medieval Irish king of southern Brega fell during a horse race ("Saints of Meath," *ODNB*). It was popularly held that William III died after his horse faltered over a molehill in Hyde Park on 21 February 1702, resulting in a broken collarbone; although the real cause of death was pulmonary fever, Jacobites like the Laird of Balmawhapple, in Scott's *Waverley*, "demanded a bumper, with the lungs of a Stentor, 'to the little gentleman in black velvet [i.e. the mole] who did such service in 1702, and may the white horse break his neck over a mound of his making!'"[23] Pope nearly drowned when Lord Bolingbroke's coach overturned crossing the River Crane in September 1726.[24] Historian and biographer Thomas Birch died after a fall from his horse on the Hampstead Road in 1766 (*ODNB*). In the following year, the Marquess of Tavistock, son of the Duke of Bedford, met a similar fate. Samuel Johnson had a couple of close calls getting off a horse, once by a "steep proclivity," in Scotland.[25] He also felt a bit ridiculous on his "little Highland steed" as "a bulky man upon one of their backs makes a very disproportionate appearance" (120). *The Universal Magazine* of March 1759 published a poem, "On K— F—'s Falling from her Horse" (152), which alluded to Kitty Fisher, the celebrated courtesan, who enjoyed riding through St. James's Park and the Mall. A broadside, *Horse and Away to St James's Park ... Who rides fastest, Miss Kitty Fisher or her Gay Gallant*, and a satirical print,

The Merry Accident ... Who rides fastest, Miss Kitty Fish–r, or her Gay Gallant, soon followed.[26] In fiction, Humphry Clinker enters the narrative just after a faltering horse causes the Bramble coach to overturn.[27]

Horse health care was a thriving subgenre in eighteenth-century bookshops. Horse culture demanded its own particular niche in publishing with elaborate title pages such as:

> The Gentleman's Compleat Jockey:
> With the Perfect Horseman, and Experienc'd Farrier. Containing,
> I. The Nature of Horses; Their Breeding, Feeding, and Management in All Paces, to Fit Them for War, Racing, Travel, Hunting; or other Recreations and Advantages.
> II. The True Method, with Proper Rules and Directions to Order, Diet and Physick the Running-Horse, to Bring him to any Match, or Race, with Success.
> III. The Methods to Buy Horses, and Prevent Being Cheated; Noting the Particular Marks of the Good and Bad Horses, in all their Circumstances.
> IV. How to Make Blazes, Stars and Snips: to Fatten a Horse with Little Charge, and to Make Him Lively and Lovely.
> V. The Whole Art of a Farrier, in Curing all Diseases, Griefs and Sorrances Incident to Horses; with their Symptoms and Causes.
> VI. The Methods of Shooing, Blooding, Roweling, Purging, and Prevention of Diseases, and Many Other Things, from Long Experience and Approved Practice.

By "A. S. gent," this guide-book was printed in London for Henry Nelme, at the Leg and Star, over against the Royal Exchange in Cornhill in 1696. *The Gentleman's Compleat Jockey* went into numerous reprints throughout the eighteenth century and would have been required reading for anyone contemplating buying a horse, breeding, dressing, and caring for it. Even then, there were specialists like Henry Bracken (1697–1764), who was the main source on horseshoes in the much-in-demand *Farriery Improved* (London, 1737).[28]

The *Encylopædia Britannica*, first published in three volumes in 1771, catered to horse owners. Articles on "Equus," "Farriery," and "Horsemanship" are among the longest in the second volume (whereas entries on "Cat" and "Dog" are noticeably shorter; elsewhere, the entry on the largest territory in the British Empire, Canada, barely merits a paragraph). The Earl of Pembroke, who is credited with covering "horsemanship," can be less than objective on occasion, treating the entries as editorials with which to censure veterinary practices *en masse*. Self-help pamphlets like *A Treatise upon the True Seat of the Glanders in Horses* (1751), translated from Étienne-Guillaume La Fosse's work, came on the market. Much secrecy surrounded treatments for horse skittishness and assorted ailments, hence the "horse whisperer" Daniel Sullivan (d. 1810) from Mallow, Cork, whose services were much in demand in England. In France, Claude Bourgelat (1712–1779), a contributor to the Éncyclopedie who was an authority on horse and cattle, started the first-ever veterinary college in Lyons around 1760. Great Britain lagged behind: the Royal Veterinary College, based in London, was founded in 1791.[29] A year later, Charles Pigott had a runaway hit with the satirical *Jockey Club*, followed by *The Female Jockey Club* in 1794. Central to the organization and regulation of the sport of horse racing from the mid-eighteenth century, the Jockey Club, or at least a gathering by the same name, had been satirized as early as the reign of Queen Anne.

Antedating the Jockey Club

Robert Black compiled the first substantial history for racing aficionados with *The Jockey Club and its Founders in Three Periods*, published by Smith and Elder of London in 1891. "It is plain," he writes, "that the Jockey Club must have been in existence as early as 1751, and probably as early as 1750" (6). He admits, "How the Club came to be founded, and at whose initiative, is a mere matter of conjecture" (7).[30] Following Roy Porter, a BBC website for a Panorama story on the Jockey Club offers 1752 as the founding date. On its own website the Jockey Club gives 1750 as the date of its origin, noting that "The first written reference to The Jockey Club came in Pond's annually published racing 'Kalendar,' which gave notice in April 1752 that there would be a race at Newmarket for 'horses the Property of the Noblemen and Gentlemen belonging to The Jockey Club.'"[31] Until now, the Maryland Jockey Club, founded in Annapolis in 1743, has predated by at least seven years the official founding of the British Jockey Club.[32]

However, a group calling itself the "Jockey Club" was noted in the London *Daily Post* of Saturday, 2 August 1729:

> The Jockey Club, consisting of several Noblemen and Gentlemen, are to meet one Day next Week at Hackwood, the Duke of Bolton's Seat in Hampshire, to consider of Methods for the better keeping of their respective Strings of Horses at Newmarket.

Four days later, another reference appears in the *Daily Post* at the end of a strange (possibly satirical) advertisement which lists "Kingston Assizes, drawing, hanging quartering among great Folks; Candidates for Scarborough, Jockey Club, a Case and Cover to a Coffin, &c." Readers of the *Daily Advertiser* on 10 March 1731 were informed of a "Picture of Lord James Cavendish's Horse, which his Lordship rode on some time since for a very considerable Wager to Windsor ... the same will be plac'd in the Jockey Club-Rooms at William's Coffee-House, St. James's." Four years later, on 26 April 1735, the *Daily Journal* announced:

> By Request of several Noblemen and Gentlemen of the Jockey-club, the Sale of those exceeding beautiful ARABIAN HORSES, which were to be sold on Thursday the 17th Instant, at Williams's Chocolate-house, St. James's, will be by Auction, on Tuesday the 29th Instant, at Mr. Cock's in the Great Piazza, Covent-garden.

The next reference comes eight years later in the *Daily Advertiser* of 14 January 1743:

Yesterday several Noblemen belonging to the Gentlemens Jockey-Club were at the White Horse Inn in Fleet-Street, to see the wonderful Gigantick Prussian Colt, and acknowledg'd it the most surprising Creature of its kind ever yet seen; and tho' so large a creature, is as nimble as a Greyhound, and gentle as a Lamb.

One hit might be regarded as a fluke, but five references in three different newspapers would seem to be well beyond the realm of accident, coincidence, or misprint. The first 1729 reference is most compelling in its triangulation of horses, humans, and locus: four-legged friends, the Duke of Bolton (a fanatical sportsman and feckless groom as mentioned above) et al, and Newmarket.

Even earlier—by 20 years—Ned Ward's eight-page pamphlet of 1709, *The History of the London Clubs*, boasts a frontispiece entitled *The Jockey Club* (see Figure 6.1).[33] In the center foreground kneels a man dressed like a jockey raising a clenched fist to the sky. On the left-hand side, the man seated at the gambling table is raking up his winnings. An animated discussion is going on behind him while a punch is about to be thrown on the other side. On the right foreground, a man is spewing into a bowl on a chair liquid vomit, which then cascades into a hat and then onto the floor. Empty bottles roll around the floor up front. Images of horses decorate the walls in the background, one showing only hind legs and cropped tail, a horse standing solo, another being ridden, and three horses in a race. No cards appear on the table; while dice may be in the background, the setting is obviously meant for gambling encounters of the equestrian kind. James Sambrook in his *ODNB* entry on Ward, with reference to *The Secret History of Clubs*, a larger satirical compilation of 32 clubs also dated 1709, states, "Most clubs satirized in this collection were fictitious, but one exception was the Kit-Cat." This illustration could be as bona fide as the map of Lilliput; on the other hand, one might ask why there wouldn't have been a Jockey Club in 1709. Jacob Tonson's Kit-Cat Club dates from the late 1690s, the Beefsteak Club from about 1705, and the short lived but satirically far reaching Scriblerus Club from 1713. Clubs, both fictitious and real, were mushrooming at this time. Howard William Troyer suggests that Ward's imaginary Atheistical Club may have inspired the real-life Hell-Fire Club.[34]

Hogarth may well have seen *The Jockey Club*, as there are striking similarities between it and the sixth plate of *A Rake's Progress* (Figure 6.2). In both images the central figure in the foreground has fallen to the floorboards on one knee with a fist clenched to the sky, having apparently lost everything at the gambling table, while the winner rakes in the coins on the table. A pair of men fight in the background while others seem to be sharing in the spoils. Hogarth's engraving omits the vomit, and no pictures of horses adorn the wall as in *The Jockey Club*.[35] In the second plate of *A Rake's Progress*, Hogarth includes a jockey on bended knee holding a whip in one hand and, in the other, a silver trophy with a scalloped rim, bearing the inscription "Won at Epsom Silly Tom" flanking an image of the winning horse and rider (Figure 6.3).

If owning a racehorse was part of Tom Rakewell's "Progress" in 1734/35, it is hardly a stretch to imagine a winner's circle, a presentation ceremony, followed

Figure 6.1　*The Jockey Club*, frontispiece, Edward Ward, *The History of the London Clubs, or, the Citizens' Pastime…*, part 1 (London: J. Bagnall, 1709). BL: 10349.bbb.25. © The British Library Board.

Figure 6.2   Detail of plate VI, 3rd state, William Hogarth, *A Rake's Progress*, 1734/35. Author's copy.

by libations, hence the need for some sort of clubhouse. Illustrations such as these suggest that there may well have been a Jockey Club in operation more than 40 years before the commonly given date of establishment.[36] Lord Lovechace wears jockey boots in Tom D'Urfey's comedy *The Bath, or, The Western Lass* (1701).[37] Peter Tillemans (1684–1734) painted a *View of a Horse-Match over the Long Course at Newmarket, from the Starting Post to the Stand* (ca. 1717–1723, Paul Mellon Collection, 99.96) with a stable centrally located and a building that could well be a clubhouse where race goers could seek sustenance, shelter from the elements, and of course, a gaming table. The town seems to be prospering in the background (Cormack 130–31).

140   *British Sporting Literature and Culture in the Long Eighteenth Century*

Figure 6.3.   Detail of plate II, 4th state, William Hogarth, *A Rake's Progress*, 1734/35. Author's copy.

By the spring of 1752, a group of horse fanciers held forth at the Star and Garter in Pall Mall, but soon moved away from London, settling on Newmarket. The coffers of the Jockey Club were sufficiently flush that it was able to lease the grounds for the building of the Coffee Room where Club members could meet and gamble at their leisure. But membership wasn't restricted to English gentry. The Jockey Club issued its first known formal fashion statement on 4 October 1762 when seven dukes, one marquis, four earls, one viscount, two baronets, another lord, and three commoners displayed the colors their jockeys would wear at Newmarket, in part to help keep track of riders during a race, especially at the finishing line. Presumably anyone with a dash of charm and some disposable cash could join: the young James Boswell wrote *The Cub at Newmarket* in 1760, mentioning in the preface its "Coffee Room, in which the author, being elected a member of the Jockey Club, had the happiness of passing several sprightly good-humoured evenings."[38] Later, after meeting Johnson, Boswell was pronounced "a very clubable man." By that time, the Jockey Club had well established its place in the world of sport. But, as the 1709 engraving and pre-1750 newspaper notices suggest, The Jockey Club may have influenced the course of horse racing much earlier than has previously been thought.

The Jockey Club and Satirical Representations of Government in *The New Foundling Hospital for Wit*

As the Jockey Club proved popular among royals, nobles, politicians, and an otherwise wealthy clientele, it wasn't long before the sport and its illustrious gamblers attracted the attention of artists, poets, and satirists. *The New Foundling Hospital for Wit*, a satirical miscellany published by the radical bookseller John Almon, and assisted by John Wilkes's notoriety, offered up some satire of dubious provenance. One example, "The Muse at a Horse-Race," satirically juxtaposes jockeying at court with country jockeys. Subtitled "A Ballad, Addressed to C—t and Country Jockies," it begins with a nod to the muse of history, whom the poet whisks away from town for a day at the races:

> When my Clio is gay,
> It is always my way,
> In my pleasures to give her a place:
> So I order'd my chaise,
> (For the muses love ease)
> And I drove her away to a race.[39]

Everyone arrives at five o'clock, a drum builds up anticipation, and after some delay, finally they're at the post, and they're off. The jockeys are brutal to their mounts in the zeal to win, using boots, spurs, and whips:

> To see poor jades so lash'd,
> So kick'd, spurr'd, and thrash'd,
> Was too sharp for soft nature, like mine;
> Yet to give them their due,
> While a plate was in view,
> Their hearts were too great to repine. (*NFHW* 1:81)

While the race looks like a mêlée as horses criss-cross one another on the course, expert commentators weigh in: "Yet, the *knowing ones* said, / (And they live by the trade) / That to see such *quick turns* was a wonder." The poet then takes a political slant, imagining George Grenville, Whig Prime Minister from 1763 to 1765, as the leader of the race ahead of "hacks of all prices, / All ages and sizes." Also invoked is "B—" or Bute, one of the very few Tory Prime Ministers of the century. Lord Bute was Grenville's predecessor as Prime Minister; although he survived for less than a year in office, satirists harangued him long afterwards. Bute was vilified in *The New Foundling Hospital for Wit* as an English-hating Scot, as the baleful force behind the Treaty of Paris and as the alleged lover of the King's mother. Bute is accused here of making dubious political appointments on the basis of "race" (i.e. Scottishness) rather than ability: "Tho' ponies or pacers, / He puffs them for racers, / And starts 'em to win the king's plate." The ballad ends cryptically:

> Since customs so base
> Sunk the name of this race,
> Good horses all pass to the leeward;
> And trust me, my friend,
> Our C—t races won't mend
> As long as l— B— is a Steward. (*NFHW* 1:82)

That is, the political climate won't improve until Lord Bute ceases to be a "Steward"—a racecourse official—or a "Stuart"—his natal name. In other words: never.

"The Analogy between Legislation and Horse-racing" highlights politicians' preference for attending the Jockey Club and Newmarket races at the expense of their parliamentary duties in the period between the Seven Years War and the War of American Independence. "The Analogy" begins

> The swift-pac'd hours convoke again
> Our senate on Newmarket's plain;
> They mind not here who's out, who's in—
> Their contest is, who most shall win.
> Here too they drop all party rage—
> Far different heats their thoughts engage. (*NFHW* 1:133)

So horse races offer an environment where political stripes and axes to grind can be momentarily forgotten. After making a jest about his Pegasus being kept on earth by the jockey's lead weight, the poet proceeds to exploit the analogy:

> I've heard there is a near alliance
> 'Twixt ev'ry lib'ral art and science;
> So the same features we may trace in
> Both legislation and horse-racing.
> Good laws require good heads to make 'em:
> And so do bets, to lay, or take 'em.
> Laws are design'd to keep rogues under;
> To save your house and purse from plunder.
> And he whose noble genius aims
> To shine at these olympic games,
> And cannot, with superior sleight,
> Out-wit the knave, the biter bite,
> Must leave the turf, or ever curse
> The mis'ries of an empty purse. (*NFHW* 1:133)

The legislators, who ought to "enact their laws for general good," instead risk squandering fortunes which might be put to better use easing the plight of starving families. "The Analogy" concludes with a plea to parliamentarians:

> Does not the saddle represent
> Taxes, clapt on by parliament?
> Nor has the nation shewn bad sport;
> We humbly thank their honours for't.
> Though some have made complaint of late,
> Their backs were gall'd with over-weight;
> And that their sides had sorely felt
> The whip and spur full freely dealt;
> Yet hope these patriot-jockies will
> At length, to shew true sportsmen's skill,
> Pull in their steeds, quite out of breath,
> Nor push the willing tits to death.
> Proceed, ye two-fold legislators
> Of horses and your fellow creatures;
> Keep well your seats, nor vote, nor ride,
> On post's or ministry's wrong side;
> So shall the purse your pockets fill,
> And grooms and statesman praise your skill. (*NFHW* 1:134)

Signing as "Vicissitudinarius," one anonymous contributor is alarmed that the location where Magna Carta was signed by King John in 1215 is now a trampling ground in "A Thought on Seeing Races Advertised for Runney-Mead":

> Shame on the age! that once so glorious place,
> Is now the scene of action for—a Race;
> Where Fraud successful drains th' unwary purse;
> And private gain becomes a public curse.
> Blotted from hist'ry, that once hallow'd ground,
> Shall shine in Walker for its turf renown'd
> Time, thou hast made a wond'rous change indeed,
> A Cow-stall of a Forum,—a Course of Runny-mead. (*NFHW* 5:121)

Having had his fill, Vicissitudinarius suggests that horse racing and the rage for gambling, legitimized somehow by B. Walker, who continued Heber's record keeping in *An Historical List of Horse-matches, Plates and Prizes, Run for in Great-Britain and Ireland* (London, 1769/70, 1771), will quickly lead to Great Britain's decline and fall.

The Jockey Club provided other forms of gambling in between races. One bit of dirty laundry, reprinted from *The London Evening Post* of 12 December 1767, was given a more enduring public airing in *The New Foundling Hospital for Wit* (1:135–6). It was a petition signed by 28 members of the Jockey Club, including the Dukes of Grafton and Ancaster, Charles Bunbury, and C. Boothby Skrymsher, blackballing one Major Brereton, possibly William Brereton (1741–1787), son of a Master of Ceremonies at Bath, who trained as an actor under Garrick and made his debut at Drury Lane in 1768. Brereton, described as "a sad vulgar" by Lady Bunbury (*née* Lady Sarah Lennox), accused Hugo Meynell and Captain Richard "Jockey" Vernon ("Oracle of Newmarket" and member of Bloomsbury Gang under the Duke of Bedford) of cheating the Duke of Northumberland at cards. The Club was able to silence Brereton on a technicality: he was "deemed" not to be a member of the Jockey Club as he had simply paid a subscription to use the Coffee Room, a backhanded method of padding Vernon's profits.[40] Founding member Augustus Henry Fitzroy, 3rd Duke of Grafton (1735–1811), spent so much time at the races, even when he was Prime Minister, that he was dubbed "Jockey" Grafton.

It is hardly surprising then that *The New Foundling Hospital for Wit* should allude to the Jockey Club, horse-mad politicians, gamblers, cheats, and other sportive rogues. Members of the Jockey Club during Brereton's expulsion included: Thomas Panton (son of chief equerry to George II, who was a horse breeder); Sir Thomas Shirley (former governor of Antigua); Richard, 6th Earl of Barrymore (horse owner, jockey, gambler); Granville Leveson-Gower (Lord President in North's administration who supported the hardline policy against the American colonists); and John Manners (Master of the Horse from 1761 to 1766).

John Almon leveled more serious charges against political horse fanatics who neglected their parliamentary duties in *A New and Impartial Collection of Interesting Letters*, published in 1767:

> Long has the public been in expectation of seeing some measure adopted to regulate the heavy price of provisions, but our expectations are not likely to be felicitated this session. Were the scenes of our grievances to be rehearsed at Newmarket, they may perhaps grow interesting, since that is the theatre for the exertion of ministerial talents; but surely if the importance of a character is not preserved with propriety in public, we have but little encouragement to hope it is maintained with dignity in private! Equally ridiculous and unbecoming is it to behold a minister of state figuring it on the Turf, as to see a Primate acting Foppington on the stage, or a Lord Chancellor jigging with a sett of milkmaids round the May-garland.... They, therefore, who frequent the Turf, and other places of dissipation, can have but little leisure for the weighty concerns of state; and as the country pays them for their time, their time ought to be wholly devoted to the services of their country.[41]

Of course, one might argue that the racecourse was the perfect place for any Member of Parliament to go, as it was there an MP was likeliest to find the Prime Minister. Too many of Lord North's advisors, it seems, were indulging their gambling addictions at Newmarket rather than tending to military stratagems at Whitehall while Britain was losing the War of American Independence.

દે દે દે

To complement a statue of William Pitt commissioned by grateful American colonists, an equestrian statue of George III, sculpted by Joseph Wilton, was shipped across the Atlantic and erected in Bowling Green, a park in Broadway, Gotham, now New York City, in 1770. Three years later, the frontispiece to the sixth and last part, *The New Foundling Hospital for Wit* (1773), dared to parody this royal equestrian statue (Figure 6.4).[42] The original was based on the equestrian statue of Marcus Aurelius in Rome, dating from 161–180 A.D., whereas in the parodic engraving, the sculptor produces the mad tyrant Nero anachronistically brandishing a pistol. With his long hair flowing, sporting bells on his cape and missing a boot, he appears, nonetheless, to have managed to put on his spur. The dark owl is poised to swoop away with the royal horseman's laurels. The figure on the lower right resembles the sort of rustic colonial who might soon be taking aim at the troops of George III. The Cap of Liberty on the Staff of Maintenance (which Hogarth had used in his 1763 engraving to satirize Wilkes), 10 years later, is being trampled by the tyrant's horse. Five days after the ink dried on *The Declaration of Independence*, the newly inspired revolutionaries toppled the equestrian statue of George III. This symbolic act of defiance had a pragmatic side as well: the king and his horse were melted into lead for an estimated 42,000 musket balls to be fired by George Washington's army against the king's soldiers.[43]

દે દે દે

James Watt's improvements upon the 1712 Newcomen engine in the 1760s changed the nature of horse power. When the automobile was introduced at the start of the twentieth century, it was commonly referred to as the horseless carriage. Swift, perhaps a protoenvironmentalist lurking behind the mask of the satirist, imagined a better world governed by horses. Much nostalgia accompanied the decline of the horse age. Booth Tarkington's 1918 novel, *The Magnificent Ambersons*, noted the passing of "the introspective horses [which] curried and brushed and whacked and amiably cursed—those good old horses switch their tails at flies no more.... The stables have been transformed.... They went quickly, yet so silently that we whom they served have not yet really noticed that they vanished." Nostalgia is aroused by an old movie about a horse-drawn fire engine in John Cheever's short story, "The Fourth Alarm," from *The World of Apples* (1973). Nicholas Evans's 1995 novel, *The Horse Whisperer*, sold more than 15 million copies, and was adapted for the screen in 1998, directed by and starring Robert Redford. Twenty-first century film

Figure 6.4   Frontispiece, *The New Foundling Hospital for Wit*, vol. 6 (London: John Almon, 1773). Author's copy.

goers have been treated to *Seabiscuit*, directed by Gary Ross in 2003, and *War Horse*, directed by Steven Spielberg in 2011, based on the play, which in turn was based on Michael Morpurgo's 1982 children's novel. The Royal Newfoundland Constabulary, which dates back to 1729, reactivated a mounted unit in 2003 with four Percherons named Vince, Fraize, Dobbin, and Townshend (named after George Townshend, 1st Marquess Townshend, who served under General James Wolfe at the Siege of Quebec in 1759, hence Fort Townshend in St. John's). While the garage has largely replaced the stable, the clip-clop of horseshoes can still be heard at certain moments in our postmodern world.

Notes

I am grateful to my graduate assistants—Jessica Pollard for sharing her considerable equestrian expertise, and Katherine (Kt) Barker for her much appreciated help with revisions.

* A version of the section "Antedating the Jockey Club" was published as "Lost Trousers" in *The Times Literary Supplement*, 26 July 2013, 14–15. The frontispiece to Ned Ward's *The History of the London Clubs* (1709), entitled *The Jockey Club* (shown below), is taken from the original, sole surviving copy in the British Library (BL: 10349.bbb.25) rather than from the less detailed reproduction in *Eighteenth Century Collections Online* (*ECCO*).

1   See John Philip Hore, *The History of Newmarket, and the Annals of the Turf, with Memoirs and Biographical Notices of the Habitués of Newmarket, and the Notable Turfites, from the Earliest Times to the End of the Seventeenth Century*, Volume II (London: A.H. Baily, 1886), 246–49.

2   Newmarket Racecourse homepage, accessed 7 January 2014, http://www.newmarketracecourses.co.uk/about-the-home-of-racing/newmarket-history/.

3   *The Twickenham Edition of the Poems of Alexander Pope*, gen. ed. John Butt, 11 vols in 12 (London: Methuen; New Haven, CT: Yale University Press, 1939–1969), *The Odyssey*, ed. Maynard Mack et al., 1967, 9:416, Book XI:639–42.

4   Jonathan Swift, *The Complete Poems*, ed. Pat Rogers (Harmondsworth: Penguin, 1983), 114, lines 47–52.

5   Robert Hogan, ed., *The Poems of Thomas Sheridan* (Cranberry, NJ: Associated University Presses, 1994), 63.

6   Angus Ross and David Woolley, eds., *Jonathan Swift* (Oxford: Oxford University Press, 1984), 6.

7   Claude Rawson and Ian Higgins, eds., *Jonathan Swift: The Essential Writings* (New York: Norton, 2010), 338.

8   Swift, *Gulliver's Travels*, introduced by Jeanette Winterson (Oxford: Oxford University Press, 1999), vii–viii.

9   Rawson and Higgins, *Jonathan Swift*, 315.

10   Matthew Kilburn, "Powlett, Charles, third duke of Bolton (1685–1754)," *Oxford Dictionary of National Biography* (Oxford: Oxford University Press, 2004), accessed 3 February 2014, http://www.oxforddnb.com/view/article/21615.

11   John Cleland, *Memoirs of a Woman of Pleasure*, ed. Peter Sabor (1985; repr., Oxford: Oxford University Press, 1999), 9. As Sabor points out, "jockey-ship" meant "trickery" because of the unsavory reputation of horse dealers; this usage predates the first *OED* example by some 15 years.

12   Laurence Sterne, *The Life and Opinions of Tristram Shandy, Gentleman*, ed. Ian Campbell Ross (Oxford: Oxford University Press, 1983), 16. In the opening chapter to *Don Quixote*, Cervantes's knight spends four days coming up with a name for his mount, thus making Rocinante one of the earliest and most celebrated horses in literature to have a name.

13   "When for Air I take my Mare," *Thomas D'Urfey's Pills to Purge Melancholy: Lewd Songs and Low Ballads from the 18th Century*, performed by the City Waits (Wotton-under-Edge, Gloucestershire, 1990), CD, track 18.

[14] Henry Fielding, *The History of Tom Jones, A Foundling*, ed. Thomas Keymer and Alice Wakely (London: Penguin, 2005), 270.

[15] The British Triple Crown is composed of the 2,000 Guineas Stakes (a one-mile race at Newmarket dating from 1809), the Epsom Derby (one mile, four furlongs, and 10 yards at Epsom Downs from 1780), and the St. Leger Stakes (one mile, six furlongs, and 132 yards at Doncaster from 1778). The other two British Classic races are the Epsom Oaks (one mile, four furlongs, and 10 yards from 1779) and the 1,000 Guineas Stakes (one-mile at Newmarket from 1814).

[16] Quoted in M. Dorothy George, *England in Johnson's Day* (1928; repr., Freeport, NY: Books for Libraries Press, 1972), 231. Also worth noting here is Jean-Bernard Le Blanc's 1745 *Letters on the English and French Nations*, translated 1747, in which he marvels at the more than 2000 spectators who will turn out to see a horse race in England (16).

[17] Roy Porter, *English Society in the Eighteenth Century* (Harmondsworth: Penguin, 1982), 254–5.

[18] Daniel Defoe, *A Tour through the Whole Island of Great Britain*, ed. Pat Rogers (Exeter: Webb and Bower, 1989); originally published in 3 vols., 1724–1726. Letter 1 in volume 1 may date from 1722 when Defoe traveled around East Anglia (9).

[19] Charles Johnstone, *Chrysal; or, the Adventures of a Guinea* (London: T. Becket, 1760 [vols. 1 and 2]; 1765 [vols. 3 and 4]), ed. Kevin Bourque; 4 vols. in 2 (Kansas City: Valancourt Books, 2011), 299–300.

[20] The first two sentences are quoted in the *ODNB* entry on Frampton, but without attribution to Defoe.

[21] Lester Piggott [*sic*] (b. 1935; retired 1995), one of the most famous British jockeys ever, comes from a long line of riders and trainers, tracing his family's involvement with horse racing back to the eighteenth century. He won 4493 races, crossed the finish line first in nine Epsom Derbies, and merited a Spitting Image puppet.

[22] Anon., *The Foundling Hospital for Wit*, 6 vols. (London, 1743–1749), 6:68.

[23] Sir Walter Scott, *Waverley* (Boston: DeWolfe, Fiske & Co., 1910), 75. Redmond Barry's only son Bryan dies after being thrown from his horse in William Makepeace Thackeray's *The Luck of Barry Lyndon*, situated in the eighteenth century, but published serially in 1844. Another later product of a troubled marriage, Eugenie Victoria "Bonnie Blue" Butler dies attempting to jump a bar on her Shetland pony in Margaret Mitchell's 1936 *Gone with the Wind*.

[24] Maynard Mack, *Alexander Pope: A Life* (1985; repr., New York and London: Norton, 1988), 446–7.

[25] James Boswell, *The Journal of a Tour to the Hebrides*, with Samuel Johnson, *A Journey to the Western Islands of Scotland*, ed. Peter Levi (Harmondsworth: Penguin, 1984), 66, 120, 281.

[26] Entry on Catherine Maria Fischer, *ODNB*.

[27] Tobias Smollett, *The Expedition of Humphry Clinker*, ed. Lewis M. Knapp (Oxford, 1966), 79–81.

[28] For a study on changing horse culture over the century, especially in relation to horses from the East, see Donna Landry, *Noble Brutes: How Eastern Horses Transformed English Culture* (Baltimore: Johns Hopkins University Press, 2008).

[29] The Dick Vet, originally the Highland Society's Veterinary School in Edinburgh, was established in 1823 by William Dick who had come from the College of Surgeons; the Royal College of Veterinary Surgeons was founded in 1844; Glasgow Veterinary College

was established in 1862; an offshoot of the University Department of Pathology in 1909, Cambridge Veterinary School wasn't founded until 1949.

[30] Black lists his sources in *The Jockey Club and its Founders* (London, 1891): "My chief authorities (necessarily so interwoven with the work that it would be impossible to give special references) are:—'Calendar of State Papers'; Horace Walpole's 'Letters'; Wraxall's 'Historical Memoirs'; 'Histories of the British Turf'; Admiral Rous's 'Horse-Racing'; Hore's 'History of Newmarket'; the Badminton Library; the Racing Calendars of Cheney, Heber, Pond, Tuting and Fawconer, B. Walker, and Weatherby; Cobbett's 'Parliamentary History,' and Hansard's 'Debates'; 'The Sporting Magazine'; 'Baily's Magazine'; works by 'The Druid'; Obituaries; and the works of Burke, Debrett, Lodge, &c, as well as a scurrilous publication called 'The Jockey Club,' by Charles Pigott (alias 'Louse' Pigott), an ex-member of the Club" (x).

[31] "Our History," the Jockey Club (which begins, "The precise origins of the Jockey Club are not known, but the first evidence of its existence came in 1752"), accessed 1 June 2013, http://www.thejockeyclub.co.uk/about/our-heritage.

[32] In the course of my writing this chapter, Richard Nash announced similar newspaper antedatings (but not the 1709 engraving) in the newly published *Cambridge Companion to Horseracing*, ed. Rebecca Cassidy (Cambridge, Cambridge University Press, 2013), 22–8. I am also grateful to Timothy Cox of the Cox Library, David Oldrey of the Jockey Club, and Mike Huggins of the University of Cumbria.

[33] The full title runs: *The History of the London CLUBS, or, the Citizens Pastime. Particularly, the Lying Club, the Beggars Club, the Yorkshire Club, the Broken Shopkeepers Club, the Thieves Club, the Basket Womans Club. With a Sermon Preach'd to a Gang of High-way-Men. Part I*, "*By the Author of the* London Spy" (London: printed for J. Bagnall, near Fleetstreet, 1709). Ward followed this up with an eight-page sequel: *The Second Part, of the London Clubs; Containing, the No-Nose Club, the Beaus Club, the Farting Club, the Sodomites, or Mollies Club. The Quacks* ... (London: J. Dutton [1709?]). He saved extensive revelations for the 170-page *The Secret History of the Calves-Head Club: or, the Republican Unmask'd* ... (London: B. Bragge, 1709). *The Secret History of Clubs: Particularly the Kit-Cat, Beef-Stake, Vertuosos, Quacks, Knights of the Golden-Fleece, Florists, Beaus, &c.* (London, 1709) filled 395 pages. The "7th" edition of *A Compleat and Humorous Account of All the Remarkable Clubs and Societies in the Cities of London and Westminster* (London, J. Wren [1756]), covered 30 clubs (none of them the Jockey Club) over 260 pages.

[34] Howard William Troyer, *Ned Ward of Grub Street* (London: Frank Cass, 1968), 162. There is no discussion of the Jockey Club or its illustration here.

[35] Tanya Cassidy notes this illustration without further elaboration in "People, Place, and Performance: Theoretically visiting Mother Clap's Molly House," *Queer People: Negotiations and Expressions of Homosexuality, 1700–1800*, ed. Chris Mounsey and Caroline Gonda (Cranbury, NJ: Associated University Press, 2007), 111, n. 26.

[36] Beyond the scope of this article, a study of contemporary letters might produce earlier "Jockey Club" references.

[37] *The Bath, or, The Western Lass. A Comedy, as it is Acted at the Theatre Royal in Drury-Lane, By His Majesty's Servants. By Mr. Durfey* (London: printed for Peter Buck, at the Sign of the Temple, at the Middle Temple Gate in Fleetstreet, 1701), 30.

[38] Boswell, *Life of Johnson*, 1:383 n.

[39] *The New Foundling Hospital for Wit* [cited as *NFHW*], 6 vols. (London: John Almon, 1768–1773), 1:80. Facsimile, 6 vols. in 3, edited by Donald W. Nichol (London: Pickering and Chatto, 2006).

[40] Robert Black, *The Jockey Club*, 154; John Tyrrel, *Running Racing: The Jockey Club years since 1750* (London: Quiller Press, 1997), 17, 154.

[41] John Almon, *A New and Impartial Collection of Interesting Letters, From the Public Papers; Many of them Written by Persons of Eminence, On a great Variety of Important Subjects, which have occasionally engaged the Public Attention: From the Accession of his present Majesty, in September 1760, to May 1767*, 2 vols., (London: John Almon, 1767), 2:172.

[42] This frontispiece is not included in *Catalogue of Prints and Drawings in the British Museum. Division I. Political and Personal Satires*, vol. 5. (1771–1783), ed. Mary Dorothy George (London, 1935), but is reproduced in Vincent Carretta's *George III and the Satirists from Hogarth to Byron* (Athens and London: University of Georgia Press, 1990), 94.

[43] David Hackett Fischer, *Liberty and Freedom* (Oxford: Oxford University Press, 2004), 176–7; Arthur S. Marks, "The Statue of King George III in New York and the Iconology of Regicide," *The American Art Journal* 13 (1981), 61. Alexander J. Wall, *The Equestrian Statue of George III and the Pedestrian Statue of William Pitt: Erected in the City of New York*, New York Historical Society, 1770.

PART III
People

Chapter 7
Boxing for England: Daniel Mendoza and the Theater of Sport

Sharon Harrow

Daniel Mendoza held the title of heavyweight Champion of England from 1792 to 1795. Arguably the most famous fighter of his time, he fought during the renaissance of bare-knuckle boxing. His rise to stardom in the late 1780s was so precipitous that one biographer wrote, "The outbreak of the French Revolution was inside-page news in the journals of 1789, because in those July days Mendoza made front page news with boxing's first literary work, *The Art of Boxing*."[1] His 1816 *Memoirs of the Life of Daniel Mendoza* was the first autobiography written by a pugilist.[2]

Mendoza was a charismatic and handsome man with dark, wavy hair that he sometimes wore long until a punishing fight with Gentleman John Jackson during which the latter pulled Mendoza's hair, pinned and pummeled him. *The Times* expressed pleasure that "the Jew appeared overpowered by the strength of the Christian."[3] Such a move had not yet been instituted as against the rules, but it was the sort of tactic Mendoza would have eschewed. His refusal to strike a clearly beaten opponent invited praise of his "humanity" in the ring.[4] Indeed, prints of him alternately depict him as fierce and sympathetic.[5]

Mendoza's "scientific" method of defense distinguished him from his contemporaries. His very use of tactics made him famous, for most fighters had been trained to stand their ground and slug at each other. By contrast, Mendoza strategized and fought defensively. As prints of him illustrate, Mendoza was muscular enough to stand his ground (see Figure 7.1). Rather than slug, he would dance, sidestep, swerve, and even strategically endure blows to exhaust his opponent. While he was quick to punch and dart, he would also parry; he revolutionized the strategy of defense. Eighteenth-century writers debated whether or not a system of fighting that foregrounded defense was sufficiently manly and therefore sufficiently English. At five feet seven inches and 160 pounds, Mendoza technically classed as a middleweight. His skill, however, enabled him to beat larger men. Like his writing, his fighting style was not plodding, but methodical, crisp, and engaging.

Alternately hailed as "The Star of Israel" and "Mendoza the Jew," Mendoza enjoyed a reputation as a "professor of pugilism" whose success in the ring as well as the popularity of *The Art of Boxing* made him a Jewish luminary. His fame is particularly impressive given the anti-Semitism that pervaded eighteenth-century England. Among the sinister pastimes favored by eighteenth-century Londoners

Figure 7.1   James Gillray. Portrait of Daniel Mendoza (1788). Etching and aquatint. © Trustees of the British Museum.

was recreational bigotry. As one historian put it: "Jew-baiting became a sport, like cock-throwing, or bull-baiting or pelting some poor wretch in the pillory."[6] Mendoza's renown as a boxer, perhaps ironically, helped to abate such violence. He refashioned the public image of Jews by marketing himself as a pugilist who worked in the service of English honor by promulgating a useful sport and by training gentlemen in what was often called a manly art. *The Art of Boxing* presented the sport as a valid "science" with "public and private utility."[7] The treatise includes rules, methods for training, a dictionary of terms, a "system of boxing" intended to train fighters, and a brief, articulate (even legalistic at times) summary of his famous 1788 fight with the acclaimed boxer Richard Humphries. Using the rhetoric of education, Mendoza calls participants "scholar" and "master," and he dubs a defensive move a "riposte." As shown in more detail below, the text endeavors to intellectualize and legitimize the sport, and in that regard *The Art of Boxing* had a measure of success, for the six-pence tract was printed twice in London in 1789, reprinted in London in 1790, and in Dublin in 1792. Some of the editions included expanded coverage of Mendoza's verbal sallies with Humphries in the popular newspaper the *World*. In both body and text, Mendoza manipulated the sports of "Jew-baiting" and boxing, and turned to his advantage the literary and social traditions from which he would have been excluded because of his ethnicity.

Jews had been banned from England since the Edict of Expulsion in 1290, and the tepid "Jew Bill" of 1753 afforded only minimal rights, mainly to wealthy Jews. Debate over the bill often centered on nationalism—and sometimes on fighting. Businessman and philanthropist Jonas Hanway opposed the bill on the grounds that Jews would not fight to defend England: "I know not upon what authority it is said, but I have been told, that a *Jew* will not fight in defence of a *Christian* country."[8] The status of Jews as religious and civil outsiders sanctioned public abuse. It did not help that both crime and punishment were abundant in the isolated Jewish communities. Todd Endelman provides a detailed account of the infamous Chelsea Murder Case of 1771, the negative consequences of which impacted Jews throughout England. By 1770, Endelman writes, hangings and transportation of Jewish criminals had doubled.[9] Temple elders maintained steady contact with Sir John Fielding, magistrate and administrator of the protopolice force the Bow Street Runners, and brother to famous novelist Henry Fielding. Sir John prosecuted the notorious Chelsea case in which a robbery perpetrated by Jewish criminals resulted in the death of an innocent servant. Newspapers widely reported the murder, negative public opinion toward Jews became rabid, and "Anglo-Jewry as a body stood convicted."[10] Jews were physically and legally harassed. Public opinion was so low, and respectable and established Jews were so outraged by what they saw as lower-class ruffianism, that efforts were made to slow immigration of poor Jews from Holland.[11] Radical reformer and social commentator Francis Place famously reported the ill-treatment of Jews: "I have seen Jews hooted, hunted, cuffed, pulled by the beard, spit upon, and so barbarously assaulted in the streets, without any protection from the passers-by or the police.... Dogs could not be used in the streets in the manner many Jews were treated."[12] In this age of bigotry and blood sports, Mendoza became a celebrity champion, and his acclaim helped to ameliorate the social situation of Jews:

> One circumstance among others put an end to the ill-usage of the Jews.... About the year 1787 Daniel Mendoza, a Jew, became a celebrated boxer and set up a school to teach the art of boxing as a science, the art soon spread among the young Jews and they became generally expert at it. The consequence was in a very few years seen and felt too. It was no longer safe to insult a Jew unless he was an old man and alone.... But even if the Jews were unable to defend themselves, the few who would [now] be disposed to insult them merely because they are Jews, would be in danger of chastisement from the passers-by and of punishment from the police.[13]

Mendoza's reputation prompted others to defend themselves from assault and mitigated the Jewish population's vulnerability. How did the Jewish boxer authorize an illegitimate and illegal sport, and himself as a writer and sports icon?

He did so largely by refashioning traditional literary principles to his rhetorical advantage and, more broadly, by capitalizing on the period's enthusiasm for sport and theater.

Mendoza was born in 1764 to Sephardic Jewish parents in Aldgate. He married a Jewish woman named Esther, with whom he raised a large family. Like numerous boxers, his profligacy outweighed his wealth. He was apprenticed to assorted tradesmen and worked at various professions, including greengrocer and glazier, but a street brawl brought him to the attention of the already-famous fighter Richard Humphries, and Mendoza pursued the more lucrative profession of the fist. In his memoirs, Mendoza describes a number of early fights for pay and an almost equal number of fights resulting from unprovoked insults. He portrays himself as a regular victim of anti-Semitic taunts and jabs. Mendoza is a charismatic figure who narrates his life with literary flair. In a scene reminiscent of Fielding's picaresque novel *Tom Jones*, Mendoza describes an incident in which he rides his horse into a "dancing room, to the surprise and entertainment of the company, chiefly consisting of sailors and their lasses, and having remained here for about two hours, and it drawing near midnight, I thought it high time to quit this place of mirth."[14] His frolic occurred after he had had three separate, spontaneous fights, all pitched during his return from Barnet Racecourse, where he had viewed a boxing match. At various times, he worked as a smuggler, a publican, a counterfeiter, and a hired hand in Covent Garden. Ironically, he also worked as a rowdy retained to oppose Parliamentary member Henry Thornton, who lobbied for Catholic emancipation. "No popery!" Mendoza was heard to have shouted at him.[15] At the height of his Championship, Mendoza was so widely acclaimed that George III is said to have summoned him to court. Mendoza's life was as theatrical as his boxing career.

Nineteenth-century boxing historian Pierce Egan describes Mendoza's stardom as so great that it challenged contemporary prejudice. In his biography of Mendoza, Egan writes:

> The name of Mendoza has been resounded from one part of the kingdom to the other; and the fame of this once-celebrated pugilist was the theme of universal panegyric—and, though not
>   The Jew
>   That Shakespeare drew—
> Yet he was that Jew, the acknowledged pride of his own particular persuasion, and who, so far interested the Christian that, in spite of his prejudices, he was compelled to exclaim—'Mendoza was a pugilist of no ordinary merit!'[16]

Egan's Shakespearian quotation underscores the theatrical nature of boxing during the eighteenth century. Moreover, writing about Mendoza, and Mendoza's *The Art of Boxing* and *Memoirs*, reflects Mendoza's sharp manipulation of neoclassical ideals as they related to sport and literature. Michael Scrivener views Mendoza's prose as characteristic of writing by British Jews during the Romantic period; he asserts that "Jewish difference makes itself fit into already existing generic conventions in much the same way that British Jews became acculturated.... These texts affirm Jewish identity with varying degrees and strategies of defiance."[17] Similarly, he claims that Mendoza's memoir and his new scientific method of fighting resulted in a "cultural hybridization" of the sport: "British boxing, because of Mendoza and other Jews, becomes Jewish, and the Jews become British."[18] Indeed, Mendoza's victories in the ring were favorably compared to "Levi's theological victory over Priestley,"[19] recorded in a print that describes David Levi as a "Jewish hero."[20] Mendoza, too, was depicted as a hero, and he realized his commercial value. His representation of the sport and of himself capitalized on the era's interest in both sports and the theater, especially as they related to civic discourse and nationalism. Such a focus is unsurprising given that his career took off during the era of the French Revolution.

Political, wartime discourse understandably affected Mendoza's public persona. Prevailing literary, theatrical, cultural, and pugilistic discourses shaped his career as well. An overview of boxing in the eighteenth century and a description of some of the literature and cultural debates surrounding the sport will set the stage for a closer look at Mendoza's writing—and for his stint at the 1809 Old Price Riots. In that role, his abilities as a sportsman and performer coalesced at the storied Covent Garden Theatre in London.

During the long eighteenth century, boxing became a formalized and fashionable sport. As sporting historian Dennis Brailsford puts it, the century saw "pugilism's emergence out of the welter of other combat sports with which it was associated and its development from a fairground knock-about into an organized affair of national interest, followed by prince and peer, ploughman and potboy alike."[21] Boxing first shone on the literal as well as literary stage in the early eighteenth century with the opening of several venues dedicated to fighting. In 1743 Jack Broughton, the "father of boxing," opened an amphitheater that was underwritten by William, the Duke of Cumberland. That same year, Broughton published "Proposals for erecting an amphitheatre for the manly exercise of boxing," a four-page treatise that begins with a quote from Virgil's *Aeneid*, lauding the British as "inheritors of the Greek and Roman virtues." Thus, Broughton adds gravitas to his subject by establishing a connection between bare-knuckle boxing and the ancients. *Broughton's Rules* became the standard code, and they were followed for over a century. Boxing had become popular, and sportsmen and writers began to professionalize the sport. Egan writes that "public challenges of the pugilists" began to be "advertised" in 1740. Before the 1740s, boxing had been bare-knuckled, brutal, unregulated, unruly, and largely unlawful. In Egan's words, "Previous to the days of Broughton, it was downright slaughtering."[22] Broughton's amphitheater followed that of James Figg, who had opened his in 1719 in order to capitalize on fair- and theater-goers' interest in staged fights and to profit from the gentry's interest in learning fisticuffs as an alternative to dueling.[23]

William Hogarth engraved boxing champion Figg's business card, included Figg's boxing booth in his engraving *Southwark Fair*, and also drew Figg into one of the plates of his *A Rake's Progress* (1735).

Broughton trained as Figg's student, and he established his reputation on multiple fronts. In his pioneering 1747 "Treatise Upon the Useful Science of Defense," Captain John Godfrey wrote biographies of sword and backsword fighters, and he included a laudatory account of Broughton.[24] By 1730, Broughton had distinguished himself by having won the Doggett's Coat and Badge, a Thames River rowing race.[25] Broughton's fame was far-reaching; Hogarth painted his portrait in the 1730s. In 1733, Broughton and Figg staged a demonstration bout for George II at Figg's Amphitheatre. Broughton's performance impressed the King and his sons, and William, Duke of Cumberland eventually became Broughton's patron. George II called on Broughton to join the Yeomen of the Guard, bodyguards to the King, and in 1743, Broughton fought alongside the King at the Battle of Dettingen, the last time a King fought in battle. Broughton's success in the ring and on the battlefield made him a prestigious figure.

Broughton was also a savvy businessman. He cashed in on the new fashion for fisticuffs by adding "muffles"—or gloves—so that upper-crust gentlemen could learn "the whole theory and practice of that truly British art" without the "inconveniency of black eyes, broken jaws, and bloody noses." So read his 1747 advertisement in the *Daily Advertiser*.[26] Broughton staged well-attended boxing performances. Since boxing was technically illegal, matches in boxing academies were to be regarded as performances or exhibitions, and spectators paid not to watch the match but ostensibly for a commemorative coin or some other such token of the event. It is paradoxical that the illegal sport was guided by Broughton's rules as well as by clear, and by all accounts legally binding, articles of agreement.[27] Illegal but trendy, boxing was in vogue through the 1740s.

The fledgling sport suffered a setback in 1750 when legitimate boxing got knocked off stage after the Duke of Cumberland lost roughly £10,000 on a fight and had a hand in closing Broughton's amphitheater. The legal details remain strangely obscure, though the moment is recorded in many boxing histories. One of the earliest histories was penned by William Oxberry, staff comic actor at Drury Lane. In his 1812 *Pancratia, Or, A History of Pugilism*, Oxberry describes the pivotal fight between Broughton and Jack Slack in 1750, which triggered the shift in legal standing of the sport. Oxberry writes that the Duke's loss of £10,000 "proved the ruin of Broughton, and he never fought again; even his old supporter, the Duke of Cumberland, forsook him, and shortly after his amphitheatre was closed by act of parliament."[28] Brailsford notes that no record of parliamentary influence has been found, but historians of the fancy ("followers of prizefighting," as Egan defines the term) generally mark 1750 as the year during which advertisement waned, organization unraveled, and prosecutions of matches increased.[29] The decline in the sport was even noted by the century's most famous intellectual and lexicographer, Samuel Johnson, whose uncle had a boxing and wrestling ring in Smithfield, and who was said to have regretted that, in the 1750s, "prize-fighting is gone out;

every art should be preserved, and the art of defense is surely important."[30] After the closing of Broughton's amphitheater, boxing venues moved to the outskirts of London and to the margins of society and legitimacy. The 1760s and 1770s did see regular fights, but the irregularity of aristocratic backing, the absence of regular performance spaces (fights were often staged at horse racing venues, such as Newmarket and Ascot), the apparent increase in bribes and thrown fights, and the absence of a celebrity boxer contributed to the slump into which organized fighting fell for about three decades.

Historians of the sport agree that the late 1780s mark the second heyday of boxing. A fight between "gentleman" boxer Richard Humphries and the "Bath Butcher" staged at Newmarket Racecourse in 1786 attracted the Prince of Wales and a crowd of nobles. The largest wager was said to have been £30,000. Humphries's style and charisma appealed to the Prince of Wales, who "added prizefighting to his itinerary of rotating pleasures."[31] Oxberry writes in *Pancratia* that after the fight "the British spirit of pugilism again revived."[32] The rise of superstar fighters in the late 1780s regalvanized the sport's legitimacy and visibility. Boxers often set matches by publishing challenges in the popular press. A 1788 press war over a contested match between Humphries and Mendoza indicates just how high profile boxing had become. In this instance, the media event even increased sales of some newspapers.[33] The publicized epistolary challenges show the fighters' business acumen, as they were able to arrange matches for great profit by fanning public interest through the press.

One account of the 1788 Humphries v. Mendoza fight in Odiham exemplifies popular excitement over the sport: "Boxing now was again at the zenith of its glory, being patronised and supported by some of the first sporting characters in the country, particularly by the Prince of Wales."[34] The fight attracted thousands of audience members and, though the gate was guarded by a veritable university of pugilistic professors (the price of admission was a prohibitive half a guinea), a "mob broke down the fences and took possession of every vacant seat."[35] Aristocratic patronage allowed boxing to regain its public profile, as Sawyer notes: "Local magistrates were understandably inclined to turn a blind eye to any illegal event at which HRH and half the nobility were present."[36] Egan captures the spirit of boxing's revival:

> Humphries and Mendoza were the rage: the modern comedies glanced at their exploits ... they rose up like a NEW FEATURE OF THE TIMES! Boxing became fashionable, followed, patronized, and encouraged. Sparring matches took place at the Theatres and Royal Circus. Schools were established for the promulgation of the art; and the *Science of SELF-DEFENCE* considered as a necessary requisite for all Englishmen.[37]

Newspaper accounts provided just one avenue through which boxing's literary popularity burgeoned.

This renewed interest in pugilism was also reflected in the proliferation of boxing manuals and treatises. In praise of *The Art of Boxing* and Mendoza's professional instruction, Egan lauds Mendoza as a superior and articulate instructor: "It has been a tolerably general expressed opinion, that no pugilist whatever, since the days of Broughton (or even Broughton himself) has ever so completely elucidated, or promulgated, the principles of boxing as Daniel Mendoza."[38] In addition to Mendoza's *The Art of Boxing*, there was *The Complete art of Boxing, According to the Modern Method* (An Amateur of Eminence, 1788), *Modern Manhood; or The Art and Practice of English Boxing* (Henry Lemoine, 1788), *The Modern Art of Boxing* (1789), *The Art of Manual Defence, or System of Boxing* (A pupil of Humphreys and Mendoza, 1784[39]), and *Boxing Made Easy* (1800). Writers endeavored to professionalize the sport through scientific codification, and they shared a common interest in the ideological work of promoting English patriotism and masculinity. Multiple boxing histories were published as well. Mendoza's career was coterminous with the revival of boxing and the specialization of boxing literature.

☙ ☙ ☙

Throughout the eighteenth century, boxing's proponents argued that the sport had social value because it promulgated the public virtues of patriotism, masculinity, and heroism. The political climate of the 1740s would have influenced writers' tendencies toward nationalism. In 1743, both the Duke of Cumberland and his father, George II, rode in the Battle of Dettingen. And Broughton's royal supporter, the so-called Butcher Duke, fought in the 1745 Jacobite rebellion. The bellicose times stand out visibly in boxing texts. Broughton's 1743 treatise, one of the first focused and popular texts on boxing, situates boxing within the lineage of classical virtues, connecting reverence for the ancients to proud militarism:

> BRITONS then who boast themselves Inheritors of the *Greek* and *Roman* Virtues, should follow their example, and by encouraging Conflicts, of this magnanimous Kind, endeavour to eradicate that *foreign Effeminacy* which has so fatally insinuated itself among us, and almost destroyed that glorious spirit of *British Championism*, which was wont to be at once the *Terror and Disgrace* of our Enemies.[40]

Broughton's treatise illustrates that, as Christopher Johnson has argued, boxing participated in "the classical model of a societ[y]" whose virtue was displayed through demonstrations of "martial prowess."[41] Other writers of the era shared Broughton's conviction that boxing cultivated manly virtues that could protect the nation from "foreign Effeminacy."[42] Throughout the century, the spirit of boxing was often credited with defending England. As John Whale put it, "the martial prowess of the English nation which has saved it from revolution and tyranny is put down to the country's manly sports."[43] This morality play was rehearsed in training manuals, performed on boxing stages, and valorized in print.

Like many eighteenth-century sporting texts, Mendoza's *Memoir* and *The Art of Boxing* employ neoclassical references to argue that boxing advanced national honor and was a boon to social health. Mendoza's preface situates his *Memoirs* and boxing literature within a neoclassical literary tradition: "That the *art* of pugilism is founded in *nature*, is so obvious a *truth*, that it scarcely requires any illustration."[44] The relationship of such terms harkens back to Pope's *Essay on Criticism*, in which he described "nature" as "At once the *Source*, the *End*, and *Test* of *Art*."[45] Pope's was a rational world ordered by natural laws. In this world, a rational mind rules over a passionate body, and science guides one to know that "the proper study of mankind is man."[46] Mendoza believed that boxing was a proper subject of study, and *The Art of Boxing* described methods of training the mind and the body. His scientific pedagogy and practice were, like Pope's, "*Nature Methodiz'd.*"[47] Mendoza lauds the "utility" of an art worthy enough to have "been highly celebrated by both ancient and modern authors."[48] He invokes the ancients in defense of the art and science of boxing:

> The high honour in which athletic exercises and contests, requiring active and vigorous exertion, were held by the ancients, is universal: witness the Olympic games which were encouraged and patronized by the most illustrious men in Greece, and recorded and celebrated by the first of their historians and poets. It is an acknowledged truth, that Greece never rose to such a height in arts and arms, as in those days, when the honours paid to the Olympic victors kindled every spark of emulation in the Grecian youth.[49]

Mendoza figures athletics as more than physical preparation for combat; they are the subject of poems and histories. Indeed, athletics foster the literary arts. Just as Pope suggests that the ancients can guide humans to be reasonable and moral social beings ("*You* then whose Judgment the right Course wou'd steer, / Know well each ANCIENT's proper *Character*"[50]), Mendoza suggests that the ancients can remind readers of boxing's personal and social value. Further, he singles out England as the sole country that has intellectualized boxing: "[N]otwithstanding the high estimation in which athletic exercises were held by the ancients, this country is the only one in which pugilism has been wrought into a regular system and elevated even to the rank of a science."[51] Boxers are the inheritors of classical virtues that must be disseminated by boxing for England.

Notably, though, Mendoza adds a sportsman's twist to his invocation of the ancients citing Anacreon:

> Anacreon, in one of his Odes, has just recently remarked, that Nature, in the distribution of her favours, has furnished all her creatures with weapons proper for their protection—the bull is guarded by his formidable horns—the steed by his powerful hoofs—the timid hare is protected by her swiftness—and man, the lord of the creation, is furnished with hands, and with reason to guide them in the hour of danger, when either his own life, or the lives of those who are dear to him, are attacked.[52]

Mendoza lionizes the boxer by elevating him to the top of the great chain of being as a creature whom Nature has made both strong and reasonable.

By using Anacreon to make that point, Mendoza also appeals to the moderns, for he wishes to take boxing seriously but to put a playful spin on the tradition in which boxing is situated. Anacreon's association with drink culture appropriately flavors the autobiography of a boxing life because of the long-standing connection between pugilism and pubs.[53] Many boxers retired from the ring to the more salubrious profession of publican, and sportsmen gathered in pubs to arrange fights. Mendoza's preface prepares the reader for literature and sport that have the authority of English tradition and the appeal of a modern sense of play.

In the preface to the *Memoirs*, Mendoza also cites contemporary writers to authorize the subject of sports in literature. Henry Fielding and Paul Whitehead are "among other British authors, who have not disdained to pay the just tribute of applause to our proficiency in this manly art."[54] Mendoza then quotes a passage from *Tom Jones*, in which the narrator concludes that boxing is a civilized method of resolving personal and national disputes.[55] In his study of boxing in the works of Fielding, Christopher Johnson argues that boxing could be figured as an epic struggle similar to the "epic structure of Fielding's new art form."[56] Mendoza concludes with a defense of boxing's social worth that trumpets the athlete's moral fiber: "The robust and athletic should never forget that excellent observation of Shakespeare: 'It is good to have a giant's strength / But merciless to use it like a giant.'"[57] This slight misquote from *Measure for Measure* avails itself of England's great Bard to close with familiar arguments in favor of boxing. This art is useful, he says. Such a claim lay at the heart of Mendoza's *The Art of Boxing*. He wishes to "disseminate ... the knowledge of an ART; which though not perhaps the most elegant, is certainly the most useful species of defence."[58] Again, he claims to have used science to triumph over nature: "I have deprived Boxing of any appearance of brutality to the learner, and reduced it into so regular a system."[59] Here, too, Mendoza contextualizes boxing within a neoclassical English literary tradition. He promises the Horatian ideal to instruct and entertain:

> The great object of my present Publication, has been to explain with perspicuity, the Science of Pugilism, and it has been my endeavour to offer no precepts which will not be brought to bear in practice, and it will give me peculiar satisfaction and pleasure, to understand, that I have attained my first object, by having taught any man an easy regular System of so useful an art as that of Boxing.[60]

The depiction of boxing as a "regular System" associates the sport with enlightened arts and sciences rather than with illegitimate and low entertainments.

Mendoza frames both of his texts with the claim that the art and science of boxing are singularly English. This exposition sets the stage for him to create a portrait of himself in his autobiography in the picaresque mode, as a kind of Tom Jones, an affable young chap who gets into scrapes, who is good-hearted, who moves from one theatrical scene to the next, fighting, riding, boxing, and dancing. He styles himself as a performer who can benefit the English citizenry by embodying and teaching English values learned in the ring: honor, courage, mastery over nature, masculinity, martial prowess, and even plainspokenness.

ぞ ぞ ぞ

Popular literary representations of Mendoza were often equally laudatory and playful. *The Sporting Magazine* made its debut in 1792 when Mendoza was already famous, so it is unsurprising that he appears frequently in its pages. One poem titled "Parody on the Celebrated Soliloquy in Hamlet By a Boxer" is indicative of Mendoza's celebrity and the magazine's propensity toward satire. Mendoza and Humphries are the central characters of the poem whose opening lines are: "To box, or not to box, that is the / question."[61] Mendoza was thus humorously memorialized. Of course, Hamlet dealt with treason, revenge, and morality—big, splashy themes that could be well metaphorized by a pitched battle in a boxing ring. Writings about Mendoza appeared in multiple forms. An 1811 edition of *The Sporting Magazine* includes an article about nationalism and civic honor in relation to boxing, and a sentimental narrative about Mendoza and other boxers who save damsels in distress. The dramatic rescue showcased the boxers' humanity. The magazine also included a reprint of a play that featured *Pancratia* author William Oxberry, references to Mendoza and African American fighter Tom Molineaux, as well as poems and songs about boxing. The play, listed under "Public Amusements," was titled *The Boarding House, or Five Hours at Brighton*, and was performed at the Lyceum Theatre, where Mendoza had run a boxing academy 20 years earlier. Mr. Oxberry was cast as Young Contract, whose speech highlights the currency of boxing in public discourse:

> Milling's [boxing] all the go now. In London, it occupies the heads and hands of dukes, lords, apprentices, and blackguards; while at Cambridge, it is not who is a senior wrangler but who is the best boxer. The Lexicon is forsaken for the slang dictionary—we cut prize poems for prize fighters—Aristotle's logic for Mendoza's knock-down arguments—and Horace, Homer, Demosthenes, and Cicero, for Crib, Gully, Molineux, and the devil.[62]

The play satirizes the fashion for the fancy and the genre of sports writing by pitting the ancients against the moderns. Years earlier, Pope had made famous this satiric comparison in his mock-heroic poem *The Dunciad*. In the above speech, the ancients remain the same, but the moderns are not hack writers, as in Pope's poem, but rather boxing champions. The embodiment of modernity was thus depicted as rugged and rough, a foil to refined ancient literary principles. In the play, young scholars do not read Pope's *Essay on Criticism*, which advises readers to imitate the intellectual and aesthetic principles of the ancients. Rather, they follow the hooks and jabs of the fancy. The play demonstrates that boxing was still modish enough in 1811 to be satirized. It also shows that the group of British champions included in its ranks a Jewish man and an African American man. This point is especially compelling given that late eighteenth-century racist discourse tied physiological difference to moral difference as a way to advocate for the superiority of white Englishmen,[63] although "white" did not include people of Irish or Jewish descent.

Boxing allowed Mendoza and Molineaux each to fight for his nation, as expressed in the poem below. The following ditty was printed in the same 1811 issue of *The Sporting Magazine*:

A Boxing We Will Go

Throw pistols, poniards, swords, aside, And all such deadly tools;
Let boxing be the Briton's pride,
The science of their schools.
Since boxing is a manly game,
And Briton's recreation;
By boxing we will raise our fame,
'Bove any other nation
Mendoza, Bully, Molineux,
Each nature's weapon wield;
Who each at Boney would stand true,
And never to him yield[64]

The poem asserts that boxing is the organizing principle behind Britain's image and might on the world stage. Of the three boxers who contribute to social value, one was Jewish and the other was African American. All three fighters elevate England's character and defend England from enemies like Napoleon Bonaparte (or the diminutive "Boney" of the poem). Mendoza and Molineaux are enlisted in the service of English national pride because they are boxers—even though they have been overwhelmingly figured elsewhere as foreigners.

Perhaps Mendoza and Molineaux appear together because they were each alternately embraced and othered in popular print. As previously demonstrated, popular boxing literature depicted non-white, non-Christian fighters equivocally, both lauding and fearing their physical prowess. A brief look at writing about Molineaux illustrates the kind of ambivalence characteristic of representations of others, especially during the French and Haitian Revolutions and the Napoleonic wars. Tom Molineaux was a former Virginian or South Carolinian slave who had boxed his way to freedom by fighting other slaves from neighboring plantations. When he came to England in 1809, he found a patron in another black fighter, Bill Richmond, "the Black Terror," a former Georgian slave who "knocked out three drunken English sailors in a bar and was given a job as a footman by the British general Early Percy."[65] Richmond became a respected "professor" of pugilism (as trainers were called), and he trained Molineaux for his 1810 fight with Tom Cribb, the heavyweight Champion of England. Molineaux became a boxing legend who inspired an enormous body of prose and poetry. Egan's excited description of him combines the rhetorics of masculinity, nationalism, and warfare. Such choices are to be expected in the literature of sport, but Egan notably uses the term "race" to signify national identity and to distinguish fighters:

Since the days of the renowned Figg, when the Venetian Gondolier, impotently threatened, on his arrival in London, to tear the Champion's cap from the British brow (but who was soon convinced of his error), it has been transferred quietly,

at various times and without murmurs, from the nob of one native to another, whose merit entitled him to its possession—but, that a foreigner should ever again have the temerity to put in a claim, even for the mere contention of obtaining the prize, much more for the honour of wearing it, or bearing it away from Great Britain, such an idea however distant, never intruded itself into the breasts of Englishmen, and reminds us, in a more extended point of view, of the animating passage in the works of our immortal bard, so truly congenial with the native characteristic spirit of the country:
England never did nor never shall
Lie at the proud foot of a conqueror.
But the towering and restless ambition of Molineaux induced him to quit his home and country, and erect his hostile standard among the British Heroes, and who dared the most formidable of her chiefs to the chance of war; when it was reserved for the subject of this memoir to chastise the bold intruder, in protecting the national practice and honour of the country, his own character from contempt and disgrace, and the whole race of English pugilists from ridicule and derision.[66]

Egan quotes Shakespeare to celebrate boxing as an institution capable of defending England's national virtue. Citing *King John*, "England never did nor never shall / Lie at the proud foot of a conqueror,"[67] Egan equates the battle for the pugilistic crown with nothing less grand than the battle for the crown of England. The tone of Egan's account also calls to mind the staunchest of nationalistic poems, James Thompson's "Rule Britannia" of 1740: "Blest isle! with matchless beauty crowned / And manly hearts to guard the fair. / Rule Britannia, Britannia rules the waves; / Britons never shall be slaves."[68] Egan's nationalistic description of fighters—"native," "foreign," "British," "Venetian"—is coupled with a pathos-laden narrative about "honour," "heroes," and "war." In this passage, Molineaux is described first as a "foreigner." Like that of the Venetian who challenged English champion Figg, Molineaux's difference is classified primarily by nationality, not by race or complexion. Molineaux's boxing career was political from the start because he traded blows for freedom and for passage to another country. As would-be Champ of England and fighter in America, and as former slave, his body was the site of several national contests at once.

The Cribb v. Molineaux fight was a lightning rod for racial fears and nationalistic jingoism. As Daniel O'Quinn has argued, the theater of public opinion about their matches is representative of a complex political and cultural ideology that arose from a view of English national and ethnic identity as unique on the world stage.[69] Like Mendoza, Cribb was featured in a Cruikshank illustration. He also appeared on Byron's dressing screen. And, like Mendoza, he could be co-opted or othered by the English. He was largely figured as a heroic boxer, but public discourse about race and national identity remained ambiguous. The following poem by Bob Gregson is more somber in its representation of race than is Egan's purple prose. In 1810 Gregson was a fighter known best for having been knocked down.[70] Unsuccessful in the ring, he opened a sporting house called The Castle Tavern, patronized by sportsmen, Covent Garden types, and the Quality. Gregson became known as "the poet-laureate to the Prize Ring."[71] He was so excited by Cribb's victory that he wrote and performed a song in his tavern:

British Lads and Black Millers

You gentlemen of fortune attend unto my ditty,
A few lines I have penn'd upon this great fight,
In the Centre of England the noble place is pitched on,
For the valour of this country, or America's delight:
The sturdy black doth swear,
The moment he gets there
The planks the stage is built on, he'll make them blaze
and smoke:
Then Cribb, with smiling face,
Says these boards I'll ne'er disgrace;
They're relations of mine, they're Old English oak.

Brave Molineaux replied, I've never been denied
To fight the foes of Britain on such planks as those:
If relationship you claim, bye-and-bye you'll know my name:
I'm the swellish milling cove that can drub my foes.
Then Cribb replied with haste,
You slave, I will you baste
As your master used to cane you, 'twill bring things to
your mind,
If from bondage you've got clear,
You'd better stopp'd with Christophe, you'll quickly find.

The garden of freedom is the British land we live in,
And welcomes every slave from his banish'd isle;
Allows them to impose on a nation good and generous,
To incumber and pollute our native soil:
But John Bull cries out aloud,
We're neither poor nor proud,
But open to all nations, let them come from where they will.
The British lads that's here,
Quite strangers are to fear:
Here's Tom Cribb, with numpers round, for he can them mill.[72]

Whereas "A-Boxing We Will Go" depicts Molineaux and Mendoza as defenders of English liberty against France, the above poem denigrates Molineaux by raising the specter of slavery that excludes him from the British "garden of freedom." England is thus figured dually as defender of liberty and as a dominating master. Molineaux is a "sturdy black," a "brave" fighter, and a "slave" who can be "cane[d]." What is to be made of the layers of prejudice in the song? Like Molineaux, Christophe was a freed black slave. But he was also leader of the Haitian Revolution and Haiti's first elected president, so it is the reference to Christophe that frames the pub song in terms of martial and political might.

While Molineaux was linked with the Haitian Revolution, he and Mendoza were mutually connected to the French Revolution, as demonstrated in

"A Boxing We Will Go." Several sections of that volume of *The Sporting Magazine* enlist Mendoza in the ranks of those whose skills could usefully represent and spread English values to France. The 1811 edition's section on pugilism cites a French General in the Revolutionary and Napoleonic Wars, General Junot, Duke d'Abrantes. A "convert to the English pugilistic system," he lauds the moral value of the sport. Boxing, he claims, is "consonant with the rules of justice and morality, as to form one of the greatest glories of the country ... an English blackguard learns more humanity and good morals in seeing a regular boxing match, than it is probable, he would, in hearing five dozen sermons."[73] In this partial reprint of *The Philosophy of Sports*, the General elevates English fighting above fighting methods of the French, Italian, and Dutch. He represents himself as a student of pugilism who even knew Broughton. And he hopes that "Mendoza would be ready, on the return of peace, to open a school in the splendid metropolis of France" (78). Reading about Mendoza and Molineaux in the context of the French and Haitian Revolutions reveals writers who vacillate between admiration and aversion. The abundance of and easy access to boxing literature not only facilitated celebrity culture, but it also helped to shape public discourse about important issues, such as ethnicity and nationalism.

While Mendoza could be figured as an English soldier, he was equally defined by his Judaism. In his biography of Mendoza, Egan writes:

> Prejudice so frequently distorts the mind that, unfortunately, good actions are passed over without even common respect; more especially, when they appear in any person who may chance to be of a different country, persuasion or color: Mendoza, in being a Jew, did not stand in so favourable a point of view, respecting the wishes of the multitude towards his success, as his brace opponent.[74]

Egan quotes from a 1794 play titled *The Jew* by famous playwright and politician Richard Cumberland so as to illustrate the deeply entrenched prejudices to which Mendoza would have been subject. But Egan also suggests that Mendoza's skill and bottom as a boxer would prevail in the theater of public opinion. Mendoza himself did not hide his difference, because in the world of boxing he did not need to do so. He was adept at reading his audience and his culture, and he not only played to his own strengths but to theirs as well.

In sum, boxing literature served several rhetorical and social purposes. Mendoza wrote within a literary tradition that did not include Jews; nonetheless, he used its terms to his advantage. Moreover, boxing literature helped not only to consolidate but to complicate the image of a heroic English fighter.

☙ ☙ ☙

As the material above has demonstrated, nationalistic ideology was dramatized in boxing matches. Such dramas naturally also took the stage in theaters. Examining Mendoza's participation in the 1809 Old Price Riots reveals how definitions of nationhood and legitimacy played out on the stage and in the pit. When boxers were enlisted to restore order, staged and spontaneous dramatic bursts of violence ensued, and the lines between reality and representation blurred.

Mendoza performed on many stages. In 1791, he opened a boxing academy at the Lyceum in the Strand to stage sparring exhibitions. He taught these principles at his successful academy, and he was engaged to perform on stage at Covent Garden. His memoirs describe a tour with a comedian; as Mendoza reports, he and the comic alternated taking the stage: "This gentleman gave recitation, and at intervals I exhibited the art of pugilism."[75] On a tour to Dublin, he performed boxing exhibitions on stage for Mr. Astley, the famous circus manager.[76] While in Dublin, Mendoza was delighted to have been recognized by a porter who remembered him as a regular of Covent Garden coffeehouse, the Finish.[77] However, not all of his theatrical engagements were pugilistic. Once, during a visit to Bury St. Edmunds, he was recognized as a famous figure, and he was asked to perform with a troop of strolling players. He did so for three weeks. During the height of Mendoza's fame, people could find his image on commemorative coins and mugs. Other artistic representations of him also abounded; Cruikshank and Gillray illustrated his fights against Humphries. In his *Memoirs*, Mendoza boasts that he was written into three plays: *The Duenna*, *The Farmer*, and *The Road to Ruin*. In 1788, a play performed at Drury Lane, *'Tis An Ill Wind Blows Nobody Good; or the Road to Odiham, a farce*, was described as "a satire on the then reigning fashion for pugilism." Mendoza's first famous fight with Humphries was in Odiham, Hampshire, in 1788.[78] Pub songs and mock-heroic poems were written about him, and interest in Mendoza's life has endured even into our own century. He is the inspiration for the protagonist of David Liss's historical novel *A Conspiracy of Paper* (2000), the subject of a graphic novel, and Mendoza even made it to Broadway as a central figure in Randy Cohen's 2010 play *The Punishing Blow*.[79]

As we know, boxing and theater were closely related in the eighteenth century; both were underwritten and patronized by members of the aristocracy and the gentry. The financial structures of pugilistic and theatrical performances bore some similarity as well: in both cases, performers primarily, though not always, came from the lower or working class. Both had superstar theater managers such as James Figg and Colly Cibber, the famous actor-manager of Drury Lane; in fact, Cibber and Figg were depicted together in Hogarth's *Southwark Fair*. Boxing and the theater each required a license, and each was subject to the political, financial, and personal tastes of its patrons and politicians. As with a play, the spectator's relationship to a fight was immediate; both crowds were known to rush the stage or assault the players. Boxing matches sometimes provided entertainment as prelude to or intermission for a performance. Indeed, in his *Essay of Dramatic Poesy* (1668), John Dryden objected to the presence of boxers and bears on stage in the middle of a play. Dryden's contemporaries and his future countrymen viewed boxing as a form of popular, if illegitimate, theater.

At the other end of the long eighteenth century, Egan saw theaters as a natural parent and parallel to boxing:

Have not our classic theatres, within the last five and twenty years, possessing all the advantages of authors the most exalted and refined, actors the most inimitable and chaste, either to extort the tear or provoke the laugh, music the most splendor, unparalleled, invited pugilism to their boards, and the names of some of the first rate boxers enriched their play-bills; and the audiences (of whom no doubt can attach to their respectability) testified their approbation by loud plaudits at the liberality of the managers in thus publicly displaying the principles of pugilism![80]

When Brailsford writes that the closing of the first boxing amphitheater in 1750 was a near death knell for the sport, he notes boxing's generic consanguinity with theater:

Pugilism's opportunity to develop, alongside the theatre, as a legitimate public entertainment was lost. Until then, the two could readily be thought of together, enjoying much of their support in common and linked together in the minds of that considerable body of people whose puritan inheritance made them equally suspicious of both.[81]

The Restoration and eighteenth century still battled some of the seventeenth-century culture wars forwarded in large part by Puritans who shuttered theaters and who objected to sports so much that they encouraged public burning of James I's *Book of Sports*.[82] For instance, disguise on stage, in the pit, and at balls facilitated an uncomfortable fluidity of class and gender boundaries. These objections were mirrored in complaints about boxing matches, the audiences for which could number in the thousands. The complaints changed little during the century. In 1698, Jeremy Collier wrote that the "dangerous principle" of the theater was that it would "[o]pen the way to all licentiousness, and confoun[d] the distinction between mirth and madness, for the stage corrupted with "profaneness and obscenity."[83] But with the relaxing of Puritan strictures, boxing matches and other sorts of sporting amusements reemerged at fairs and at loosely arranged public venues. In 1720, George I himself ordered the setup of a boxing ring in Hyde Park, and 101 years later, George IV outfitted pugilists as pages at his coronation.

By Mendoza's lifetime, boxing had moved from side show to center stage, its popularity facilitated by the association with legitimate theater, as well as its success as a form of illegitimate theater. Theater had long skimmed the line between licit and illicit. In 1737, Prime Minister Robert Walpole passed the Licensing Act, which subjected plays to censorship and effectively barred a certain kind of politics from mainstream theaters. The Act also reinstated vagrancy laws, classing performers of illegitimate theater with vagabonds.[84] As we saw in Mendoza's writing, generic and cultural legitimacy were bound together. In Jane Moody's study of the origins of illegitimate theatre, she focuses on the connection between generic and cultural (il)legitimacy. She explains that the two patents issued to Drury Lane and Covent Garden created a "system of dramatic classification based ... on theatrical genres."[85] While comedy and tragedy were lawful, certain kinds of entertainment such as "pantomime and Italian opera" were viewed as bad for England's social health and nationalistic autonomy, thereby disdained as "immigrant cultural forms."[86] Moody reads the theater in relation to "Britain's resurgent national self-consciousness" as seen, for example, in the first performance of the song "Rule Britannia" in 1740. Moody describes writer Richard Steele's critique of generic adulteration: "[T]his critique of [generic] monstrosity now demanded an absolute and inviolable distinction between a text-based canon of English drama (defined by Richard Steele as 'Shakespeare's Heroes, and Jonson's Humourists') and a miscellaneous realm of non-textual, physical entertainment allegedly imported from Bartholomew Fair ('Ladder-dancers, Rope-dancers, Juglers, and mountebanks')."[87] She might easily have added boxers to that playbill list.

Furthermore, in a move to literally silence illegitimate theater, speech itself was banned from fringe theaters. Physical methods of speaking supplanted actual speech. It is as if the body became a proxy language, and one can imagine sport as a muffled drama of epic narratives disallowed on the legitimate stage. Illegitimate theaters circumnavigated the Licensing Act in ways similar to those used by boxers, who were permitted to perform sparring exhibitions but not actual fights: playhouses would charge for an alternate performance, such as music, and offer the play for free.[88] According to Moody, the Licensing Act and the 1752 act regulating public order at unlicensed playhouses created an ironic space of performative freedom, for "how could a system of censorship be imposed on performances for which no texts existed?"[89] While playhouses used scrolls to replace the spoken word, boxing combined the pantomime of revolution and war with newly established sports journalism to create a two-part performance of national identity. Given that most fighters were identified by country of origin or ethnicity, and given that boxing styles were characterized by national identity, the discourse of patriotic competition was as bare as the boxers' chests.

During the 1790s, the height of Mendoza's fame, English theater was a staging ground for contests over revolutionary discourses, both home grown and imported from France. (No wonder, then, that sports writing appealed to nationalist sentiments.) Moody points out that, following the fall of the Bastille, "revolution and war now provided the scripts for an illegitimate theatre of peril, danger, and spectacular illusion."[90] Arguing that there was "political anxiety surrounding mixed genres," she locates the emergence of the term "'legitimate' as a category of dramatic classification during the late 1790s."[91] Genre itself became a battleground of political discord. One year after the publication of Mendoza's *The Art of Boxing*, Edmund Burke wrote *Reflections on the Revolution in France*, a text that dramatized the battle over legitimate monarchy. Moody sees this battle as one staged at the theater: "Throughout the 1790s, the language of cultural nationalism began to be appropriated in the case of theatrical war between two apparently irreconcilable kinds of dramaturgy."[92] Illegitimate theatrics represented "a lawless disregard for morality, decorum and dramatic tradition."[93] These debates over legitimacy, genre, and nationalism were still heated when Mendoza played a role in the Old Price Riots at Covent Garden.

Mendoza was at home in the patent theaters, and he was certainly well versed in theatrical controversies about legitimacy and morality that emerged during the Old Price Riots. The riots were primarily a response to admission and seating changes, but people also objected to changes in genre, which were depicted as a profanation of traditional English theater. When Covent Garden reopened after a fire, manager John Philip Kemble increased space for expensive seats, raised the price for cheap gallery tickets, and altered the gallery space so as to make it more difficult for the audience to see the stage. Objectors were vociferous. Rioters shouted down players at the opening night performance of *Macbeth*. After a week of protests, Kemble hired a faculty of pugilistic professors to squelch the mob. Mendoza was among them. Objections to the Jewish hired hand echoed complaints that patent theaters had grossly corrupted traditional theater by staging illegitimate genres (anything other than comedy or tragedy—opera, for instance) and by employing Italians to sing in English theaters. One protest sign read:

> The Drama's laws no longer are respected
> Its 'patrons' are abused, insulted, and neglected;
> But—Englishmen have laws they will not lose
> Tho' trampled on by thieftakers and Jews.[94]

The purity of genre and national identity are depicted as equally vulnerable to degradation. Another objector who identified as "A True Briton" complained that "The Italian Frenchified operas have ruined the British drama, and will ultimately ruin the British constitution."[95] One newspaper reporter writes that the theater has been transformed into chaotic corruption: "The Pit has been metamorphosed into a pugilistic arena where all the blackguards of London, the Jew prize-fighters, Bow Street runners, hackney-coach helpers and vagabonds returned from transportation have ranged themselves on the side of the managers."[96]

Among the criminals identified as actors in this scene of disorder, Jews were especially excoriated. It is not surprising since, as Marc Baer claims, anti-Semitism at the time "was more widespread than anti-Catholicism." (Theater manager Kemble was Catholic.) Newspapers, pamphlets, and theatergoers' signs were venomously anti-Semitic. One placard read "Oppose Shylock and the whole tribe of Israel."[97] Protestors connected ideas about legitimate theater to national political pride buttressed by xenophobia. Anti-French sentiments abounded as well; Baer writes that "the national effort against France was transferred to the war in Covent Garden."[98] To combat the growing mob of protestors, theater managers instructed the hired fists to stage a fight and thereby divert the crowd (Figure 7.2). Baer describes one placard depicting a number of "ruffians," one of whom is "recognizably Jewish, a character—the boxer Daniel Mendoza—who exclaims: 'Down down to H-l with all OPs & say t'was *Dan* that sent the[e] there.'"[99]

One pamphleteer favored King Edward I's strategy of dealing with Jews: hang or expel them.[100] Thus for Mendoza, the possibility of turning prejudice to account was not entirely successful. When signs of cultural difference were displayed

Figure 7.2 George Cruikshank, *Killing no murder. As performed at the Grand National Theatre* (1809). Print. © Trustees of the British Museum.

as placards in Covent Garden and in newspapers, Mendoza's efforts toward legitimacy in the theater of public opinion were undercut.

While Mendoza felt at home on stage and in theaters, his relationship with that home was complex. He both shone upon and was hissed off of stages, pugilistic and theatrical. He peddled his sport as moral muscle to the social body, but he used that strength for unprincipled purposes if the pay were good enough. He was famous and infamous. Mendoza walked the line between legitimate and illegitimate, and the multiple narratives of his exploits suggest that he did so intentionally. The story of how he managed that balancing act made him a celebrity.

܀ ܀ ܀

Eighteenth-century texts about boxing reveal a cultural ambivalence toward the status of the sport as well as the civic status of fighters. Boxing writing by turn was didactic, satiric, political, theatrical, and neoclassical. No matter the genre, these texts participated in Enlightenment discourses about nationalism, morality, art and science. And, for a time, at the center of this stage, moving with both physical and literary skill among efforts to intellectualize and legitimize his sport, attempting to entertain and educate his audience, and trying to make a living, Mendoza played a pioneering role in shaping popular ideas about nationalism, theater, and sport.

Notes

[1] Daniel Mendoza, *The Memoirs of the Life of Daniel Mendoza*, ed. Paul David Magriel (London: B.T. Batsford, 1951), 8–9.

[2] Kasia Boddy suggests that the memoir was "ghost-written." *Boxing: A Cultural History* (London: Reaktion Books, 2008), 38.

[3] Quoted in John Ford, *Prizefighting: The Age of Regency Boximania* (South Brunswick, NJ: Great Albion Books, 1971), 117. The fight with John Jackson took place in 1795.

[4] Pierce Egan, *Boxiana: or, Sketches of ancient and modern pugilism from the days of the renowned James Figg and Jack Broughton to the heroes of the later milling era Jack Scroggins and Tom Hickman*, ed. John Ford (London: The Folio Society, 1976).

[5] For example, see a portrait of Mendoza painted by Robineau and engraved by Kingsbury. Under his portrait are the words "the most SCIENTIFFIC BOXER ever KNOWN." The image is held by the British Library: http://www.britishmuseum.org/research/collection_online/collection_object_details/collection_image_gallery.aspx?assetId=945824001&objectId=1526456&partId=1.

[6] M. Dorothy George, *London Life in the Eighteenth Century* (New York: Harper, 1964), 132.

[7] Daniel Mendoza, *The modern art of boxing as practised by Mendoza, Humphreys, Ryan, Ward, Wason, Johnson, and other eminent pugilists. To which are added, the six lessons of Mendoza, as published by him, for the use of his scholars; and a full account of his last battle with Humphreys* (London: printed [for the author] and sold at No. 42, Little Britain, and by all Booksellers and news carriers in town and country, 1789). *Eighteenth-Century Collections Online*. The text was reprinted in 1790 and 1792.

[8] Jonas Hanway, *A Review of the Proposed Naturalization of the Jews* (London: J. Waugh, 1753), 78, quoted in Frank Felsenstein, *Anti-Semitic Stereotypes: A Paradigm of Otherness in English Popular Culture, 1660–1830* (Baltimore: Johns Hopkins University Press, 1995), 230.

[9] Todd M. Endelman, *The Jews of Georgian England, 1714–1830: Tradition and Change in a Liberal Society* (Ann Arbor: University of Michigan Press, 1999), 198.

[10] Endelman, *The Jews of Georgian England*, 200.

[11] Endelman, *The Jews of Georgian England*, 201–2. For a full discussion of the case and its impact on the Jewish community, see his chapter "Pickpockets and Pugilists."

[12] Quoted in George, *London Life in the Eighteenth Century*, 132.

[13] George, *London Life in the Eighteenth Century*, 132.

[14] Mendoza, *Memoirs*, 22.

[15] Henry Thornton was an abolitionist who played a major role in founding the Sierra Leone Company, which established a colony for freed American slaves. See Endelman, *The Jews of Georgian England*, 221. See also Mendoza's *Memoirs* (20) for a description of Mendoza's work as a smuggler.

[16] Egan, *Boxiana*, 38.

[17] Michael Scrivener, "British-Jewish Writing of the Romantic Era and the Problem of Modernity: The Example of David Levi" in *British Romanticism and the Jews*, ed. Sheila A. Spector (New York: Palgrave, 2002), 159.

[18] Scrivener, "British-Jewish Writing," 160.

[19] Scrivener, "British-Jewish Writing," 167.

[20] See Endelman, *The Jews of Georgian England*, 220.

[21] Dennis Brailsford, *Bareknuckles: A Social History of Prizefighting* (Cambridge: Lutterworth Press, 1988), 2–3.

[22] Egan, *Boxiana*, 24.

[23] Christopher Johnson, "'British Championism': Early Pugilism and the Works of Fielding," *The Review of English Studies* 47, no. 187 (1996): 332. See also chapter 3, "The Status of Sport," in Dennis Brailsford, *A Taste for Diversions: Sport in Georgian England* (Cambridge: Lutterworth Press, 1999). Tom Sawyer writes in *Noble Art: An Artistic and Literary Celebration of the Old English Prize-Ring* (North Sydney, Australia: Allen and Unwin, 1989) that the "years of Broughton's ascendancy had coincided with a period in which the sword had ceased to be a fashionable dress accessory among the English gentry" (21).

[24] John Godfrey, *A Treatise on the Useful Science of Defence: Connecting the Small and Back-sword, and Shewing the Affinity between Them: Likewise Endeavouring to Weed the Art of Those Superfluous, Unmeaning Practices Which Over-run It ...: With Some Observations upon Boxing ...* (London: T. Gardner, 1747).

[25] Brailsford, *Bareknuckles*, 3.

[26] Quoted in Sawyer, *Noble Art*, 21.

[27] Brailsford, *Bareknuckles*, 8. Of the three most popular sports, (boxing, horse racing, and cricket), boxing was the last to develop a set of rules. See also chapter 2 in *Bareknuckles*, "Illegal, Immoral and Injurious."

[28] William Oxberry, *Pancratia, or, a History of Pugilism. Containing a Full Account of Every Battle of Note from the Time of Broughton and Slack, Down to the Present Day* (London: Published and Sold by W. Oxberry, 1812), 47.

[29] An ECCO search revealed no primary texts that connect the Duke to Broughton and the outlawing of boxing. I have not searched all Parliamentary documents for relevant years. For a discussion of the illegality of boxing, see, for instance, Brailsford, *Bareknuckles*, especially chapter 1, "Jack Broughton's Rules," chapter 2, "Illegal, Immoral and Injurious," and chapter 5, "The Sport and the Law"; Ford, *Prizefighting*, chapter 5, "Development and Promotion"; Bob Mee, *Bare Fists: The History of Bare-Knuckle Prize-Fighting* (New York: The Overlook Press, 2001), especially chapter 2, "Life After Figg," and chapter 3, "The Golden Years."

[30] James Boswell, *Boswell's Life of Johnson. Including Boswell's Journal of a Tour to the Hebrides and Johnson's Diary of a Journey into North Wales*, ed. G.B. Hill (Oxford: Clarendon Press, 1934–1964), 5:229. Thanks to Jack Lynch for this reference. One boxing historian claimed that Johnson, that "harmless drudge, knocked down an impudent bookseller in Covent Garden!" Sawyer, *Noble Art*, 56.

[31] Arthur E. Bilodeau, "Pugilistic Rhetoric in Eighteenth and Nineteenth Century England" (PhD dissertation, Indiana University, 2001), 40.

[32] William Oxberry, *Pancratia*, 68.

[33] Egan, *Boxiana*, 17–18. See also Brailsford, *Bareknuckle*s, chapter 3, "A Fashionable Sport." Stan Shipley writes, "The professional sport exploded into popularity in the 1790s with the interaction of manufacturing, deep coal-mining, busy ports, the city as premier marketplace, and a Jewish lad from Whitechapel, named Daniel Mendoza" (78). See also Shipley's chapter 3, "Boxing," in *Sport in Britain: A Social History*, ed. Tony Mason (Cambridge: Cambridge University Press, 1989), 78–115.

[34] Oxberry, *Pancratia*, 74.

[35] Oxberry, *Pancratia*, 74.

[36] Sawyer, *Noble Art*, 22.

[37] Quoted in Bilodeau, "Pugilistic Rhetoric," 42.
[38] Egan *Boxiana*, 46.
[39] WorldCat has a question mark following the 1784 edition. Several editions followed in the 1780s and 1790s.
[40] Jack Broughton, *Proposals for Erecting an Amphitheatre for the Manly Exercise of Boxing: By John Broughton, Professor of Athletics* (London, 1743), 1.
[41] Johnson writes: "The existence of classical precedents for gladiatorial combats seems in the eyes of many to have legitimized their reappearance in the eighteenth century, and to have made their violence even seem laudable, the natural by-product of a virile, heroic society" ("British Championism," 335).
[42] David Higgins offers a valuable reading of effeminacy and pugilism in Regency England in his article "Englishness, Effeminacy, and the New Monthly Magazine: *Hazlitt's* 'the Fight' in Context," *Romanticism: The Journal of Romantic Culture and Criticism* 10, no. 2 (2004): 173–90.
[43] John Whale, "Daniel Mendoza's Contests of Identity: Masculinity, Ethnicity and Nation in Georgian Prize-fighting." *Romanticism* 14, no. 3 (December 2008): 260. The article offers an interesting reading of Mendoza in the context of Georgian era boxing discourses, which Whale connects to discourses surrounding other blood and combat sports, as well as to discourses about ethnicity and Englishness.
[44] Mendoza, *Memoirs*, ix (my emphasis).
[45] Pope, *Essay on Criticism*, line 73
[46] Pope, *Essay on Man*, epistle 2, line 2.
[47] Pope, *Essay on Criticism*, line 89.
[48] Mendoza, *Memoirs*, xi.
[49] Mendoza, *Memoirs*, ix.
[50] Pope, *Essay on Criticism*, lines 118–19.
[51] Mendoza, *Memoirs*, ix–x.
[52] Mendoza, *Memoirs*, ix.
[53] "Drink poetry was generally performed to music at all-male gatherings, whether the Greek symposium or the medieval and early modern tavern" (318). Marty Roth, "'Anacreon' and Drink Poetry; or, the Art of Feeling Very Very Good," *Texas Studies in Literature and Language* 42, no. 3 (2000): 314–45. Egan includes a collection of pub songs and a list of "Sporting Houses Kept by Pugilists" in *Boxiana*.
[54] Mendoza, *Memoirs*, x.
[55] See Henry Fielding, *The History of Tom Jones, a Foundling* (New York: Norton, 1995), 454. First published 1749 by A. Millar, London.
[56] Johnson, "British Championism," 332.
[57] Mendoza, *Memoirs*, xi.
[58] Mendoza, *The Art of Boxing*, vi.
[59] Mendoza, *The Art of Boxing*, viii.
[60] Mendoza, *The Art of Boxing*, 9.
[61] *The Sporting Magazine: Or, Monthly Calendar of the Transactions of the Turf, the Chase, and the Temples devoted to the Fickle Goddess* (December 1792): 10. Photocopy from the New York Public Library.
[62] *Sporting Magazine: Or, monthly calendar of the transactions of the turf, the chase and every other diversion interesting to the man of pleasure, enterprise, and spirit*, 38 (April 1811): 263.

63   See Roxann Wheeler, *The Complexion of Race: Categories of Difference in Eighteenth Century British Culture* (Philadelphia: University of Pennsylvania Press, 2000); and Felicity A. Nussbaum, *Torrid Zones: Maternity, Sexuality, and Empire in Eighteenth-Century English Narratives* (Baltimore: Johns Hopkins University Press, 1995).

64   *Sporting Magazine: Or, monthly calendar of the transactions of the turf, the chase and every other diversion interesting to the man of pleasure, enterprise, and spirit*, Vol. 38 (April 1811): 295.

65   Bob Mee, *Bare Fists*, 60. Richmond also schooled William Hazlitt in the "sweet science." Hazlitt writes about Richmond in his essay "The Fight" (*The New Monthly Magazine*, 1822).

66   There are five volumes of *Boxiana*, the last of which was published in 1828. All references are to the first volume. Egan, *Boxiana*, 108.

67   Shakespeare, *King John*, V.vii.112–13.

68   James Thompson, *Rule Britannia*, lines 33–6. http://www.poetryfoundation.org/poem/174671.

69   For a trenchant discussion of the fights between Thomas Molineaux and then Champion of England Thomas Crib (the spelling of his last name is not consistent), see Daniel O'Quinn, "In the Face of Difference: Molineaux, Crib, and the Violence of the Fancy," in *Race, Romanticism, and the Atlantic*, ed. Paul Youngquist (Surrey: Ashgate, 2013), 213–35.

70   Egan said of him: "Bob's character as a boxer reminds us of the anecdote mentioned in the House of Commons, by the late right honourable Charles James Fox, who observed of the fighting Austrian, General Clairfayt, who had been for several years engaged in one and twenty battles in the cause of his country, that the general might be compared to a drum: for he was never heard of but when he was beaten!" (159).

71   Egan, *Boxiana*, 160.

72   Egan, *Boxiana*, 160–61.

73   *The Sporting Magazine*, 1811, 37–8.

74   Egan, *Boxiana*, 44.

75   Mendoza, *Memoirs*, 94.

76   Mendoza, *Memoirs*, 76–7, 69, chapter 5, "Engagements in the Theatre."

77   Mendoza, *Memoirs*, 70.

78   Walley Chamberlain Oulton, *The History of the Theatres of London ... From the Year 1771 to 1795*, vol. 2 (London: Martin and Bain, 1796), 9.

79   See David Liss, *A Conspiracy of Paper: A Novel* (New York: Random House, 2000); and Ronald Schechter and Liz Clarke, *Mendoza the Jew: Boxing, Manliness, and Nationalism, A Graphic History* (New York: Oxford University Press, 2014). *The Punishing Blow* by Randy Cohen was performed at the Clurman Theater, Theater Row, New York City. The play addressed anti-Semitism, and the central character discusses Daniel Mendoza. On 22 August 2010, I was a guest speaker at the "talk back" following that night's performance.

80   Egan, *Boxiana*, 17.

81   Brailsford, *Bareknuckles*, 13.

82   See Semenza, *Sport, Politics, and Literature in the English Renaissance* (Newark: University of Delaware Press, 2003), 59, for a brief discussion of the burning of *The Book of Sports*.

83   Jeremy Collier, "A Short View of the Immorality and Profaneness of the English Stage," in *The Broadview Anthology of British Literature* (Ontario: Broadview Press, 2006), 3:538.

[84] Jane Moody, *Illegitimate Theatre in London, 1770–1840* (New York: Cambridge University Press, 2000), 16.
[85] Moody, *Illegitimate Theatre in London*, 11.
[86] Moody, *Illegitimate Theatre in London*, 12.
[87] Moody, *Illegitimate Theatre in London*, 13.
[88] Moody, *Illegitimate Theatre in London*, 17.
[89] Moody, *Illegitimate Theatre in London*, 18.
[90] Moody, *Illegitimate Theatre in London*, 27–8.
[91] Moody, *Illegitimate Theatre in London*, 50, 51.
[92] Moody, *Illegitimate Theatre in London*, 53.
[93] Moody, *Illegitimate Theatre in London*, 54.
[94] Marc Baer, *Theatre and Disorder in Late Georgian London* (New York: Oxford University Press, 1992), 216.
[95] *A True Briton, Strictures on the Engagement of Madame Catalani ... and on the Italian Opera* (London: Cox and Baylis, 1809), 3; *Political Review* (28 October 1809), quoted in Moody, *Illegitimate Theatre in London*, 64, n. 38.
[96] *Examiner*, 15 October 1809, quoted in Baer, *Theatre and Disorder*, 216.
[97] Baer, *Theatre and Disorder*, 215.
[98] Baer, *Theatre and Disorder*, 217. He also writes: "Jews and Frenchmen were equally useful as foils, regardless of political persuasion." See chapter 6, "John Bull in Covent Garden."
[99] Baer, *Theatre and Disorder*, 216.
[100] Baer, *Theatre and Disorder*, 215.

Chapter 8
Rehearsing Leander: Byron and Swimming in the Long Eighteenth Century

Jack D'Amico

The event alluded to in the title of this essay, Lord Byron swimming the Dardanelles in 1810, obviously took place some distance from the Britain of more ordinary recreational pastimes. Preparation for the swim, however, began in 1807 in London where Byron swam under the watchful eye of a trainer and the skeptical eye of the writer Leigh Hunt: "The first time I saw Lord Byron, he was rehearsing the part of Leander, under the auspices of Mr. Jackson, the prizefighter. It was in the river Thames, before his first visit to Greece."[1] In his *Autobiography* (1850), written long after Byron had crossed the strait formerly known as the Hellespont, Hunt uses the theatrical metaphor "rehearsing the part" to poke fun at Byron's role-playing, something Byron himself did in his letters and in the poem "Written after Swimming from Sestos to Abydos" (9 May 1810).[2] In the poem, the young lord describes himself as a "degenerate modern wretch" who completes the swim half dead. And when Byron writes to Francis Hodgson and says "I plume myself on this achievement more than I could possibly do on any kind of glory, political, poetical, or rhetorical," he uses "plume" as a variation on both the classical victory wreath and the modern feather.[3]

The letters show that Byron expected his readers to be aware of the literary tradition, dating from at least the fifth century B.C., according to which Leander swam from the Asian city of Abydos to join his beloved Hero, a priestess of Venus who resided in a tower on the opposite shore outside Sestos. After repeated nightly crossings, Leander drowned on a stormy winter's night. Seeing his body on the rocks below, Hero threw herself from the tower to join her beloved in death.[4] The early modern retellings of the Hero and Leander legend are antiheroic, wittily so in Christopher Marlowe's poem "Hero and Leander" and more farcical in Ben Jonson's play *Bartholomew Fair*, where Leander is made "a dyer's son, about Puddle-wharf; and Hero a wench o'the *Bank-side*" (V.iii.114–15).[5] By describing himself as a "degenerate modern wretch," Byron sets his poem squarely in the antiheroic tradition.

Hunt made his observation after a less vigorous bathe in the Thames where, he reports, there used to be a "bathing-machine stationed on the eastern side of Westminster Bridge" (not far from Puddle-Warf). Standing on this portable hut adjusting his clothes, Hunt noticed "a respectable-looking manly person, who was eyeing something at a distance" (Hunt, 374). This person was none other than Gentleman John Jackson, the boxing instructor whose "pupil," Hunt tells us, was "swimming with somebody for a wager."[6] Byron's competitor remains anonymous. Hunt recalls that Jackson spoke of his pupil "in terms of praise" but adds that he himself

> saw nothing in Lord Byron at that time, but a young man who, like myself, had written a bad volume of poems; and though I had a sympathy with him on this account, and more respect for his rank than I was willing to suppose, my sympathy was not an agreeable one; so, contenting myself with seeing his lordship's head bob up and down in the water, like a buoy, I came away.[7]

By comparing the breaststroking Byron to a common buoy, Hunt cuts the pretensions of the young man of rank caught rehearsing in the Thames.

Whether in the Thames, the Tagus or the Grand Canal, Byron enjoyed open water swimming throughout his life, often competing for a token wager, or bragging rights. His swimming fits the definition of amateur sport as a form of competition that requires physical exertion and skill, freely engaged in by participants who agree on certain rules and objectives and, unlike Byron, do not gamble. Many such sporting activities were related to military skills mastered for survival or display. Byron's interest in sport included elite, as well as more common, pastimes. At Harrow he had taken lessons from the popular fencing master Henry Angelo, and it was through Angelo that Byron was probably introduced to the pugilist Jackson (*BLJ* 1:92). In his *Detached Thoughts*, 15 October 1821, Byron reviews his sporting life while reflecting on what he considered the inapt comparisons made between himself and Rousseau, who

> could never ride nor swim 'nor was cunning of fence'—I was an excellent swimmer—a decent though not at all a dashing rider ... was 'sufficient of fence'—particularly of the Highland broadsword—not a bad boxer—when I could keep my temper—which was difficult—but which I strove to do ever since I knocked down Mr. Purling and put his knee-pan out (with the gloves on) in Angelo's and Jackson's rooms in 1806 during the sparring, and I was besides a very fair Cricketer—one of the Harrow Eleven when we play[ed] against Eton in 1805. (*BLJ* 9:12)

Swimming boxing, fencing, riding, and marksmanship were manly sports with an aristocratic, military history that attracted Byron's interest and his competitive spirit. Because of his lame foot he could not run, and each of these activities allowed him to overcome, or escape entirely from, his disability.

Hunt's account fits what Byron reports in two of his letters to Elizabeth Bridget Pigot. On 13 July 1807, he writes, "The Intelligence of London cannot be interesting to you who *have rusticated* all your life, the annals of Routs, Riots, Balls & Boxing matches, Dowagers and demireps, Cards & Crim-con, Parliamentary Discussion,

Political Details, Masquerades, Mechanics, Argyle Street Institution & Aquatic races" (*BLJ* 1:127). The playful balance and antithesis mirrors the life Byron was leading in London at that time, a mixture of the social high life he mocks and the low-life associations that included Jackson, the retired boxing champion who gave Byron lessons, sponsored boxing matches, and supervised at least one of Byron's "aquatic races." The letter of 11 August brings us closer to the scene Hunt describes: "Last week I swam in the Thames from Lambeth through the 2 Bridges Westminster & Blackfriars, a distance including the different turns & tacks made on the way, of 3 miles!! you see I am in excellent training in case of a *squall* at Sea" (*BLJ* 1:132).

Swimming meant many things to Byron—it anticipated his travels, it provided the competition he enjoyed, it allowed him to show off, and it created a bond with some of his closest friends. As Charles Sprawson asserts, "Swimming was a bond that united Byron with his friends, and acted as a catalyst for his emotional attachments. He swam with the boys who attracted him, across the Piraeus with Nicolo Giraud and in Falmouth harbour with a youth to whom he gave the name L'Abbé Hyacinth."[8] On the other hand, we know that Byron had many strong emotional attachments to women, though the opportunity to swim with females would have been limited. Perhaps to counter any sexual ambiguities, Hunt carefully describes the other observer along the Thames as a "respectable-looking, manly person." As a competitive exercise, or as a form of relaxation, swimming is a uniquely sensual activity; the poem Byron wrote about his most famous swim across the Hellespont gives equal attention to the demands of swimming and lovemaking.

The "bathing machine" Hunt mentions was a device Tobias Smollett calls "a small, snug, wooden chamber, fixed upon a wheel-carriage, having a door at each end."[9] Popular at seaside resorts and obviously also employed along the Thames, it allowed bathers to enter at one end, undress, and exit through the other into the water. Men generally swam naked and women, often dipped in the sea by an assistant, changed into a bathing costume of some kind. For men and women, a bathe was commonly more therapeutic than competitive. Henry Long provides us a glimpse of Byron as a more playful but still competitive swimmer who made use of a bathing machine. Long describes being carried on Byron's back "like Orion [*sic*] on the Dolphin" and watching Byron and his brother Edward jump into the river from the pier at Little Hampton, where they are carried out to sea "to such a distance as I could barely discern their heads, popping up and down like little ducks upon the sea," where they swim out with the tide and finally return safely "at the spot where the machine was prepared to receive them."[10] As in Hunt's description, the swimmers are bobbing up and down while doing the breaststroke. The reference to a bathing machine creates an amusing picture of the young men spontaneously jumping naked into the sea (like Leander) and then making use of the bathing machine for a more decorous exit into the public space of the pier.

≈ ≈ ≈

Through his association with men like Gentleman John Jackson, Byron the aristocratic sportsman came to know something of the underworld of London sporting and criminal life. Swimming, with its blend of competition and sensuality, was literally and figuratively outside the conventional social sphere Byron gently mocks in his 13 July letter to Elizabeth Pigot.[11] Ever alert to the ironies of high and low forms of recreation, Byron uses alliteration to play with opposites— fashionable routs may end in riots, vigorous balls resemble boxing matches, many dowagers are little better than demireps, and a game of cards may lead to "Crim-con."[12] He knows the language of both common and elite pastimes. While Byron may be posing when he represents himself as swimming in order to prepare for some adventure, such as a *"squall* at Sea," he had been educated in an aristocratic tradition that saw activities like swimming as preparation for life's adventures, as the acquisition of a skill that might be required to survive a shipwreck, to cross a river or a bay, or to confront the swift current of the Dardanelles. He spoke the London slang, or "flash," of Jackson, but he also knew the waters of the Cam and the literary language of Cambridge.

Swimming had its place within the humanist tradition that Byron would have known from his school years. For example, in his *Book of the Courtier*, Baldassare Castiglione includes swimming among the pastimes and exercises recommended for the courtier:

> It is meete for him also to have the arte of swimming, to leape, to runne, to cast the stone: for beside the profit that he may receave of this in the warres, it happeneth to him many times to make proofe of him selfe in such thinges, whereby hee getteth him a reputation, especially among the multitude, unto whom a man must sometime apply him selfe.[13]

Castiglione's ideal courtier was expected to master practical skills and to perform them with *sprezzatura*, the seemingly effortless style that could draw the attention and admiration of the multitude, where needed, and more importantly of the prince. It was, in the realm of sport, an art that concealed art, the swim that concealed the rehearsing. We can imagine that a voracious reader like Byron might have identified with the spontaneous swimming contest described in act I of Shakespeare's *Julius Caesar* where Cassius recounts how he was challenged by Caesar to swim "to yonder point," whereupon both men plunged into the Tiber:

> The torrent roar'd, and we did buffet it
> With lusty sinews, throwing it aside
> And stemming it with hearts of controversy.
> But ere we could arrive the point propos'd,
> Caesar cried, "Help me, Cassius, or I sink!"
> (I.ii.106–10)

The image of the two men leaping into the Tiber fully dressed, or "Accoutred," fits the Roman tradition of swimming as a form of military training. Nicholas Orme discusses "the qualities required of Roman soldiers and the methods used to train them" as enumerated in the *Epitoma Rei Militaris* of Vegetius (AD 383–395).[14] Vegetius stresses the practical uses of swimming, and the poet Horace, among others, makes reference to young Romans swimming in the Tiber near the military training ground of Campus Martius (see Odes 1:8 and 3:7).[15] But Shakespeare dramatizes a head-to-head competition that has more to do with ego than usefulness. He may have expected some in his audience to note that the anecdote recreated by Cassius contradicts both Plutarch and Suetonius, who record how Julius Caesar swam heroically to escape from the Egyptians in the harbor of Alexandria.[16] The English humanist Sir Thomas Elyot used Caesar's exploit as an example of how swimming offers both "recreation and profit."

> How much profited the feat in swimming to the valiant Julius Caesar, who at the battle of Alexandria, on a bridge being abandoned of his people for the multitude of his enemies, which oppressed them, when he might no longer sustain the shot of darts and arrows, he boldly leapt into the sea, and, diving under the water, escaped the shot and swam the space of two hundred paces to one of his ships, drawing his coat armour with his teeth after him, that his enemies should not attain it. And also that it might somewhat defend him from their arrows. And that more marvel was, holding in his hand above the water certain letters which a little before he had received from the Senate.[17]

Shakespeare the dramatist (or Cassius the conspirator) invents a scene that gives his audience the essence of sport—challenge and fierce competition; Elyot, the humanist educator, recommends swimming as a pleasurable form of recreation that prepares a leader to act resourcefully when others panic. The literary character of this anecdote builds up to the "marvel" of Caesar having the presence of mind and aquatic skill required to escape under attack while keeping the senatorial dispatches dry. Though clearly in the heroic mode, the details of Elyot's description fit what we can imagine of Caesar as a world class swimmer using a formidable sidestroke, head up and teeth fasted to his armor, one arm and the kick working underwater while the free arm holds up the dispatches. As a literary hero/swimmer Caesar was not alone. In Ariosto's *Orlando Furioso* the hero Orlando swims like a fish (canto 29, st. 48, line 2, canto 30, st. 5, line 1), as does Artegall in Spenser's *The Faerie Queene* (bk. 5, canto 2, st. 16). And Spenser lists among Sir Philip Sidney's accomplishments that he was "In wrestling nimble, and in renning swift, / In shooting steddie, and in swimming strong" ("Astrophel" lines 73–4). The literary model of the swimmer as hero anticipates the inclusion of swimming in military training to build character and, as Elyot says, to provide both recreation and profit.[18]

In England, swimming instruction, whether for military preparedness or recreation, did not become popular until the second half of the nineteenth century.[19] Michael West argues that Everard Digby's *De Arte Natandi* (1587) did much to remove the imputation that swimming was ungentlemanly.[20] As Vybarr Cregan-Reid puts it, "What makes Byron's devotion to swimming so unusual is the fact that in the early 1800s, swimming as a sport received almost no publicity of any kind."[21] Perhaps the best known essay on swimming from this period was Benjamin Franklin's letter to Oliver Neave, "Learning to Swim," written in London in the late 1760s. Franklin's letter focuses on a practical and still useful method of inducing beginners to experience the natural buoyancy of their bodies. Additionally, his *Autobiography* includes a description of his swim down the same stretch of the Thames between Lambeth and Blackfriars where Byron swam. In a less practical vein, Franklin recounts how he "stript & leapt into the River, & swam from near Chelsea to Blackfryars, performing on the Way many Feats of Activity both upon & under Water." Having studied "Thevenot's Motions and Positions," Franklin exhibits a form of American *sprezzatura* "aiming at the graceful & easy, as well as the Useful."[22]

In the period from 1750 to 1830, swimming was primarily regarded as a useful skill or a therapeutic activity. Not until the late 1830s do we find reports of the British Swimming Society organizing races.[23] Charles Sprawson outlines the literary context of organized swimming in the early nineteenth century: "The first Swimming Society in England, formed by a group of Old Etonians in 1828, was inspired by the classical example.... They adopted as their motto the opening line of Pindar's Olympian odes—'ariston men hudor'—water is best—and their records in the college library reveal the rivers, lakes, and streams of Europe bathed in by various members, with their comments, often classical: the Cam 'at Grantchester passable, elsewhere vile'; the Rhine 'kathara rei'—flows sweetly; Loch Achray 'achraees'—useless" (82–3). Rupert Brooke evokes something of this Byronic culture of swimming, sensuality, and classicism in his poem *The Old Vicarage, Grantchester*:

> Still in the dawnlit waters cool
> His ghostly Lordship swims his pool,
> And tries the strokes, essays the tricks,
> Long learnt on Hellespont, or Styx.[24]

Leslie Marchand recounts that while still at Cambridge in 1805–1806, "Riding out to the weir above Grantchester (still called Byron's pool) with his friend Long, he could escape the depression of spirits that followed the nightly carousing with his too hospitable companions."[25] Though less given to "nightly carousing," Brooke too sought out the pool to cure his spiritual malaise: "It may be there is a herb growing at the bottom of the river just above the pool at Grantchester, & that if I dive & find it & bring it up—it will heal me. I have heard so. I do not know. It seems worth trying."[26] Sadly, Roger Deakin reports that today Byron's Pool is "ruined as a swimming hole by an ugly concrete weir and the constant drone of the M11 a few hundred yards away."[27]

Though Byron was a gentleman schooled in the humanist tradition, he never lost the flair and sporting showmanship associated with Jackson and the London of 1807. He boasted about his aquatic victories and enjoyed the pure fun of swimming and diving. In a letter to John Murray, Byron introduces an example of aquatic play when discussing the current in the Hellespont: "An amusement in the small bay which opens immediately below the Asiatic fort was to *dive* for LAND tortoises which we flung in on purpose—as they amphibiously crawled along the bottom" (*BLJ* 8:83, 16 February 1821). Sport is never far removed from games, but the schoolboy character of this "amusement" has its serious side, as revealed in a striking recollection from the same period that appears in Byron's *Ravenna Journal* of 12 January 1821. He begins, "How strange are my thoughts," and then records how reading the song "Sabrina fair …"[28] from Milton's masque *Comus* brought back memories of Cambridge and his close friend Edward Noel Long, who drowned while serving with the Guards:

> We were rival swimmers—fond of riding—reading—and of conviviality. We had been at Harrow together; but—*there*, at least—his was a less boisterous spirit than mine. I was always cricketing—rebelling—fighting—*rowing* (from *row*, not *boat*-rowing, a different practice), and in all manner of mischiefs; while he was more sedate and polished. At Cambridge—both of Trinity—my spirit rather softened, or his roughened, for we became very great friends. The description of Sabrina's seat reminds me of our rival feats in *diving*. Though Cam's is not a very "translucent wave," it was fourteen feet deep, where we used to dive for, and pick up—having thrown them in on purpose—plates, eggs, and even shillings. I remember, in particular, there was the stump of a tree (at least ten or twelve feet deep) in the bed of the river, in a spot where we bathed most commonly, round which I used to cling, and "wonder how the devil I came there." (*BLJ* 8:23–4)

Byron did not shy away from the combative world of the British public school. But competition in the submarine world of the Cam helped to form a friendship which, with a "violent, though *pure*, love and passion [probably for John Edleston] … were the then romance of the most romantic period of my life" (*BLJ* 8:24). Like the reading that triggers the recollection, swimming combined adventure, escape, play and magic. Byron no doubt identified the "seat" beneath the "translucent wave" with Sabrina's role as surrogate poet whose charm breaks the spell cast by the evil Comus.

This identification of underwater play with something poetic and magical appears in Byron's closet drama *The Two Foscari* and his poem *The Island*.[29] The Doge's son Jacopo Foscari contrasts the pain he has experienced under torture with what he once felt as a boy swimming in Venice, "plunging down" into the "green and glassy gulfs" of the waves to bring back shells and seaweed, "tokens" that showed how he had "search'd the deep" (*The Two Foscari* I.i.112–17).[30]

Byron conveys the sensual play between the swimmer and the elements when Jacopo speaks of "Flinging the billows back from my drench'd hair, / And laughing from my lip the audacious brine, / Which kiss'd it like a wine-cup" (I.i.107–9). Similarly in the concluding section of his poem *The Island* (1823), drawn from "*the Mutiny of the Bounty in the South Sea, (in 1789),*" Torquil, "the nursling of the northern seas," follows the "liquid steps" of his island love Neuha to an underwater cave "Whose only portal was the keyless wave" (canto 4, line 122). In a poem that celebrates the Romantic ideal of revolution, swimming becomes the means of escape not from a tempest or a shipwreck but from the tyranny represented by the British fleet. Neuha recounts how a young chief "Diving for turtle in the depths below" (196) discovered the underwater cave where he sheltered the daughter of a hostile tribe and then made her his "Mermaid bride" (214). Once the British sails have vanished, Neuha and Torquil emerge from their "amphibious lair" (375) to join a society rededicated to "such happy days / As only the yet infant world displays" (419–20).

Bernard Blackstone describes the underwater world of poems like *The Island* as a paradise exempt from the time-space coordinates of everyday experience ("Landscape" 16–17). The recollection triggered by "Sabrina fair" includes the youthful paradise identified with diving in the Cam, as well as the sense of loss associated with the passage of time and Edward Long's death by drowning. But the youthful Byron treats Leander's death and his own fatigue lightly: "For he was drown'd, and I've the ague" ("Written After" line 20). When he archly celebrates his accomplishment in verse or repeatedly announces it in prose, Byron assumes his readers know the Hero and Leander legend and will appreciate the danger faced by anyone swimming across that particular strait. In his letter to Francis Hodgson he writes, "I shall begin by telling you, having only told it you twice before, that I swam from Sestos to Abydos. I do this that you may be impressed with proper respect for me, the performer; for I plume myself on this achievement more than I could possibly do on any kind of glory, political, poetical, or rhetorical" (Constantinople, 4 July 1810 *BLJ* 1:253). I have said that Byron had not been consciously "rehearsing the part of Leander" in 1807, but the word "performer," used in the first sense of one who has performed a feat, connotes something theatrical when combined with the phrase "I plume myself." In 1810 Byron had not achieved poetical glory—he was yet to be made famous by the publication of *Childe Harold's Pilgrimage* in 1812 and would leave the political/rhetorical arena for good after his maiden speech to the House of Lords that same year. But the swim was in a sense a rehearsal for the emergence of his public persona, someone who challenges nature and takes his place among heroes ancient and modern.[31] He dates "Written after Swimming from Sestos to Abydos" precisely 9 May 1810, six days after he had completed the swim, as though he were recording an Olympic event. The first two stanzas address the "broad Hellespont" and set his swim in the context of the legend:

>   1.
> If in the month of dark December,
> Leander, who was nightly wont
> (What maid will not the tale remember?)
> To Cross thy stream, broad Hellespont!
>   2.
> If when the wintry tempest roar'd
> He sped to Hero, nothing loth,
> And thus of old thy current pour'd,
> Fair Venus! how I pity both!

Time, place, and conditions are important. Byron faced the same powerful current (if "of old" it was the same) and, as we will see, defended himself against the accusation that he swam not against but with the strong current of the Dardanelles. Wiser, or luckier, he swims "in the genial month of May" and barely survives, while Leander drowned during a winter storm. Having been educated in the humanist tradition, Byron would think of moderns as being dwarfed by the ancients, hence the mock heroic tone. But as a modern he also wants to challenge the legend. He both questions what took place "According to the doubtful story" and mocks the suffering of the modern performer with his off rhyme:

> Sad mortals! thus the Gods still plague you!
> He lost his labour, I my jest:
> For he was drown'd, and I've the ague.

Despite his irony, Byron wants the poem to stand as the record of a significant athletic accomplishment.

By the early nineteenth century the definition of sport had begun to shift from recreation (Byron diving for tortoises) to a competitive activity that required physical exertion, skill, and preparation. Leander swam the Hellespont for love, not as a demonstration of his aquatic prowess.[32] The modern swimmer competes against wind and currents to challenge a record or as a test of endurance and usually does so after a period of training and careful planning.[33] Byron did not train like a modern long distance swimmer, but determined to succeed, he learned from his experience: "I attempted it a week ago and failed owing to the North wind and the wonderful rapidity of the tide, though I have been from my childhood a strong swimmer, but this morning being calmer I succeeded and crossed the 'broad Hellespont' in an hour and ten minutes" (*BLJ* 1:237).

As the first modern on record to complete the swim, Byron created a legend others still try to equal or surpass. In addition to its annual competition held on Turkish Victory Day (30 August), the Canakkle Rotary Club sponsored an event on 3 May 2010 to commemorate Byron's crossing. Each year the swimmers set off from the European shore at Eceabat, near what was Sestos, and finish at a dock near the fortress of Kal-i-Sultanije in Canakkle, the modern Abydos. Accompanied by a flotilla of fishing boats, they follow a course that fits Byron's observation on the current, which he points out "is favourable to the Swimmer on neither side—but may be stemmed by plunging into the Sea—a considerable way above the opposite point of the coast which the Swimmer wishes to make, but still bearing up against it; it is very strong but—if you *calculate* well you may reach land" (21 February 1821, *BLJ* 8:81). Byron deservedly "plumed" himself on this swim since the best swimmers today complete the crossing in little better than his time of one hour and 10 minutes.

Byron's observation on the current comes from a letter he wrote a decade after his famous swim when his accomplishment was questioned by the traveler William Turner in his *Journal of a Tour in the Levant* (1820).[34] Turner, who was attached to the Embassy in Constantinople, had attempted but failed to complete the swim from Abydos, where Leander began his nightly journey to Hero's tower. Turner maintained that Byron and Ekenhead had benefited from swimming *with* the current by departing from the opposite shore. Byron defended his reputation in a letter to John Murray that concludes, "Mr. T. may find what fault he pleases with my poetry—or my politics—but I recommend him to leave aquatic reflections—till he is able to swim 'five and twenty minutes' without being '*exhausted*' though I believe he is the first modern Tory who ever swam '*against* the Stream' for half the time" (*BLJ* 8:83).[35] In addition to the jibe at Turner's conservative politics, Byron asserts that his own swim was accomplished very much against, not with the current, and he records the time exactly, just as he had done in 1810: "Mr. Ekenhead & myself both succeeded—the one [Byron] in an hour and ten minutes—the other in one hour and five minutes" (*BLJ* 8:80). It is important for the modern adventurer not only to attempt the swim but to complete it with witnesses, preferably *English*. In the 1821 letter to Murray, Byron identifies "the four instances on record" of a successful crossing: "a Neapolitan—a young Jew—Mr. Ekenhead—& myself—the two last done in the presence of hundreds of *English* witnesses" (*BLJ* 8:81).[36] Byron's companion John Cam Hobhouse served as official time keeper and recorded the event to the minute in his diary: "This instant 3 m[inutes] p[ast] 10 a.m. wrote this in the Dardanelles, at anchor. Byron and Ekenhead ... now swimming across the Hellespont—Ovid's Hero to Leander open before me."[37] The timepiece and the diary represent the time-space coordinates of athletic competition, while the *Heroides* recalls the legend and its literary tradition.

In the response to Turner, Byron cites some of his other notable swims—crossing the Tagus in three hours (which Hobhouse considered a more demanding swim), as well as his triumph over the Italian "Chevalier Mengaldo" and Alexander Scott in 1818 when the trio set out from the Lido in Venice and only Byron reached the end of the Grand Canal: "I had been in the water by my watch without help or rest—and never touching ground or boat *four hours* and *twenty* minutes" (*BLJ* 8:81). Though precise regarding time, conditions and the witness (consul General Hoppner), the public response to Turner omits a sexual boast Byron felt compelled to include when he described the Venice competition to his friend Hobhouse in 1818, "I was in the sea from half past *4*—till a quarter past *8*—without touching or resting.—I could not be much fatigued having had a *piece* in the forenoon—& taking another in the evening at ten of the Clock" (*BLJ* 6:55). Byron, the man of rank jealous of his fame, was never far from the London sportsman who swam the Thames, knew the world of demireps and "Crim-con" and liked to brag about his sexual exploits. The sportsman treats the amatory side of the "old story" with humor, as when he remarks that the current is so strong "that I doubt whether Leander's conjugal powers must not have been exhausted in his passage to Paradise" (*BLJ* 1:237), or when he jokes to his mother about his "humble imitation of *Leander* of amorous memory" (*BLJ* 1:244). Charles Sprawson speculates that "Byron was attracted by Leander's combination of nocturnal swimming and dangerous loving" (123). Beneath the jocular tone, did Byron identify with the tragic story of Hero and Leander because it mirrored the dangers of his forbidden love for his half-sister Augusta?

These deeper implications do not fit the mock-heroic tone of "Written after Swimming from Sestos to Abydos," but when Byron returned to London after his eastern sojourn he used the "broad Hellespont" as the setting for one of his oriental tales, *The Bride of Abydos* (1813). Before the tragic conclusion of that tale, Byron's narrator alludes to Hero and Leander:

> The winds are high on Helle's wave,
> As on that night of stormy water
> When Love—who sent—forgot to save
> The young, the beautiful, the brave,
> The lonely hope of Sestos' daughter.
>   (canto 2, lines 1–5)[38]

Byron sets his tale in Abydos where, the poem recalls, his eye fixed on the light from Hero's lamp (14–15), Leander defied the threatening December storm. Selim does not swim the Hellespont, but the lamp that glimmers in Zuleika's tower (61) inspires him to challenge fate. The fact that Byron initially conceived of the lovers Selim and Zuleika as brother and sister gives added meaning to the assertion that the old tale of Hero and Leander may "nerve" young hearts (18–19), like Byron's own, to risk the dangers of a forbidden love. Though Byron prudently decided to alter the "consanguinity" of Selim and Zuleika and "confine them to cousinship,"[39] he interrupts his narrative to remind the reader of a personal connection between the poet and the tale. Byron the voyager, swimmer and lover had visited the Asiatic shore near Troy, "The desert of old Priam's pride" (24), where he says: "These feet have press'd the sacred shore, / These limbs that buoyant wave hath borne" (29–30). The poet/wanderer who explored Troy and swam in imitation of Leander addresses the "Minstrel" Homer, happy to have traced the "undoubted scene" where "Thine own 'broad Hellespont' still dashes" (35–6). Byron was convinced, correctly it turned out, that he had explored the "undoubted scene" of Homer's ancient Troy.[40] In a more sarcastic vein he appends a footnote to line 36 on the appropriateness of applying the Homeric epithet "broad Hellespont" to a *narrow* strait: "I have even heard it disputed on the spot; and not foreseeing a speedy conclusion to the controversy, amused myself with swimming across it in the mean time, and probably will again, before the point is settled." Byron likes to have it both ways and from both sides of the strait. As poet, he recalls his Homer "on the spot" where Troy once stood and where Leander set off from Abydos; as man of action, he swims from European Sestos while the pedants wrangle. The poem takes forbidden love seriously, while the footnote returns to the offhand, jaunty tone of the letters.

For Byron, experience determines whether Leander's swim was practicable, whether the term "broad" fits the strait, whether it is named the Hellespont or the Dardanelles, and whether he was on the very site of ancient Troy: "Who will persuade me, when I reclined upon a mighty tomb, that it did not contain a hero?—its very magnitude proved this" (*Ravenna Journal*, 11 January 1821, *BLJ* 8:22). The modern who swims for "Glory" rather than Love has the certainty of experience on his side. In this regard Byron is very much the athlete measured by performance in the sea or on the field. As he says of his antagonist Turner, "The secret of all this is—that Mr. Turner failed and that we succeeded—and he is consequently disappointed—and seems not unwilling to overshadow whatever little merit there might be in our Success" (*BLJ* 8:83).

Though legends were important to Byron, including his own, it is also surprising that he would bother to respond to Turner in 1821. His love affair with Teresa Guiccioli had brought him to Ravenna and put him in contact with the Liberal/Carbonari movement in the Romagna through Teresa's father, Count Ruggero Gamba, and her brother Pietro. Why would he care how his swim was remembered when he could write in his *Ravenna Journal*, "To-morrow is my birthday—that is to say, at twelve o' clock, midnight, i.e. in twelve minutes, I shall have completed thirty and three years of age!!!—and I go to my bed with a heaviness of heart at having lived so long, and to so little purpose" (20 January 1821, *BLJ* 8:31). Did his recollection of the year when he equaled the youthful Leander, and did so in record time, ease Byron's sense of futility 12 minutes before the stroke of midnight?

When he responded to Turner, Byron was in some ways the aging athlete, "ten years older in time and twenty in constitution" (*BLJ* 8:82) after the years of dissipation in Venice that had doubled his effective age. Swimming the Dardanelles had played a key role in the youthful Byron's construction of his personal version of the grand tour, where facing "perils" in an exotic setting replaced the more conventional pursuits of young men crossing the Alps to study and relax in Italy. From the *Salsette* frigate off Abydos he writes to Francis Hodgson:

> We have undergone some inconveniences and incurred partial perils, but no events worthy of commemoration unless you will deem it one that two days ago I swam from Sestos to Abydos.—This with a few alarms from robbers, and some danger of shipwreck in a Turkish Galliot six months ago, a visit to a Pacha, a passion for a married woman at Malta, a challenge to an officer, an

attachment to three Greek Girls at Athens, with a great deal of buffoonery and fine prospects, form all that has distinguished my progress since my departure from Spain. (*BLJ* 1:240)

The young lord who ran with the Dandies in London and trained with Jackson constructs himself as a version of Leander, stripping off the conventions of his contemporaries and taking the plunge into a world most of them would never see and certainly would not explore in quite the way he did. As we have seen, his bravado requires that Byron invoke the threat of death and then treat it lightly—as another jest, like Leander's death, or his own ague.

Byron certainly became more than the young man of 1807 who had produced "a bad volume of poems" and spent his days rehearsing Leander's swim in the Thames. Did he believe he would achieve lasting fame as a swimmer? A few months after his Hellespont swim, Byron wrote to John Cam Hobhouse: "A Bolognese physician is to be presented to me tomorrow at his own petition having heard that I am the *celebrated aquatic genius* who swam across the Hellespont when he was at Abydos. I believe the fellow wants to make experiments with me in diving" (Athens, 26 November 1810, *BLJ* 2:30). In 1810 Byron was not a famous poet; that fame would come two years later. But the phrase *celebrated aquatic genius* neatly sums up the combination of self-advertisement, physical accomplishment and intellect that turned the swim into a modern legend. Additionally, the physician conducting experiments on the poet's lung capacity anticipates scientific studies of athletic performance. Byron presents the anecdote as a joke, but we can sense, behind the irony, considerable pride in the fact that in 1810 the term *genius* fit the swimmer, as it would one day fit the poet.

Notes

[1] *The Autobiography of Leigh Hunt*, ed. Edmund Blunden (1850; London: Oxford University Press, 1928), 374.

[2] All of Byron's poetry quoted from *The Complete Poetical Works*, ed. Jerome J. McGann, 7 vols. (Oxford: Clarendon Press, 1980–1993).

[3] *Byron's Letters and Journals*, ed. Leslie A. Marchand, 12 vols. (Cambridge: Harvard University Press, 1973–1994), 1:253, hereafter *BLJ*.

[4] The most important literary sources of the legend are Musaeus, *Hero and Leander*, fifth century AD; Virgil, *Georgics* 233–71, 29 BC; Ovid, *Heroides* (18 and 19), 25–16 BC; and Christopher Marlowe, "Hero and Leander," 1598. On the influence of Musaeus in modern times, see Musaeus, *Hero and Leander*, ed. Thomas Gelzer (Cambridge: Loeb Classical Library, 1975), 323–6.

[5] Ben Jonson, *Bartholomew Fair*, ed. E.A. Horsman (Cambridge: Harvard University Press, 1960). See also Hunt's poem "Hero and Leander," *Hero and Leander and Bacchus and Ariadne* (London: C. and J. Ollier, 1819).

[6] In a note on canto 11, st. 19 of *Don Juan*, Byron refers the reader who needs help with the London slang of his early years "to my old friend and corporeal pastor and master, John Jackson, Esq., Professor of Pugilism."

[7] Hunt, *Autobiography*, 374; see also ch. 5, 137: "My father collected the verses, and published them [in 1802, under the title of *Juvenilia*], with a large list of subscribers.... I was as proud, perhaps, of the book at that time as I am ashamed of it now." Byron's first collection of poems offered to the public was *Hours of Idleness*, which appeared in June of 1807. It was most probably in the summer of 1807 that Hunt saw Byron swimming in the Thames.

[8] Charles Sprawson, *Haunts of the Black Masseur: The Swimmer as Hero* (1992; Minneapolis: University of Minnesota Press, 2000), 109.

[9] Smollett tells us that the person who uses the bathing machine "being stripped, opens the door to sea-ward." See *The Expedition of Humphrey Clinker*, ed. André Parreaux (New York: Houghton Mifflin, 1968), 162.

[10] Quoted in Leslie A. Marchand, *Byron: A Biography*, 3 vols. (New York: Alfred Knopf, 1957), 1:115–16. Professsor Marchand's "sic" reminds us that it was the singer Arion, not Orion, who was carried to shore on a dolphin's back.

[11] See Gary Dyer, "Thieves, Boxers, Sodomites, Poets: Being Flash to Byron's *Don Juan*," *PMLA* 116 (2001): 564; see note 6 above.

[12] "Crim-con," the abbreviation of criminal conversation, originally a legal term, was eighteenth-century slang for adultery.

[13] Baldassare Castiglione, *The Book of the Courtier*, trans. Sir Thomas Hoby (1561; New York: J.M. Dent, 1928), 42.

[14] Nicholas Orme, *Early British Swimming, 55 BC–AD 1719* (Exeter: Short Run Press, 1983), 7.

[15] See Gregory M. Colon Semenza, "Sport, War, and Contest in Shakespeare's *Henry VI*," *Renaissance Quarterly* 54 (2001): 1258.

[16] Sir Thomas North, *Plutarch's Lives of the Noble Grecians and Romans*, 7 vols. (1579; repr., New York: AMS Press, 1967), 5:51–2; and Philemon Holland, *Suetonius, History of Twelve Caesars*, 2 vols. (1606; repr., New York: AMS Press, 1967), 1:61, and Orme, *Early British Swimming*, 59.

[17] Sir Thomas Elyot, *The Booke named The Governour*, ed. S.E. Lehmberg (1531; New York: Dutton, 1962), 62–3.

[18] Thomas A.P. van Leeuwen speculates that the popularity of floating baths and barges in the Seine may have contributed to "French hegemony on the battlefield" in the nineteenth century, which inspired the Austrians and Prussians to promote swimming instruction as a part of military training. See Thomas A.P. van Leeuwen, *The Springboard in the Pond* (Cambridge: MIT Press, 1998), 27.

[19] Nicolas Orme traces the limited influence of Everard Digby's *De Arte Natandi* (1587) via Christopher Middleton's translation and abridgement entitled *A Short Introduction for to Learne to Swimme* (1595), William Percey's unacknowledged adaptation entitled *The Compleat Swimmer* (1658), and the popular, unacknowledged French translation of Digby by M. Thévenot, *L'Art de nager* (1696). See Orme, *Early British Swimming*, 94, 104–5.

[20] Michael West, "Spenser, Everard Digby, and the Renaissance Art of Swimming," *Renaissance Quarterly* 26 (1973): 17.

[21] Vybarr Cregan-Reid, "Water Defences: The Arts of Swimming in Nineteenth-Century Culture," *Critical Survey* 16, no. 3 (2004): 36.

[22] "To Oliver Neave," 840–43; *The Autobiography*, part 1, 1351. Digby is the rare writer who provides some instruction in aquatic fun, with illustrations of how to play above the water with one foot, or show one's toes (see Orme, *Early British Swimming*, 168–71). Benjamin Franklin, *Writings*, ed. J.A. Leo Lemay (New York: Viking Press, 1987).

[23] See Ralph Thomas, *Swimming: With Lists of Books* (London: Sampson Low, 1904), 250–53.

[24] *The Collected Poems of Rupert Brooke* (New York: Dodd Mead, 1915), lines 50–53.

[25] Marchand, *Byron: A Biography*, 1:105.

[26] *The Letters of Rupert Brooke*, ed. Geoffrey Keynes (New York: Harcourt Brace, 1968), to Geoffrey Keynes, 24 June 1912, 389.

[27] Roger Deakin, *Waterlog: A Swimmer's Journey through Britain* (New York: Vintage, 1999), 43.

[28] "Sabrina fair / Listen where thou art sitting / Under the glassy, cool, translucent wave" (*Comus* lines 859–61).

[29] On water and magic, see Bernard Blackstone, "Byron and the Levels of Landscape," *Ariel* 5, no. 4 (1974): 14–19.

[30] On diving for "tokens," see Byron's letters to Octavius Gilchrist, 8 September 1821 (*BLJ* 8:203) and to the Earl of Blessington, 23 May 1823 (*BLJ* 10:183).

[31] See his letter to John Hanson, 23 May 1810: "I believe I mentioned in my last that I had visited the plains of Troy, and swam from Sestos to Abydos in the Dardanelles, any of your classical men (Hargreaves or Charles) will explain the meaning of the last performance and the old story connected with it" (*BLJ* 1:243).

[32] See Musaeus, "Hero and Leander," lines 240–50.

[33] Lynne Cox, *Swimming to Antarctica: Tales of a Long-Distance Swimmer* (New York: Harcourt, 2004), provides an excellent example of modern endurance swimming, and for swims directly inspired by Byron, see Richard Halliburton, *The Glorious Adventure* (New York: Bobbs-Merill, 1926), 131–47; and Sprawson, *Haunts of the Black Masseur*, 124–32.

[34] See *BLJ* 8:80, n. 1.

[35] The letter to John Murray, from Ravenna, 21 February 1821, was published in the *Monthly Magazine*, April 1821, and the *Traveller*, 3 April 1821 (see *BLJ* 8:83, n. 3).

[36] See Marchand, *Byron* 1:239, n. 3.

[37] Quoted in Marchand, *Byron* 1:238.

[38] Nephele provided a flying, golden-fleeced ram for her children Helle and Phrixos to escape from their cruel stepmother Ino, but Helle fell from the ram and drowned in the strait then named Hellespont, hence Byron's "Helle's wave."

[39] See his letters to Daniel Clarke, 15 December 1813 (*BLJ* 3:199) and to John Galt, 11 December 1813 (*BLJ* 3:196): "I meant to have gone on with the story, but on *second* thoughts, I thought myself *two centuries* at least too late for the subject; which, though admitting of very powerful feeling and description, yet is not adapted for this age, at least this country."

[40] On Byron's attitude toward the learned dispute over the location of Ilium, see Benita Eisler, *Byron: Child of Passion, Fool of Fame* (New York: Random House, 1999), 256–7.

Bibliography

Addison, Joseph. "No. 44, Friday, April 20, 1711." *The Spectator: A New Edition Reproducing the Original Text both as First Issued and as Corrected by its Authors, Volume 1*. London: George Routledge and Sons, 1881. http://www.gutenberg.org/files/12030/ 12030-h/SV1/Spectator1.html#section44.

Alexander, David. "Kauffman and the Print Market in Eighteenth-Century England." In *Angelica Kauffman: A Continental Artist in Georgian England*. Edited by W.W. Roworth, 341–78. London: Reaktion, 1992.

Almon, John. *A New and Impartial Collection of Interesting Letters, From the Public Papers; Many of them Written by Persons of Eminence, On a great Variety of Important Subjects, which have occasionally engaged the Public Attention: From the Accession of his present Majesty, in September 1760, to May 1767*. 2 vols. London: John Almon, 1767.

Amendt, Adreas, Christian Wacker, Stephan Wassong, and Qatar Olympic and Sports Museum. *Olympics Past and Present*. Munich, London, New York: Prestel Verlag, 2013.

Annals of gaming; or complete directions for whist, quadrille, piquet, billiards, ... in which is contained, the method of playing ... Including the laws of the several games. London: printed for William Lane, et al, n.d.

Anon. *Lords and Ladies who deal in the Sport: The Pleasures of 1722*. London: Songs, 1722.

———. *Observations on Some of the Popular Amusements of this Country, Addressed to the Higher Classes of Society*. London, 1827.

———. *Popular Pastimes, Being a Selection of Picturesque Representations of the Customs and Amusements of Great Britain*. London, 1816.

———. *The Foundling Hospital for Wit*. 6 vols. London, 1743–1749.

Aspin, Jehosaphat. *Ancient Customs, Sports, and Pastimes of the English*. London, 1832.

Atkins, J.R. *The Book of Racquets. A Practical Guide to the Game and its History, and to the Different Courts in which it is Played*. London: Frederick Warne, 1872.

Baer, Marc. *Theatre and Disorder in Late Georgian London*. New York: Oxford University Press, 1992.

Bailey, Peter. *Leisure and Class in Victorian England. Rational Recreation and the Contest for Control, 1830–1885*. 2nd ed. London: Methuen, 1987.

Bajot, M. *Eloge de la paume et de ses avantages sous le rapport de la santé et du développement des facultés physiques*. Paris: Bachelier, Nepveu, 1824.

Banks, Sophia. Extracts from newspapers, advertisements, etc. illustrative of archery. MS Add.6314–20. British Library.

Barker, Hannah. "Women, Work and the Industrial Revolution: Female Involvement in the English Printing Trades, c. 1700–1784." In *Gender in Eighteenth-Century England: Roles, Representations and Responsibilities*. Edited by Hannah Barker and Elaine Chalus. London: Longman, 1997.

Baxter, Richard. *A Christian Directory: Or, a Summ of Practical Theologie and Cases of Conscience*. London, 1673.

Bermingham, Ann. "Old Masters of the Hunt." *Times Literary Supplement* (4–10 August 1989), 840.

Berners, Dame Juliana. *The Book of St Albans*. Edited by Joseph Haslewood. New York: Abercrombie and Fitch, 1966.

———. *The Treatyse of Fysshynge Wyth An Angle, reprinted from The Book of St Albans 1496*. Edited by George Van Siclen. New York: James L. Black, 1875.

Best, David. *The Royal Tennis Court: A History of Tennis at Hampton Court Palace*. Oxford: Ronaldson Publications, 2002.

Bilodeau, Arthur E. "Pugilistic Rhetoric in Eighteenth and Nineteenth Century England." PhD dissertation, Indiana University, 2001.

Birley, Derek. *A Social History of English Cricket*. London: Aurum, 2003.

———. *Sport and the Making of Britain*. Manchester and New York: Manchester University Press, 1993.

Black, Robert. *The Jockey Club and its Founders*. London, 1891.

Blackall, Ofspring. *The Lawfulness and the Right Manner of Keeping Christmas, and Other Christian Festivals: A Sermon*. London, 1705.

Blackstone, Bernard. "Byron and the Levels of Landscape." *Ariel* 5, no. 4 (1974): 3–20.

Boddy, Kasia. *Boxing: A Cultural History*. London: Reaktion Books, 2008.

Boffey, Julia. "Berners [Bernes, Barnes], Juliana (fl. 1460), supposed author and prioress of Sopwell." In *Oxford Dictionary of National Biography*. Oxford: Oxford Dictionary of National Biography, 2004. Accessed 9 October 2013. http://www.oxforddnb.com/index/2/101002255.

Booth, Douglas. *The Field: Truth and Fiction in Sports History*. Abingdon, Oxford: Routledge, 2005.

Borlase, William. *The Natural History of Cornwall*. Oxford, 1758.

Boswell, James. *Boswell's Life of Johnson. Including Boswell's Journal of a Tour to the Hebrides and Johnson's Diary of a Journey into North Wales*. Edited by G.B. Hill. Oxford: Clarendon Press, 1934–1964.

———. *The Journal of a Tour to the Hebrides*, with Samuel Johnson, *A Journey to the Western Islands of Scotland*. Edited by Peter Levi. Harmondsworth: Penguin, 1984.

———. *The Life of Johnson*. Edited by George Birkbeck Hill. Revised by L.F. Powell. 6 vols. Oxford: Clarendon Press, 1934–1950.

Bourne, Henry. *Antiquitates Vulgares; or, the Antiquities of the Common People*. Newcastle, 1725.

Bowstead, John. *The Village Wake, or the Feast of the Dedication, its Religious Observance a Bond of Union between the Higher and Lower Classes. A Sermon.* London, 1846.

"Boxing and Prizefighting." In *Early Eighteenth-Century Newspaper Reports: A Sourcebook*. Edited by Rictor Norton. Last modified 31 December 2005. http://rictornorton.co.uk/grubstreet/boxing.htm.

Brailsford, Dennis. *Bareknuckles: A Social History of Prizefighting*. Cambridge: Lutterworth Press, 1988.

———. *A Taste for Diversions: Sport in Georgian England*. Cambridge: Lutterworth Press, 1999.

Bright, James W., and Wilfred P. Mustard. "Pan's Pipe, Three Pastoral Eclogues, with Other Verses, by Francis Sabie (1595)." *Modern Philology* 7, no. 4 (April 1910): 433–64.

Brooke, Rupert. *The Collected Poems of Rupert Brooke*. 1915. New York: Dodd, Mead, 1944.

———. *The Letters of Rupert Brooke*. Edited by Geoffrey Keynes. New York: Harcourt Brace, 1968.

Brookes, Dr. William Penny. *The Salopian Journal*, 19 September 1852. Shrewsbury: Printed by J. and W. Eddowes, 1794–1843.

Broughton, Jack. *Proposals for Erecting an Amphitheatre for the Manly Exercise of Boxing: By John Broughton, Professor of Athletics*. London: n.p., 1743.

Burder, George. *Lawful Amusements*. London, 1805.

Burke, Peter. *Popular Culture in Early Modern Europe*. London: Temple Smith, 1978.

Burney, Frances. *Early Journals and Letters of Fanny Burney*. Vol. 5: *1782–83*. Edited by Lars E. Troide and Stewart J. Cooke. Montreal: McGill-Queens University Press, 2012.

Burns, Francis. *Heigh for Cotswold! A history of Robert Dover's Olimpick Games. A new and revised edition*. Chipping Camden: The Robert Dover Society, 2000.

Byron, George Gordon. *Byron's Letters and Journals*. Edited by Leslie A. Marchand. 12 vols. Cambridge, MA: Harvard University Press, 1973–1994.

———. *The Complete Poetical Works*. Edited by Jerome J. McGann. 7 vols. Oxford: Clarendon Press, 1980–1993.

Carretta, Vincent. *George III and the Satirists from Hogarth to Byron*. Athens and London: University of Georgia Press, 1990.

Cassidy, Rebecca, ed. *Cambridge Companion to Horseracing*. Cambridge: Cambridge University Press, 2013.

Cassidy, Tanya. "People, Place, and Performance: Theoretically visiting Mother Clap's Molly House." In *Queer People: Negotiations and Expressions of Homosexuality, 1700–1800*. Edited by Chris Mounsey and Caroline Gonda. Cranbury, NJ: Associated University Press, 2007.

Castiglione, Baldassare. *The Book of the Courtier*. Translated by Sir Thomas Hoby. New York: J.M. Dent, 1928. First published in 1561.

Castle, Terry. "The Culture of Travesty: Sexuality and Masquerade in Eighteenth-Century England." In *Sexual Underworlds of the Enlightenment*. Edited by Roy Porter and George Rousseau. Chapel Hill: University of North Carolina Press, 1988.

———. *Masquerade and Civilization: The Carnivalesque in Eighteenth-Century Culture and Fiction*. Stanford: Stanford University Press, 1986.

Chandler, Richard. *Abyssinia Mythical and Historical ... Reprinted from St. James's Magazine, Illustrated with map of the seventeenth century*. London: C.J. Skeet, 1870.

———. *Inscriptiones antiquæ, pleræque nondum editæ: in Asia Minori et Græcia, præsertim Athenis, collectæ. Cum appendice*. Oxonii: E Typographeo Clarendoniano, 1774.

———. *Travels in Asia Minor and Greece*. Edited by Nicholas Revett. Oxford: Clarendon Press, 1825.

———. *Travels in Greece: or, an Account of a tour made at the expense of the Society of Dilettanti*. Dublin: Price, 1776.

Chandler, R., N. Revett, and W. Pars. *Ionian Antiquities published, with permission of the Society of Dilettanti*. London: Society of Dilettanti, 1769.

Chandler, Richard, with Nicholas Revett. *Travels in Asia Minor: or, an Account of a tour made at the expense of the Society of Dilettanti*. Oxford: Clarendon Press, 1775.

Clarkson, Christopher. *The History and Antiquities of Richmond in the County of York*. Richmond, 1821.

Clayton, John. *Friendly Advice to the Poor*. Manchester, 1755.

Clayton, Timothy. *The English Print 1688–1802*. New Haven and London: Yale University, 1997.

Cleland, John. *Memoirs of a Woman of Pleasure*. Edited by Peter Sabor. Oxford: Oxford University Press, 1999. First published 1985.

Coigney, Rodoplhe L. *Izaak Walton: A New Bibliography 1653–1987*. New York: James Cummins, 1989.

Collections Towards a Parochial History of Berkshire, Being the Answers Returned to Mr. More's Circular Letters and Queries. London, n.d., ca. 1783.

Colley, Linda. *Britons: Forging the Nation 1707–1837*. New Haven and London: Yale University Press, 1992.

Collier, Jeremy. "A Short View of the Immorality and Profaneness of the English Stage." In *The Broadview Anthology of British Literature*. Ontario: Broadview Press, 2006.

Cone, Carl. *Hounds in the Morning: Sundry Sports of Merry England*. Lexington: University Press of Kentucky, 1981.

Congreve, William. *Love for Love*. London, 1695.

Cook, Theodore. *The Field, the Farm, the Garden, the Country Gentleman's Newspaper, Letter to Sir Sidney Lee, Windsor House, Bream's Buildings*. London, 24 February 1916.

Cox, Lynne. *Swimming to Antarctica: Tales of a Long-Distance Swimmer.* New York: Harcourt, 2004.

Credland, Arthur G. "Archery and its Art in Britain." *British Sporting Art Trust* 26 (January 1994): 1–8.

———. "The Grand National Archery Meetings 1844–1944 and the Progress of Women in Archery." *Journal of the Society of Archer-Antiquaries* 43 (2000): 68–104.

Cregan-Reid, Vybarr. "Water Defences: The Arts of Swimming in Nineteenth-Century Culture." *Critical Survey* 16, no. 3 (2004): 33–47.

Crown, Patricia. "Clothing the Modern Venus: Hogarth and Women's Dress." In *Studies in Eighteenth Century Art and Culture.* Edited by Elise Goodman. Newark: University of Delaware Press, 2001.

———. "William Hogarth's Images of Working Women and Commerce." In *The Other Hogarth: The Aesthetics of DiVerence.* Edited by Bernadette Fort and Angela Rosenthal. Princeton: Princeton University Press, 2001.

D'Urfey, Thomas. *The Bath, or, The Western Lass. A Comedy, as it is Acted at the Theatre Royal in Drury-Lane, By His Majesty's Servants. By Mr. Durfey.* London: printed for Peter Buck, at the Sign of the Temple, at the Middle Temple Gate in Fleetstreet, 1701.

Daniel Mendoza. Painted by J. Robineau. Engraved by H. Kingsbury. London, 1789. Held by the British Museum. http://www.britishmuseum.org/research/collection_online/collection_object_details/collection_image_gallery.aspx?assetId=945824&objectId=1526456&partId=1.

Deakin, Roger. *Waterlog: A Swimmer's Journey through Britain.* New York: Vintage, 1999.

Defoe, Daniel. *A Tour through the Whole Island of Great Britain.* Edited by Pat Rogers. Exeter: Webb and Bower, 1989. Originally published in 3 vols., London, 1724–1726.

Delves, Anthony. "Popular Recreation and Social Conflict in Derby, 1800–1850." In *Popular Culture and Class Conflict, 1590–1914: Explorations in The History of Labour and Leisure.* Edited by Eileen Yeo and Stephen Yeo, 89–127. Brighton: Harvester Press, 1981.

Deuchar, Stephen. *Sporting Art in Eighteenth-Century England: A Social and Political History.* New Haven and London: Yale University, 1988.

The Diary, or, Woodfall's Register. London: Printed by William Woodfall, No. 62 Dorset-Street, Salisbury-Square, 1789–1793.

Dodd, James William. *Ballad of Archery.* London: Evans, 1818.

Donald, Diana. *The Age of Caricature: Satirical Prints in the Reign of George III.* New Haven and London: Yale University Press, 1996.

Dougal, Alistair. *Charles I, The Book Of Sports And Puritanism In Tudor And Early Stuart England.* Liverpool: Liverpool University Press, 2011.

Dover, Robert. *Annalia Dubrensia: Upon the yeerly celebration of Mr Robert Dovers Olimpick Games upon Cotswold Hills.* London: Robert Raworth for Matthew Walbancke, 1636.

Dunkin, John. *The History and Antiquities of Bicester*. London, 1816.
During, Simon, ed. *The Cultural Studies Reader*. London: Routledge, 1993.
Dyer, Gary. "Thieves, Boxers, Sodomites, Poets: Being Flash to Byron's *Don Juan*." *PMLA* 116 (2001): 562–78.
Edwards, C.B. *The "Tox" Story*. Canterbury: for the Royal Toxophilite Society, 1968.
Edwards, Edward. *Anecdotes of Painters Who Have Resided or Been Born in England*. London: Cornmarket, 1970. First published 1808.
Egan, Pierce. *Tom & Jerry: Life in London, or, The Day and Night Scenes of Jerry Hawthorn, esq. and His Elegant Friend Corinthian Tom, in Their Rambles and Sprees through the Metropolis*. London, 1821.
Egan, Pierce. *Boxiana: or, Sketches of ancient and modern pugilism from the days of the renowned James Figg and Jack Broughton to the heroes of the later milling era Jack Scroggins and Tom Hickman*. Edited by John Ford. London: The Folio Society, 1976. First published 1812.
Egerton, Judy. *British Sporting and Animal Paintings 1655–1867* in the Paul Mellon Collection. London: The Tate Gallery for the Yale Center for British Art, 1978.
Einberg, Elizabeth. "Catalogue Raisonné of the Work of George Lambert." *Walpole Society* 63 (2001): 116.
Eisler, Benita. *Byron: Child of Passion, Fool of Fame*. New York: Random House, 1999.
Elyot, Sir Thomas. *The Booke named The Governour*. Edited by S.E. Lehmberg. New York: Dutton, 1962. First published 1531.
Endelman, Todd M. *The Jews of Georgian England, 1714–1830: Tradition and Change in a Liberal Society*. Ann Arbor: University of Michigan Press, 1999.
Farey, John. *General View of the Agriculture of Derbyshire*. 3 vols. London, 1811–1817.
Felsenstein, Frank. *Anti-Semitic Stereotypes: A Paradigm of Otherness in English Popular Culture, 1660–1830*. Baltimore: Johns Hopkins University Press, 1995.
Fielding, Henry. *The History of Tom Jones, a Foundling*. New York: Norton, 1995. First published 1749 by A. Millar, London.
———. *The History of Tom Jones, A Foundling*. Edited by Thomas Keymer and Alice Wakely. London: Penguin, 2005.
Fischer, David Hackett. *Liberty and Freedom*. Oxford: Oxford University Press, 2004.
Fishing and hunting. London: Thomas Bailey, n.d.
Forby, Robert. *The Vocabulary of East Anglia*. 2 vols. London, 1830.
Ford, John. *Prizefighting: The Age of Regency Boximania*. South Brunswick, New Jersey: Great Albion Books, 1971.
Franklin, Benjamin. *Writings*. Edited by J.A. Leo Lemay. New York: Viking Press, 1987.
Fuller, John. *The History of Berwick-upon-Tweed*. Edinburgh, 1799.

Fyffe, Alexander. *The Tragedy of the Royal Martyr, K. Charles I.* 2nd ed. Edinburgh, 1712.

Gardiner, E. Norman. *Athletics in the Ancient World.* Oxford: Oxford University Press, 1930; Devon: Dover, 2002.

Garsault, M. de. *Art du Paumier-Raquetier, et de la Paume.* Paris: chez Saillant and Nyon, chez Desaint, 1767. Translated as *The Art of the Tennis-Racket-Maker and of Tennis.* Privately printed, 1938.

Gau, Colleen. "Stella Blum Grant Report: Physiologic Effects of Wearing Corsets: Studies with Reenactors," *Dress: The Annual Journal of the Costume Society of America* 26 (1999).

The Gentleman's Magazine. London: Bradbury, Evans, 1868–1907.

George, Mary Dorothy, ed. *Catalogue of Prints and Drawings in the British Museum. Division I. Political and Personal Satires*, vol. 5. (1771–1783). London, 1935.

———. *England in Johnson's Day.* Freeport, NY: Books for Libraries Press, 1972. First published 1928.

———. *From Hogarth to Cruikshank: Social Change in Graphic Satire.* New York: Walker, 1967.

———. *London Life in the Eighteenth Century.* New York: Harper, 1964.

———. "Phaetona or Modern Female Taste." In *Catalogue of Political and Personal Satires. Preserved in the British Museum.* Vol. 2. Edited by F.G. Stephens and M.D. George. London: British Museum, 1870–1954.

Gibson, Geoffrey. "Origins of William Tell." *Journal of the Society of Archer-Antiquaries* 18 (1975): 6–8.

Giles, Rev J.A. *History of the Town and Parish of Bampton.* Bampton, 1848.

Gillmeister, Heiner. *Tennis: A Cultural History.* London: Leicester University Press, 1997.

Glover, Stephen. *The History and Gazateer of the County of Derby.* 2 vols. Derby, 1831.

Godfrey, John. *A Treatise on the Useful Science of Defence: Connecting the Small and Back-sword, and Shewing the Affinity between Them: Likewise Endeavouring to Weed the Art of Those Superfluous, Unmeaning Practices Which Over-run It ...: With Some Observations upon Boxing ...* London: T. Gardner, 1747.

Golby, J.M., and A.W. Purdue. *The Civilisation of the Crowd: Popular Culture in England, 1750–1900.* Revised edition. Stroud: Sutton Publishing, 1999.

Grant, M.H. *Chronological History of the Old English Landscape Painters.* Leigh-on-Sea: F. Lewis, 1958.

"Great Windmill Street Area." *Survey of London: volumes 31 and 32: St James Westminster, Part 2* (1963): 41–56. Accessed 22 July 2013. http://www.british-history.ac.uk/report.aspx?compid=41453.

Griffin, Emma. *England's Revelry: A History of Popular Sports and Pastimes, 1660–1830.* Oxford: Oxford University Press for the British Academy, 2005.

———. "Popular Culture in Industrializing England." *Historical Journal* 45, no. 3 (2002): 619–35.

Grosart, Rev. Alexander B. *Occassional Issues of Unique and Very Rare Books in Seventeen Volumes. Vol. 5*. Manchester: C.E. Simms, 1877.

Guttmann, Allen. "English Sports Spectators: The Restoration to the Early Nineteenth Century." *Journal of Sport History* 12, no. 2 (Summer, 1985): 103–25.

Halliburton, Richard. *The Glorious Adventure*. New York: Bobbs-Merill, 1926.

Hansard, George Agar. *Book of Archery*. London: Henry G. Bohn, 1841.

Hanway, Jonas. *A Review of the Proposed Naturalization of the Jews*. London: J. Waugh, 1753. Quoted in Frank Felsenstein, *Anti-Semitic Stereotypes: A Paradigm of Otherness in English Popular Culture, 1660–1830*. Baltimore: Johns Hopkins University Press, 1995.

Hargreaves, John. *Sport, Power and Culture: A Social and Historical Analysis of Popular Sports in Britain*. Cambridge: Polity Press, 1986.

Hargrove, Ely. *Anecdotes of Archery from the Earliest Ages to the Year 1791*. York: for the author, 1792.

Harvey, A.D. *Sex in Georgian England: Attitudes and Prejudices from the 1720s to the 1820s*. New York: St. Martin's, 1994.

Harvey, Adrian. *The Beginnings of a Commercial Sporting Culture in Britain: 1793–1850*. Burlington, VT: Ashgate, 2004.

Haslewood, Joseph. "Anecdotes of Archery: A Thing of Shreds and Patches." MS Osborn d.20. Beinecke Library, Yale University.

Hatcher, John. "Labour, Leisure and Economic Thought before the Nineteenth Century." *Past and Present* 160, no. 1 (1998): 64–115. doi:10.1093/past/160.1.64.

Hazlitt, William. "The Fight." *The New Monthly Magazine*, 1822.

———. "On the Qualifications Necessary to Success in Life." In *The Plain Speaker*, vol. 8 of *The Selected Writings of William Hazlitt*. Edited by Duncan Wu. London: Pickering and Chatto, 1998.

Heath, E.G. *History of Target Archery*. Newton Abbot: David and Charles, 1973.

Henricks, Thomas S. *Disputed Pleasures: Sport and Society in Pre-Industrial England*. New York: Greenwood Press, 1991.

Henslow, J.S. *Suggestions Towards an Enquiry into the Present Condition of the Labouring Population of Suffolk*. Hadleigh, 1844.

Heylin, Peter. "To Mr Rob. Dover on his Pastorall and Wandering Jewe Presented before SR J.W." In *Collected Verses*. London, 1925.

Higgins, David. "Englishness, Effeminacy, and the New Monthly Magazine: Hazlitt's 'the Fight' in Context." *Romanticism: The Journal of Romantic Culture and Criticism* 10, no. 2 (2004): 173–90.

Hill, Jeffrey. *Sport and the Literary Imagination: Essays in History, Literature, and Sport*. Oxford: Peter Lang, 2006.

Hill, Jeffrey, and Jean Williams. "Introduction." *Sport in History* 29, no. 2 (2009): 127–31.

Hird, Ben. *The Antient Scorton Silver Arrow*. Edited by E.G. Heath. London: Society of Archer-Antiquaries, 1972; rpt. PDF e-book, 2002.

History of the Royal Toxophilite Society. Taunton: for the society, 1867.

Holcroft, Thomas. *The Road to Ruin. A comedy. As it is acted at the Theatre Royal, Covent-Garden*. London: printed for J. Debrett, 1792.

Holland, Philemon. *Suetonius, History of Twelve Caesars*. 2 vols. Reprint, New York: AMS Press, 1967. First published 1606.

Hollander, Anne. *Sex and Suits*. New York: Knopf, 1994.

Holme, Randle. *The Academy of Armory*. Chester: Printed for the author, 1688.

Holt, Richard. *Sport and the British: A Modern History*. Oxford: Oxford University Press; New York: Clarendon Press, 1989.

Hone, William. *The sports and pastimes of the people of England; including the rural and domestic recreations, may games, mummeries, shows, processions, pageants and pompous spectacles from the earliest period to the present time*. Edited by Joseph Strutt. London: Tegg, 1845.

Hore, John Philip. *The History of Newmarket, and the Annals of the Turf, with Memoirs and Biographical Notices of the Habitués of Newmarket, and the Notable Turfites, from the Earliest Times to the End of the Seventeenth Century, Volume II*. London: A.H. Baily, 1886.

Hoyle's Games Improved. Revised and corrected by Charles Jones, Esq. London: printed for J. Rivington and J. Wilki St. Paul's Church-Yard, 1775.

Hunt, Leigh. *The Autobiography of Leigh Hunt*. Edited by Edmund Blunden. Reprint, London: Oxford University Press, 1928. First published 1850.

Hunt, Lynn, and Margaret Jacob. "The Affective Revolution in 1790s Britain." *Eighteenth-Century Studies* 34 (2001): 491–521.

Hunter, Michael. *John Aubrey and the Realm of Learning*. London: Duckworth, 1975.

Hutton, Ronald. *The Rise and Fall of Merry England: The Ritual Year, 1400–1700*. Oxford: Oxford University Press, 1994.

Interesting Anecdotes, Memoirs, Allegories, Essays, and Poetical Fragments, Tending to Amuse the Fancy, and Inculcate Morality. By Mr. Addison, vol. 3. London: printed for the author, 1794.

Jamieson, W. Allan. "Archery at Kilwinning and Irvine." *Archer's Register for 1895–96*. Edited by Fred Follett. London: Horace Cox, 1895.

Jenkins, David Clay. "The James Street Theatre at the Old Tennis-Court." *Theatre Notebook* 23 (1969): 143–50.

Johnes, Martin. "Archery, Romance and Elite Culture in England and Wales, *c*. 1780–1840." *History* 89 (2004): 194–208.

Johnson, Anthony W. "Tennis in Early Modern Poetry." In Martin Gill et al. *Language, Learning, Literature. Studies Presented to Håkan Ringbom*. Turku: Åbo Akademi University Press, 2001.

Johnson, Christopher. "'British Championism': Early Pugilism and the Works of Fielding." *The Review of English Studies* 47, no. 187 (1996): 332–57.

Johnson, Samuel, and George Steevens. *Supplement to the edition of Shakespeare's plays published in 1778. Vol. 1: Supplemental observations.* London: C. Bathurst, W. Strahan et al, 1778.

Johnstone, Charles. *Chrysal; or, the Adventures of a Guinea.* London: T. Becket, 1760 (vols. 1 and 2); 1765 (vols. 3 and 4). Edited by Kevin Bourque. 4 vols. in 2. Kansas City: Valancourt Books, 2011.

Jonson, Ben. *Bartholomew Fair.* Edited by E.A. Horsman. Cambridge: Harvard University Press, 1960.

———. "An Epigram to my Jovial Good Friend." In *A New Edition of Annalia Dubrensia.* Edited by Christopher Whitfield. London: Sotheran, 1962.

Kelly, Jason M. "Society of Dilettanti (act. 1732–2003)." In *Oxford Dictionary of National Biography.* Oxford University Press, 2006; online ed., May 2013. Accessed 31 October 2013. http://www.oxforddnb.com/view/theme/92790.

Kench, Tony. "Sir William Wood (1609–91) and the Society of Finsbury Archers." *Worshipful Company of Bowyers.* http://www.bowyers.com/bowyery_finsbury Archers.php.

Kennett, White. *Parochial Antiquities attempted in the History of Ambrosden and Burcester in the Counties of Oxford and Bucks.* 2 vols. Oxford, 1695.

Kilburn, Matthew. "Powlett, Charles, third duke of Bolton (1685–1754)." In *Oxford Dictionary of National Biography.* Oxford: Oxford University Press, 2004. Accessed 3 February 2014. http://www.oxforddnb.com/view/article/21615.

Knight, Stephen. *Robin Hood: A Complete Study of the English Outlaw.* Oxford: Blackwell, 1994.

Kruger, Arnd, and John Marshall Carter. *Ritual and Record: Sports Records and Quantification in Pre-Modern Societies.* Westport, CT: Greenwood Press, 1990.

Kunzle, David. *Fashion and Fetishism: A Social History of Tight Lacing and Other Forms of Body Sculpture in the West.* Totowa: Rowman and Littlefield, 1982.

Lake, Robert J. "Real Tennis and the Civilising Process." *Sport in History* 29, no. 4 (2009): 553–76.

Landry, Donna. *Noble Brutes: How Eastern Horses Transformed English Culture.* Baltimore: Johns Hopkins University Press, 2008.

Latham, William. Collection for a history of archery, toxographia, anecdotes of archery. MS Add.29788–29791. British Library.

Laws of the Toxophilite Society ... Revised and altered in the year MDCCXCI. London: for the society, 1791.

Le Sage, Alain René. *The Adventures of Gil Blas of Santillane. A new translation, by the author of Roderick Random.* London: J. Osborn, 1750.

Leach, Michael. "The Scorton Shoot of 1948: A Recollection." *Journal of the Society of Archer-Antiquaries* 49 (2006): 19–27.

Leeuwen, Thomas A.P. van. *The Springboard in the Pond.* Cambridge: MIT Press, 1998.

Lemire, Beverly. *Dress, Culture and Commerce: The English Clothing Trade before the Factory, 1660–1800.* New York: St. Martin's, 1997.

A Letter to the Rev. George Burder, Occasioned by his Sermon on Lawful Amusements. London, 1805.

Liss, David. *A Conspiracy of Paper: A Novel*. New York: Random House, 2000.

Longman, C.J., and H. Walrond. *Archery*. Badminton Library of Sports and Pastimes. London: Longmans, Green, 1901.

Love, James. *Cricket. An Heroic Poem Illustrated with the Critical Observations of Scriblerus Maximus*. London, 1770.

Lowerson, John. "Fishing." In *Sport in Britain: A Social History*. Edited by Tony Mason. Cambridge: Cambridge University Press, 1989.

Lukin, Robert. *A Treatise on Tennis*. Oxford: Ronaldson Publications, 1991. First published in 1882.

L'Utilité qui provient du jeu de la paume au corps et à l'esprit. Traduict du grec de Galien en François. Paris: impr. de T. Sevestre, 1599.

Luze, Albert de. *A History of the Royal Game of Tennis*. Translated by Richard Hamilton. Kineton: The Roundwood Press, 1979.

Macaulay, Rev. Aulay. *The History and Antiquities of Claybrook*. London, 1791.

Malcolmson, Robert W. *Popular Recreations in English Society 1700–1850*. Cambridge: Cambridge University Press, 1973.

Mandelbaum, Allen. *The Aeneid of Virgil: A Verse Translation*. New York: Bantam Books, 1981. http://www.worldcat.org/title/aeneid-of-virgil-a-verse-translation/oclc/8250495/viewport.

Manevieux, M. de. *Traité sur la connaissance du royal jeu de paume*. Neuchâtel: n.p., 1783.

Manners, Lord John. *A Plea for National Holy Days*. London, [1843?].

Marchand, Leslie A. *Byron: A Biography*. 3 vols. New York: Alfred Knopf, 1957.

Marinière, Denis de la. *La Maison academique, contenant les jeux du picquet, du hoc, du tric-trac, du hoca, de la guerre, de la paulme, du billard, du palle-mail, divers jeux de cartes, qui se joüent en differentes facons ... & autres jeux facetieux & divertissans*. Paris: chez Etienne Loison, 1659.

Marks, Arthur S. "The Statue of King George III in New York and the Iconology of Regicide." *The American Art Journal* 13 (1981): 61–82.

Marshall, Julian. *Annals of Tennis*. London: Horace Cox, 1878.

Maynard Mack, *Alexander Pope: A Life*. New York and London: Norton, 1988. First printed 1985.

McTaggert, Peter. "Some Aspects and Use of Non-Fashionable Stays." *Strata of Society*, *The Annual Volume of the Costume Society* (1973), 20–28.

Mee, Bob. *Bare Fists: The History of Bare-Knuckle Prize-Fighting*. Woodstock, NY: The Overlook Press, 2001.

Melville, Whyte, Kate Coventry Surtee, and the Honourable Crasher. *The Art of Teaching in Sport: Designed as a Prelude to a Set of Toys for Enabling Ladies to Instil the Rudiments of Spelling, Reading, Grammar, and Arithmetic under the idea of Amusements*. London: John Marshall, 1770.

Mendoza, Daniel. *The Memoirs of the Life of Daniel Mendoza*. Edited by Paul David Magriel. London: B.T. Batsford, 1951. First published 1812.

―――. *The modern art of boxing as practised by Mendoza, Humphreys, Ryan, Ward, Wason, Johnson, and other eminent pugilists. To which are added, the six lessons of Mendoza, as published by him, for the use of his scholars; and a full account of his last battle with Humphreys*. London: printed for the author and sold at No. 42, Little Britain, and by all Booksellers and newscarriers in town and country. 1789. *Eighteenth-Century Collections Online*. The text was reprinted in 1790 and 1792.

Montaigne, Michel de. *Essais*. Edited by Jean Balsamo, Michel Magnien and Catherine Magnien-Simonin. Paris: Gallimard, 2007. First published 1789.

Moody, Jane. *Illegitimate Theatre in London, 1770–1840*. Cambridge: Cambridge University Press, 2000.

Moor, Edward. *Suffolk Words and Phrases*. London, 1823.

Morgan, Roger. "A Fifteenth-Century Tennis Court in London." *The International Journal of the History of Sport* 13, no. 3 (1996): 418–31.

―――. *Tennis: The Development of the European Ball Game*. Oxford: Oxford University Press, 1995.

Moseley, Walter. *An Essay on Archery*. Worcester: Hall, 1792.

Muir, Kenneth, ed. *The Oxford Shakespeare: Troilus and Cressida*. Oxford: Oxford University Press, 1982.

Mullan, John, and Christopher Reid, eds. *Eighteenth-Century Popular Culture: A Selection*. Oxford and New York: Oxford University Press, 2000.

Musaeus. *Hero and Leander*. Edited by Thomas Gelzer. Cambridge: Loeb Classical Library, 1975.

Names of the Members of the Toxophilite Society for the Year MDCCXCII. London: for the society, 1792.

Newmarket Racecourse homepage. Accessed 7 January 2014. http://www.newmarketracecourses.co.uk/about-the-home-of-racing/newmarket-history/.

Nichol, Donald W. "Lost Trousers." *The Times Literary Supplement*, 26 July 2013.

―――. *The New Foundling Hospital for Wit*. Facsimile, 6 vols. in 3. London: Pickering and Chatto, 2006. First published 1768–1773, London: John Almon.

Nichols, J., and G. Steevens. *The Genuine Works of William Hogarth*. London, 1808–1817.

North, Sir Thomas. *Plutarch's Lives of the Noble Grecians and Romans*. 7 vols. New York: AMS Press, 1967. First published 1579.

Nussbaum, Felicity A. *Torrid Zones: Maternity, Sexuality, and Empire in Eighteenth-century English Narratives*. Baltimore: Johns Hopkins University Press, 1995.

Nussbaum, Felicity A., and Laura Brown, eds. *The New 18th Century: Theory, Politics, English Literature*. New York: Routledge, 1988.

The Odes of Pindar. Translated and edited by Maurice Bowra. Harmondsworth: Penguin Classics, 1969.

O'Quinn, Daniel. "In the Face of Difference: Molineaux, Crib, and the Violence of the Fancy." In *Race, Romanticism, and the Atlantic*. Edited by Paul Youngquist, 213–35. Surrey: Ashgate, 2013.

Oldfield, Henry G. *Anecdotes of Archery, Ancient and Modern*. London: for the author, 1791.

Oldys, William. *The Life of Sir Walter Ralegh*. London: printed for the booksellers in town and country, 1740.

"The Olympic Games in Antiquity." *The Olympic Museum*. 2nd ed. Lausanne: IOC Museum, 2007. http://www.olympic.org/Documents/Reports/EN/en_report_658.pdf.

Oppé, Adolf Paul. *English Drawings, Stuart and Georgian Periods, in the Collection of His Majesty the King at Windsor Castle*. London: Phaidon, 1950.

Orme, Nicholas. *Early British Swimming 55 BC–AD 1719*. Exeter: Short Run Press, 1983.

Ormerod, George. *The History of the County Palatine and City of Chester*. London, 1819.

Oulton, Walley Chamberlain. *The History of the Theatres of London ... From the Year 1771 to 1795*. Vol. 2. London: Martin and Bain, 1796.

Oxberry, William. *Pancratia, or, a History of Pugilism. Containing a Full Account of Every Battle of Note from the Time of Broughton and Slack, Down to the Present Day*. London: Published and Sold by W. Oxberry, 1812.

Parkyns, Sir Thomas. *The Inn-Play: or Cornish Hugg Wrestler*. London, 1727.

Parr, Susie. *The Story of Swimming*. Stockport: Dewi Lewis Media, 2011.

Paulson, Ronald, ed. *The Analysis of Beauty*. New Haven and London: Yale University Press, 1992.

Penny, Nicholas. *Reynolds*. New York: Abrams, 1986.

Pickering, William, ed. *The Treatyse of Fysshynge Wyth An Angle, Attributed to Dame Juliana Berners reprinted from The Book of St Albans 1496*. London: John Baskerville, 1827.

Pilkington, James. *A View of the Present State of Derbyshire*. 2 vols. London, 1789.

Pindar. *The Pythian Odes*. Translated by H.T. Wade-Gery. and C.M. Bowra. London: The Nonesuch Press, 1928.

Pitcher, Edward W.R. *The Magazine Sources for Interesting Anecdotes, Memoirs, Allegories, Essays, and Poetical Fragments ... By Mr. Addison*. Lewiston: The Edwin Mellen Press, 2004.

Pointon, Marcia. *Strategies of Showing: Women, Possessions and Representation in English Visual Culture 1665–1800*. Oxford: Clarendon, 1997.

Polley, Martin. *The British Olympics: Britain's Olympic Heritage 1612–2012*. London: English Heritage, 2012.

Pope, Alexander. *An Essay on Criticism*. London: Printed for W. Lewis, 1711.

Porter, Roy. *English Society in the Eighteenth Century*. Harmondsworth: Penguin, 1982.

Potter, Jeremy. *Tennis and Oxford*. Oxford: Oxford Unicorn Press, 1994.

Prestzler, Maria. *Pausanias: Travel Writing in Ancient Greece*. London: Duckworth, 2007.

"Proclamation 'Enforcing Statues on Archery, Handguns, Unlawful Games, Reforming High Grain Prices'" (4 December 1528). In *Tudor Royal*

Proclamations. Edited by Paul L. Hughes and James F. Larkin. New Haven and London: Yale University Press, 1964.

Pseudo-Bunyan. *Meditations on the Several Ages of Man's Life: Representing, the Vanity of it, from his Cradle to his Grave*. London: printed for J. Blare, 1700–1701.

The Punishing Blow. By Randy Cohen. Clurman Theater, Theater Row, New York City, 22 August 2010.

Purchas, Anne. "Revett, Nicholas (1721–1804)." In *Oxford Dictionary of National Biography*. Oxford University Press, 2004; online ed., May 2006. Accessed 31 October 2013. http://www.oxforddnb.com/view/article/23395.

Raikes, George Alfred. *History of the Honourable Artillery Company*. 2 vols. London: Bentley, 1878.

Records of the Honourable Society of Lincoln's Inn: Volume One: Admissions from A.D. 1420 to 1799. London: Lincoln's Inn, 1896.

Records of the Woodmen of Arden from 1785 with Roll of Members of the Society. Edited by William Kirkpatrick Riland Bedford. Edinburgh: privately printed, 1885.

Redgrave, Richard. *A Dictionary of Artists of the English School: with critical notices of their works, and an account of the progress of art in England*. London: George Bell, 1878.

Redhead, Steve. *Post-Fandom and the Millennial Blues: The Transformation of Soccer Culture*. London: Routledge, 1997.

Regulations of the Society of Royal British Bowmen. Wrexham: for the society, 1787.

Reid, Heather, and Christos Evangeliou. "Ancient Hellenic Ideals and the Modern Olympic Games." In *Olympic Studies Reader: Multidisciplinary and Multicultural Research Guide. Vol. 1*. Edited by Hai Ren et al. Beijing: Beijing Sport University, 2009.

Rendell, Jane. *The Pursuit of Pleasure: Gender, Space, and Architecture in Regency London*. London: Continuum, 2002.

Rhodes, Ernest L. "Me thinks this stage shews like a Tennis Court." *Renaissance Papers* (1968): 21–8.

Ribeiro, Aileen. *The Dress Worn at Masquerades in England, 1730 to 1790 and Its Relation to Fancy Dress in Portraiture*. New York and London: Garland, 1984.

Richardson, Samuel. *Letters Written to and for Particular Friends on the most important Occasions*. London, 1741.

———. *Pamela*. Edited by Thomas Keymer and Alice Wakely. Oxford: Oxford University Press, 2001.

Rizzo, Betty. "Equivocations of Gender and Rank: Eighteenth-Century Sporting Women." *Eighteenth-Century Life* 26, no. 1 (2002): 70–93.

Roberts, Thomas. *The English Bowman; or Tracts on Archery*. London: for the author, 1801.

Rogers, Pat. "Burney, Frances (1752–1840)." In *Oxford Dictionary of National Biography*. Oxford University Press, 2004; online ed., September 2013. Accessed 31 October 2013. http://www.oxforddnb.com/view/article/603.

Rolls, Philip. "A Brief History of the Society of Archers." *The Society of Archers and the Antient Silver Arrow*. Accessed 15 February 2015. http://www.scortonarrow.com /history/history1.htm.

Ross, Angus, and David Woolley, eds. *Jonathan Swift*. Oxford: Oxford University Press, 1984.

Roth, Marty. "'Anacreon' and Drink Poetry; or, the Art of Feeling Very Very Good." *Texas Studies in Literature and Language* 42, no. 3 (2000): 314–45.

Rules and Orders of the Toxophilite Society ... Together with the By-Laws of the Society. London, 1784.

Rules and Regulations of the Hainault Foresters. London: for the society, 1789.

Rules of the Society of Royal Kentish Bowmen. London: for the society, 1789.

Sainsbury, John. "Wilkes and Libertinism," *Studies in Eighteenth-Century Culture* 26 (1998): 151–74.

The St. James's Chronicle, or The British Evening-Post. London: Printed by Henry Baldwin, at the Britannia printing-office, White-Friars, Fleet-Street, where advertisements are taken in, and letters to the author received, 1761–1800.

Sauer, K.C. *Allegemeines Künstlerlexikon; Die Bildenden Künstler aller Zeiten und Volker*. Munich and Leipzig: Sauer, 1992–2000.

Sawyer, Tom. *Noble Art: An Artistic & Literary Celebration of the Old English Prize-Ring*. North Sydney, Australia: Allen and Unwin, 1989.

Scaino, Antonio. *Scaino on Tennis*. Translated by W.W. Kershaw. London: Strangeways Press, 1951.

Schechter, Ronald, and Liz Clarke. *Mendoza the Jew: Boxing, Manliness, and Nationalism, A Graphic History*. New York: Oxford University Press, 2014.

Schleiner, Winfried. "We Who Are All Players:" Constructing Early Modern Tennis." *Aethlon* 22, no. 1 (Fall 2004): 15–31.

Scrivener, Michael. "British-Jewish Writing of the Romantic Era and the Problem of Modernity: The Example of David Levi." In *British Romanticism and the Jews*. Edited by Sheila A. Spector. New York: Palgrave, 2002.

Semenza, Gregory M. Colon. *Sport, Politics, and Literature in the English Renaissance*. Newark: University of Delaware Press, 2003.

———. "Sport, War, and Contest in Shakespeare's *Henry VI*." *Renaissance Quarterly* 54 (2001): 1251–1272.

The Servants Calling: With Some Advice to the Apprentice. London, 1725.

Shakespeare, William. *Henry V*. Edited by T.W. Craik. London: Routledge, 1995.

———. *King Henry VI Part 3*. Edited by John D. Cox and Eric Rasmussen. London: Bloomsbury Arden Shakespeare, 2001.

Shaw, Stebbing. *The History and Antiquities of Staffordshire*. 2 vols. London, 1798–1801.

Shipley, Stan. "Boxing." In *Sport in Britain: A Social History*. Edited by Tony Mason, 78–115. Cambridge: Cambridge University Press, 1989.

Sloan, Kim. "A Cozens Album in the National Library of Wales, Aberystwyth." *Walpole Society* 1, no. 7 (1993–1994): 101.
Smith, Adam. *An Inquiry into the Nature and Causes of the Wealth of Nations*. Vol. 2. Edited by Edwin Cannan. London: Methuen, 1961.
Smollett, Tobias. *The Adventures of Roderick Random*. Introduction and notes by James G. Basker, Paul-Gabriel Boucé, Nicole A. Seary. Edited by OM Brack, Jr. Athens and London: University of Georgia Press, 2012. First published in 1746.
―――. *The Expedition of Humphry Clinker*. Edited by Lewis M. Knapp. Oxford, 1966.
―――. *The Expedition of Humphrey Clinker*. Edited by André Parreaux. New York: Houghton Mifflin, 1968.
Soar, Hugh D.H. *Romance of Archery: A Social History of the Longbow*. Yardley, PA: Westholme, 2008.
Southey, Robert. *Letters from England*. London, 1807.
Sprawson, Charles. *Haunts of the Black Masseur: The Swimmer as Hero*. Minneapolis: University of Minnesota Press, 2000, 1992.
"Sport." In *Oxford English Dictionary Online*. Accessed 1 October 2013. http://www.oed.com /viewdictionaryentry/Entry/187478.
"Sporting Girl or Woman." In *Oxford English Dictionary Online*. Accessed 1 March 2012. http://www.oed.com/view/Entry/187490.
The Sporting Magazine: Or, Monthly Calendar of the Transactions of the Turf, the Chase, and the Temples devoted to the Fickle Goddess. London: printed for the proprietors, and sold by J. Wheble, no. 23, Warwick Lane, near St. Paul's; by the booksellers at Newmarket; and in every principal town in the Kingdom, [1792]–1870.
Staveley, Thomas. *The History of the Churches in England*. London, 1773.
Steele, Richard. "No. 12, From Thursday, May 5, to Saturday, May 7, 1709. May 5." *The Tatler, Volume 1, 1899*. Edited by George A. Aitken. Teddington, Middlesex: The Echo Library, 2006. http://books.google.com//books?id=R--2AAAAIAAJ&dq=No.%2012%2C%20From%20Thursday%2C%20May%205%2C%20to%20Saturday%2C%20May%207%2C%201709&pg=PA106#v=onepage&q&f=false. (NewYork: Hadley & Mathews, London: Duckworth & Co., 1899).
Stephen, James Kenneth. "Parker's Piece, May 19, 1891," *Cambridge Review* (May 1891).
Sterne, Laurence. *The Life and Opinions of Tristram Shandy, Gentleman*. Edited by Ian Campbell Ross. Oxford: Oxford University Press, 1983.
Storch, R.D., ed. *Popular Culture and Custom in Nineteenth-Century England*. London: Croom Helm, 1982.
Stot, Joseph. *A Sequel to the Friendly Advice to the Poor of Manchester*. Manchester, 1756.
Strutt, Joseph. *The sports and pastimes of the people of England; including the rural and domestic recreations, may games, mummeries, shows, processions,*

pageants and pompous spectacles from the earliest period to the present time. London: Tegg, 1810.
Stukeley, William. *Itinerarium Curiosum.* London. 1724.
Styan, J.L. *The English Stage. A History of Drama and Performance.* Cambridge: Cambridge University Press, 1996.
Swift, Jonathan. *The Complete Poems.* Edited by Pat Rogers. Harmondsworth: Penguin, 1983.
———. *Jonathan Swift: The Essential Writings.* Edited by Claude Rawson and Ian Higgins. New York: Norton, 2010.
———. *Gulliver's Travels.* Introduced by Jeanette Winterson. Oxford: Oxford University Press, 1999.
———. *The Poems of Jonathan Swift.* 2 vols. Edited by William Ernst Browning. London: Bell, 1910.
Thelwall, John. *The Peripatetic.* Edited by Judith Thompson. Detroit: Wayne State University Press, 2001.
Thomas, Ralph. *Swimming: With Lists of Books.* London: Sampson Low, 1904.
Thompson, E.P. *Customs in Common.* London: Penguin, 1991.
———. *The Making of the English Working Class.* New York: Vintage Books, 1966.
Throsby, John. *The History and Antiquities of the Ancient Town of Leicester.* London, 1791.
Timmers, Margaret. *A Century of Olympic Posters.* London: V&A Publishing, 2012.
Tranter, Neil. *Sport, Economy and Society in Britain 1750–1914.* Cambridge: Cambridge University Press, 1998.
Troost, Linda. "Diana's Votaries; or, The Fair Toxophilites." *East-Central Intelligencer* 10, no. 1 (1996): 9–15.
———. "Robin Hood Musicals in Eighteenth-Century London." In *Robin Hood in Popular Culture: Violence, Transgression, and Justice.* Edited by Thomas Hahn. Cambridge: Brewer, 2000.
Trowsdale, T. Broadbent. "Glimpses of olden England." *The Warwick and Warwickshire Advertiser & Leamington Gazette,* 29 July 1882.
Troyer, Howard William. *Ned Ward of Grub Street.* London: Frank Cass, 1968.
A True Briton, Strictures on the Engagement of Madame Catalani ... and on the Italian Opera. London: Cox and Baylis, 1809.
Turner, J.G. "The Properties of Libertinism." In *Unauthorized Sexual Behavior during the Enlightenment,* special issue of *Eighteenth Century Life,* n.s., 9, no. 3 (1985): 75–88.
Tyerman, Christopher. *A History of Harrow School, 1324–1991.* Oxford: Oxford University Press, 2000.
Tyrrel, John. *Running Racing: The Jockey Club Years Since 1750.* London: Quiller Press, 1997.
Underdown, David. *Revel, Riot, and Rebellion: Popular Politics and Culture in England, 1603–1660.* Oxford: Oxford University Press, 1985.

Vyvyan, E.R., ed. *Cotswold Games: Annalia Dubrensia*. London: Tabard Press, 1970.

Walbancke, Matthew. *Annalia Dubrensia 1636*. Edited by Bent Juel-Jensen. Yorkshire: first edition facsimile reprint, 1973.

Wall, Alexander J. *The Equestrian Statue of George III and the Pedestrian Statue of William Pitt: Erected in the City of New York*. New York Historical Society, 1770.

Walton, Izaak. *The Art of Angling*. Edited by Marjorie Swann. Oxford: Oxford University Press, 2014. First published in 1676.

Walton, Izaak, and Charles Cotton. *The Compleat Angler Part 1 and 2*. Edited by John Buchan. Oxford: Oxford University Press, 1935.

Ward, Edward. *A Compleat and Humorous Account of All the Remarkable Clubs and Societies in the Cities of London and Westminster* ... London: J. Wren, 1756.

———. *The History of the London CLUBS, or, the Citizens Pastime. Particularly, the Lying Club, the Beggars Club, the Yorkshire Club, the Broken Shopkeepers Club, the Thieves Club, the Basket Womans Club. With a Sermon Preach'd to a Gang of High-way-Men. Part I*. London: printed for J. Bagnall, near Fleetstreet, 1709.

———. *The Second Part, of the London Clubs; Containing, the No-Nose Club, the Beaus Club, the Farting Club, the Sodomites, or Mollies Club. The Quacks* ... London: J. Dutton [1709?].

———. *The Secret History of the Calves-Head Club: or, the Republican Unmask'd* ... London: B. Bragge, 1709.

———. *The Secret History of Clubs: Particularly the Kit-Cat, Beef-Stake, Vertuosos, Quacks, Knights of the Golden-Fleece, Florists, Beaus, &c.* London, 1709.

Waring, Jr, Thomas. *A Treatise on Archery; or The Art of Shooting with the English Bow* (1814). 4th ed. London: for the author, "sold only by him at his Archery," 1822.

Weatherill, Lorna. "A Possession of One's Own: Women and Consumer Behavior in England, 1600–1740." *Journal of British Studies* 15 (1986): 150–55.

Webster, John. "The Duchess of Malfi." In *The Works of John Webster*. Edited by David Gunby, David Carnegie, Antony Hammon, and Doreen DelVecchio. Cambridge: Cambridge University Press, 1995.

West, Michael. "Spenser, Everard Digby, and the Renaissance Art of Swimming." *Renaissance Quarterly* 26 (1973): 11–22.

Whale, John. "Daniel Mendoza's Contests of Identity: Masculinity, Ethnicity and Nation in Georgian Prize-fighting." *Romanticism* 14, no. 3 (December 2008): 259–71.

Wheeler, Roxann. *The Complexion of Race: Categories of Difference in Eighteenth Century British Culture*. Philadelphia: University of Pennsylvania Press, 2000.

"When for Air I take my Mare." In *Thomas D'Urfey's Pills to Purge Melancholy: Lewd Songs and Low Ballads from the 18th Century*. Performed by the City Waits. Wotton-under-Edge, Gloucestershire: Saydisc, 1990.

Whitaker, Rev John. *The History of Manchester*. 2 vols. London, 1771–1775.

Whitfield, Christopher. *A History of Chipping Camden and Captain Robert Dover's Olympick Games*. Windsor: Shakespeare Head Press, 1958.

———. *A New Edition of Annalia Dubrensia*. London: Sotheran, 1962.

William Nelson Letter Book, 1766–1775. Manuscript Collection, Library of Virginia, Richmond.

"William Prynne, from *Histrio-Mastix: The Player's Scourge; or, Actor's Tragedy*." *The Norton Anthology of English Literature, Norton Topics Online*, "The Early Seventeenth Century: Topics: Civil Wars of Ideas: Texts and Contexts." Accessed 22 July 2012. http://www.wwnorton.com/college/english/nael/17century/topic_3/prynne.htm.

Williams, Iolo. *Early English Watercolours*. Bath: Kingsmead Reps., 1970.

Williams, Jean. "The Curious Mystery of the Cotswold 'Olimpick' Games: Did Shakespeare Know Dover … and Does it Matter?" *Sport in History* 29, no. 2 (2009): 150–70.

Wingfield, Mary Ann. *Sport and the Artist*. London: Antique Collectors Club, 1988.

Wodehouse, P.G. *Love Among the Chickens*. London: Everyman, 2011. First published 1906, London.

Wolf-Dieter, Heilmeyer, Nikolaos Kaltsas, Hans-Joachim Gehrke, Georgia E Hatzi, and Susanne Bocher, eds. *Mythos Olympia-Kult und Spiele*. Munich: Prestel-Verlag, 2012.

Wood, Anthony. *The Life and Times of Anthony Wood, Antiquary, of Oxford, 1632–1695, described by Himself*. Edited by Andrew Clark. Vol. 19. Oxford: Printed for the Oxford Historical Society, 1891.

Wroth, W.W. "Chandler, Richard (bap. 1737, d. 1810)," Rev. R.D.E. Eagles. In *Oxford Dictionary of National Biography*. Oxford University Press, 2004; online ed., May 2006. Accessed 31 October 2013. http://www.oxforddnb.com/view/article/5108.

Index

Page numbers in **bold** type indicate illustrations.

Act to Restrain and Prevent the Excessive Increase of Horse Races, An 133
Actress at her Toilet, or Miss Brazen just Breecht, An (Collet), *see* Collet, John
Addison, Joseph, concern about staged executions 7
Adventures of Roderick Random, The, see Smollett, Tobias
advertising/adverts
    boxing 157, 158
    Cotswold games 42
    horse racing 143–4
    mass marketing and spread of sport culture 1–2
    mass marketing of football (soccer) 50
African-Americans, *see* Molineaux, Tom; race and national identity
Almon, John
    charges against political horse fanatics 144
    publisher of *New Foundling Hospital* 141
"Amazon, The" (anonymous poem) 46
Anacreon cited by Mendoza 161–2
"Analogy between Legislation and Horse racing" 142–3
ancients vs. moderns
    context for Byron's swim 186–7
    Oxberry's play on boxing champions 126–7
    Swift's *Battle of the Books* 126–7
Anecdotes of Archery, Ancient and Modern, see Oldfield, Henry
Anecdotes of Archery, From the Earliest Ages to 1791, see Hargrove, Ely
Angelo, Henry 180
angling 38–40

Annalia Dubrensia (poems on Dover's Cotswold games) 43–4
Annals of Gaming 94
Annals of Tennis, see Marshall, Julian
anti-Semitism, *see* Jews/Judaism
antiheroic tradition, Byron's poem in 179
Antiquitates Vulgares (Bourne), *see* Bourne, Henry
Apollo, depiction as horseman 126
apple shooting plot theme 118–19
Arcadia (Sidney), *see* Sidney, Sir Philip
archery
    antiquarianism and history 13, 107, 119–21
    clubs and societies 105–11, 117–18
    Henry VIII blamed decay on tennis and other games 85
    portrayed in theater 118–19
    women's participation in 111–16
Ariosto, Ludovico, on swimming in *Orlando Furioso* 183
Art du Paumier-Raquetier, et de la Paume, see Garsault, François de
Art of Boxing, The (Mendoza), *see* Mendoza, Daniel
Ascham, new edition of *Toxophilus* published 1788 107, 119, 120
Aspin, Jehoshaphat (pseud.), on May customs 27
athletics, *see* sport
Aubrey, John, interest in popular custom 25

Baer, Marc, on anti-semitism 171, 177n98
Baines, Edward, on Leeds Races 28–9
Banks, Sophia, collection of archery ephemera 116–17, 122n26, 122n27
Barcellon, Joseph ("English Barcellon") 84
Barcellon, Pierre, *Règles et principes de la Paume* 87
Barrington, Daines, "Observations on the Practice of Archery in England" 119

Bartholomew Fair, see Jonson, Ben
Bath, Earl of (William Pulteney), *World* column on language of horse racing 130
Bath, or, The Western Lass, The (D'Urfey), see D'Urfey, Thomas
bathing-machines 179, 181
Bathos, The (Hogarth), see Hogarth, William
Battle for the Breeches, The (Newton), see Newton, Richard
Battle of the Books (Swift), see Swift, Jonathan
Baxter, Richard, moralist warning against sports 4, 23, 32n24
Bell's Weekly Messenger, first newspaper with sporting leanings 10
Berkshire parsons and rectors ignorant of popular customs 25–6, 30
Berners, Dame Juliana, *Treatyse of Fysshynge wyth an Angle* 38–40
Betterton, Thomas, restoration of Tennis Court in Lincoln Inn Fields 97
betting, *see* gambling
Bickerstaff, Isaac, *see* Steele, Richard
billiards, relationship with tennis 83, 95
Birch, Thomas, death after fall from horse 134
Black, Robert, *The Jockey Club and its Founders in Three Periods* 135–6
Blackstone, Bernard, on underwater world as exempt from time and space 186
Blackstone's *Commentaries on the Laws of England*, on taking game 71
blood sports
  daily adverts for 2
  and England's reputation 5–9
  popular along with boxing and other forms of violence 45
Blount, Thomas 25
Boarding House, or Five Hours at Brighton, The (Oxberry), see Oxberry, William
Bolton, 3d Duke of (Charles Powlet/Paulet) 128
Book of Sports (James I), see James I (king)
Borlase, William, arguments in favor of parish feasts 21
Boswell, James, *The Cub at Newmarket* 141

Bourgelat, Claude, founder of first-ever veterinary college 135
Bourne, Henry
  Antiquitates Vulgares devoted to popular culture 25
  on lawful vs. sinful popular traditions 22–3
Bowles, Carrington, publisher of Collet 68
Bowman's Glory or Archery Revived, The (Wood), see Wood, Sir William
Bowmen of the Wye 117
Bowstead, John, on recreation for laborers 28
"To box, or not to box …" 163
boxing
  as allegory for political debates 5
  attendees at Figg-Sutton match 2–3
  eighteenth-century history 157–60
  financial support by Parkyns 21
  Mendoza's popularity 153–7
  objectionable due to excesses of large crowds 8, 169
  relationship with theater 156, 167–72
  role in shaping English attitudes and nationalism 13, 160–67
  rules 174n27
"Boxing We Will Go, A" 164, 166–7
Bracken, Henry, supplier of horseshoes 135
Bradford, Thomas, collector of Collet's works 68
Brailsford, Dennis
  on boxing 157, 158, 169
  on defining sport 45
  on sports press coverage 10
breeches worn by women 71–3, 75–7
Brereton, Major (William?), blackballed by Jockey Club 144
Bride of Abydos (Byron), see Byron, Lord
British Triple Crown 147n15
Brockman Family, The (Haytley), see Haytley, Edward
Brome, Richard, reference to Dover's Cotswold games 43
Brooke, Rupert, on swimming in *The Old Vicarage, Grantchester* 184
Broughton Archers 107
Broughton, Jack 157–9, 160
Brown, Laura, *see New 18th Century: Theory, Politics, English Literature, The*

Budgell, Eustace, on love and marriage as natural effects of feasts 21
Bunbury, Sarah, cricket playing and her reputation 62–3
Burder, George, arguments in *Lawful Amusements* refuted by anonymous pamphlet 30
Burke, Edmund, *Reflections on the Revolution in France* 170
Burke, Peter, on gulf between elite and popular culture 26
Burney, Fanny, on athletic activities at British "Olympic" events 47
Burney, Frances, unimpressed by archers' skills 108
Burns, Robert, *Tam O-Shanter* one of greatest literary chase scenes 134
Butcher Duke, *see* Cumberland, Duke of (William Augustus)
Bute, 3rd Earl of (John Stuart) 142
Byron, Lord
    letters
        to Elizabeth Bridget Pigot 180–81, 182
        to Francis Hodgson 179, 186, 190–91
        to John Murray 185, 188
    swimming 13, 179–93
    works
        Bride of Abydos 189–90
        Detached Thoughts 180
        Hours of Idleness 192n7
        The Island 186
        Ravenna Journal 185, 190
        The Two Foscari 185–6
        "Written after Swimming from Sestos to Abydos" (Byron) 179, 186–7, 189

Canakkle Rotary Club, events commemorating Byron's swim 187–8
Cannock Chase joint archery meeting 114
Canonical Beau, or Mars in the Dumps, The (Collet), *see* Collet, John
caricatures produced by high-ranking ladies 68
Castiglione, Baldassare, *Book of the Courtier* 182
Castle, Terry, on cross-dressing 71

Catholicism, emancipation opposed by Thornton 156
"In celebration of the yearley Preserver of the Games at Cotswald" 44
censorship, *see* Licensing Act controlling theaters
Cervantes, Miguel de, *see Rosinante (Don Quixote's* horse)
Chandler, Richard, Olympic legacy and 36–7, 47–8, 50
Charles I (king)
    as keen tennis player 85
    reissue of *Book of Sports* 4, 40
Charles II (king)
    enjoyment of sports 40–41
    popular rejoicing upon his Restoration 20
    renovation of tennis court at Hampton Court 85
    support for science, arts and sport 1, 5
Chaucer, Geoffrey, valued almost as much as Edward III's horse 128
cheating, *see* gambling; race-fixing
Cheevers, John, "The Fourth Alarm" 145
Chelsea Murder Case of 1771 155
Christian Directory (Baxter), *see* Baxter, Richard
Christophe, Henri, *see* Haitian Revolution
Chrysal (Johnstone), *see* Johnstone, Charles
Chudleigh, Elizabeth, comments on Iphigenia costume at masquerade 71–2
Cibber, Colly 168
City Chanters, The (Collet), *see* Collet, John
Clarkson, Christopher, on including customs in local histories 26
classical education, English translations of Greek and Roman writers 36–7
classical ideals and sports training 8–9
Clayton, John, *Friendly Advice to the Poor* 24
Cleland, John, *Memoirs of a Woman of Pleasure (Fanny Hill)* 46, 128–9
clothing
    archery uniforms 108, 109–12, 117–18
    "muffles" or boxing gloves 158
    sword ceased to be fashionable dress accessory 174n23

for women's sports 9–10, 13, 55–80, 111–16
clubs, fictitious and real 137; *see also* archery
Collet, John
   prints of women in sports 13, 55–80
   works
      An Actress at her Toilet, or Miss Brazen just Breecht 72, **73**
      An Actress in her Dressing Room, or Miss Brazen Just Breecht 68
      The Canonical Beau, or Mars in the Dumps 69–70
      The City Chanters clearly pro-Wilkes 72
      The Country Vicar going to Dine with the Squire 69
      The Discovery 55–6
      Essay on Women, allusion to obscene poem by Wilkes 72
      The Female Bruisers 64, 65
      The *Female Fox Hunter* 56–7, **58**
      The Female Orators 56
      The Guards of the Night Defeated 74–5
      The Joys of the Chase, or The Rising Woman and Falling Man 56–7, 65
      Miss Tipapin Going for All Nine 60, **62**
      Miss Wicket and Miss Trigger 63–4
      Modern Love (Courtship, Elopement, Honeymoon, Discordant Matrimony) 64, **66–7**
      A Morning Frolic, or the Transmutation of Sexes 75, **76**
      An Officer in the Light Infantry driven by his Lady to Cox Heath 60, **61**, 65
      The Quiet Husband 69–70
      The Refusal 56
      The Rival Milliners 55, **56**, 75
      The Shop-Lifter Detected 56, **57**
      Troops Fording a Brook 56
      View of Calais; taken from the side of the canal leading from thence to St. Omer's 65
Colley, Linda, on anxiety over women wearing pseudo-masculine dress 75, 77

Compleat Angler, The (Walton), *see* Walton, Izaac
Cone, Carl, on sports press coverage 10
conflicts, tennis court as place of enactment of 84
Congreve, William, *Love for Love*, tennis associations 97
Constable, Philip, transfer of trophies to Toxophilites 107
Cook, Theodore, letter to Sir Sidney Lee on Shakespeare 41
Cornelys, Theresa, establishment of female archery society 113
Cotswold Olympick Games 42–4, 49
Country Vicar going to Dine with the Squire, The (Collet), *see* Collet, John
courtiers, swimming a pastime recommended for 182
Cregan-Reid, Vybarr, on Byron's swimming 184
Crespigny, Mrs., hostess of archery parties 112, 113
Cribb, Tom 164, 165–6
cricket
   changing attitudes toward women players 62–3
   compared to tennis 88, 90
   as propagating spirt of idleness 24
   women players 9–10
cross-dressing 71, 75, **76**
Cruikshank, George
   boxing illustrations 165, 168
   Killing no murder **172**
Cub at Newmarket, The, see Boswell, James
cultural primitivism and medievalism, revival of interest 120
Cumberland, Duke of (William Augustus) 157–9, 160
Cumberland, Richard, *The Jew* 167
Cunliffe, Sir Foster 110
Cunningham, Hugh, on popular sports under attack 19

d'Abrantes, Duke (General Junot), lauding moral value of boxing 167
Daily Advertiser
   Broughton's boxing advertisement 158
   reference to Jockey Club 136

Daily Journal, The
   adverts for blood sports 2
   reference to Jockey Club 136
   warned against bellicose sports 7
Daily Post, references to Jockey Club 136
damage and destruction to site of Olympia 36
Dardanelles, *see* Hellespont
Darlington Archers 106
Davenant, William
   published poem on Cotswold games 44
   theater company's use of Lisle's Tennis Court 95, 97
Dawes, William
   friendship with Collet 64–5
   The Hen Peckt Husband 65
De Arte Natandi (Digby), *see* Digby, Everard
Deakin, Roger, on ruining of Byron's Pool 184
Declaration of Sports, *see* James I (king), *Book of Sports*
Defoe, Daniel, on his day at the Newmarket races 131
Dekker, Thomas, *Lust's Dominion* likens stage to tennis court 95
Detached Thoughts (Byron), *see* Byron, Lord
Deucher, Stephen, suggestion of lesbian relationship between Misses Wicket and Trigger 63–4
Devis, Arthur, *John, Anne and William Orde* (portrait) 64
Devonshire, Duchess of, wearing of modified riding habit 57
"Diana costume" 71
Diary or Woodfall's Register 114, 116
Dibdin, Charles, *Robin Hood*, play and songs about archery 117, 119
Digby, Everard, *De Arte Natandi* 183–4
Discovery, The (Collet), *see* Collet, John
disport 3, 14, 45
divorce, freedom of women's fashion as cause of 71
Dorset, Duke of, 1803 letter to *Sporting Magazine* 10
Dover, John, *The Roman Generals, or the Distressed Ladies* 43
Dover, Robert, and Cotswold Olympick Games 41–4

Dover, Thomas (Quicksilver Doctor) 43–4
Drama Brought to the Test of Scripture, and Found Wanting, The 30
Draughtsman's Assistant; or, Drawing Made Easy … (Sayer), *see* Sayer, Robert
drink poetry and culture 162, 175n53
Dryden, John 7, 168
Duchess of Malfi, The, *see* Webster, John
Dudley, Henry Bate, *The Woodman* 119–20
dueling, staged fights as alternative to 157
Dunciad, The (Pope), *see* Pope, Alexander
Dunkin, John, on Whitsun ales 27
D'Urfey, Thomas
   The Bath, or, The Western Lass 139
   "When for Air I take my Mare" 130

Easter celebrations 27
Edinburgh Review, response to evangelical sermon 30
education, sport as part of children's development 45
Edward I (king), strategy against Jews 171
Edwards, Edward, on lack of moral purpose in Collet's humor 64
Egan, Pierce
   on advertising boxing matches 157
   on Bob Gregson 176n70
   on "followers of prizefighting" 158
   Life in London 48
   on Mendoza 156, 160, 167
   on Molineaux 164–5
   on spirit of boxing's revival 159
   on theater as natural parallel to boxing 168–9
elites, *see* recreation; social class
Eloge de la paume (Bajot, M.) 90
Elyot, Sir Thomas, on Caesar and swimming 183
Encyclopedia Britannica, articles related to horses 135
Endelman, Todd, on Chelsea Murder Case of 1771 155
English Bowman; or Tracts on Archery, The (Roberts), *see* Roberts, Thomas
English Chronicle or Universal Evening Post, The, on archery 110
Epinician Odes 37

Epitoma Rei Militaris (Vegetius), *see* Vegetius
Essay of Dramatic Poetry (Dryden), *see* Dryden, John
Essay on Criticism, *see* Pope, Alexander
Essay on Women (Collet), *see* Collet, John
ethics, *see* morality
Evans, Nicholas, *The Horse Whisperer*, book and film 145
Evelyn, John 5

Fagg, Sir R., in Defoe's description 132
Fanny Hill (Cleland), *see* Cleland, John
Farey, John, on wakes in Derbyshire 28
Farriery Improved 135
fatalities from riding horses 134–5
Fawkes, Isaac, and Fawkes's Theatre 97
Female Bruisers, The (Collet), *see* Collet, John
Female Connoiseur [sic], *The* 68
Female Fox Hunter, The, *see* Collet, John
Female Orators, The (Collet), *see* Collet, John
Festival of Britain 42, 49
Field, The (newspaper) 41, 48
Fielding, Henry
  on loss of time and neglect of business 24
  Tom Jones 130, 156
  Tom Jones cited by Mendoza 162
Fielding, Sir John, prosecuted Chelsea Murder Case 155
Figg, James 2–3, 157–8, 165, 168
Finsbury Archers, first revival of archery 105–6, 107
Fisher, Catherine Maria (Kitty), poem and print on courtesan's fall from horse 134–5
fishing, *see* angling
Fitzroy, August Henry, *see* Grafton, 3d Duke of (August Henry Fitzroy)
"fives" or "hand-tennis" 84–5
football
  literary treatment and marketability of soccer 50
  matches as form of social regulation 4–5
Forbet l'Aisné, *L'Utilité qui provient du Jeu de Paume au corps et à l'esprit* 86–7

Forster, Richard, brief contribution to Berkshire questionnaire 26
Four Stages of Cruelty (Hogarth), *see* Hogarth, William
"Fourth Alarm, The," *see* Cheevers, John
Frampton, Tregonwell, loss when race-fixing backfired 132–3
France; *see also* tennis
  Burke's *Reflections on the Revolution in France* 170
  Mendoza and Molineaux both connected to French Revolution 166–7
  swimming contributing to battlefield success 192n18
  Tennis Court Oath 93
  war transferred to war at Covent Garden 171–2
Franklin, Benjamin, references to swimming 184
Free Society of Artists, exhibits of Collet's works 56, 64, 65, 68, 69
Friendly Advice to the Poor (Clayton), *see* Clayton, John

Galen, tennis as most beneficial game for health 84, 86, 88
gambling
  addiction associated with card games 133
  connection with horse racing 131–3, 137, 143–5
  tennis as opportunity for betting and cheating 93–5
game laws 70–71
garlands (Robin Hood anthologies) 118, 119
Garsault, François de, *Art du Paumier-Raquetier, et de la Paume* 87–8, **89**
genius of Byron, aquatic and poetic 191
genre, theatrical 169–71
Gentleman's Compleat Jockey, The 135
Gentleman's Magazine
  on Collet as worthy successor to Hogarth 65, 68
  on cricket propagating spirit of idleness 24
  metaphor between horse breeding and cultural miscegenation 8
  on provocative quality of women in military dress 71

on reforming rather than suppressing wakes 22
writers careful in expressing reservations on wakes and games 23–4
George I (king) 3, 85, 169
George III (king)
  parody and destruction of equestrian statue 145
  said to have summoned Mendoza to court 156
George IV (as Prince of Wales)
  early adoption of archery 110
  encouragement of boxing 159, 169
  as important sports patron 5
  portrait in archery costume **111**
George, M. Dorothy, on caricatures of courtesans 60
Gil Blas (Lesage), *see* Lesage, Alain-René
Giles, J., on recreation for laborers 28
Gillray, James 5, **154**, 168
Gilpin, William, defeated at archery by Miss Littledale 116
Gloucester Journal, advertisement for Cotswold games 42
Glover, Stephen, on Derbyshire 27, 28
Godfrey, John, "Treatise Upon the Useful Science of Defense" 158
Goldar, John, offer of subscription to prints of *Modern Love* 68
Grafton, 3d Duke of (August Henry Fitzroy) 144
Gregson, Bob 165–6, 176n70
Grenville, George, favored in *New Foundling Hospital* 142
Grosart, Alexander B., *Occasional Issues of Unique or Very Rare Books* 44
Guards of the Night Defeated, The (Collet), *see* Collet, John
Guiccioli, Teresa, Byron's love affair with 190
Gulliver's Travels (Swift), *see* Swift, Jonathan

Hainault Archers/Foresters 112, 119
Haitian Revolution 165–6, 167
Hampton Court tennis court 85
"hand-tennis" 84–5
Hanway, Jonas, believed Jews would not fight for England 155

Hargrove, Ely, *Anecdotes of Archery, From the Earliest Ages to 1791* 120
harpastè/harpastum (tennis) 84
Harrow, student archery competition 106
Harvey, Adrian, on emergence of sporting literature 10
Haytley, Edward, *The Brockman Family* 57–8
Hazlitt, William, on tennis 90–91
health care of horses 135
Hellespont 179, 182, 185–90
The Hen Peckt Husband (Dawes), *see* Dawes, William
Henry V (Shakespeare), *see* Shakespeare, William
Henry VI, Part 3 (Shakespeare), *see* Shakespeare, William
Henry VIII (king) 85, 94
Henslow, J.S., on recreation for laborers 28
Hero and Leander, *see* Byron, Lord; Marlowe, Christopher
Heroides, *see* Hero and Leander
Hertfordshire Archers 116
Higginson, Thomas, tennis court attached to gaming-house 97
Hill, Jeffrey, on reluctance of historians to take up literature 12
Histrio-Mastix: The Player's Scourge; or, Actor's Tragedy (Prynne), *see* Prynne, William
"hobby-horse" as prostitute 129–30
Hobhouse, John Cam 188, 190–91
Hogarth, William
  The Bathos 126
  Cap of Liberty on Staff of Maintenance 145
  Collet as worthy successor or "second Hogarth" 55, 68, 69
  Collet's copy of plate from *A Harlot's Progress* 60
  on hunting, shooting, and fishing 69
  relationship with James Figg 2, 158
  riding habit in *Country Dance* 57
  works
    Marriage-a-la-Mode 64
    A Rake's Progress 137, **139**, **140**, 158
    Second Stage of Cruelty 8, **9**
    Southwark Fair 158, 168

Holcroft, Thomas
    The Noble Peasant 118–19
    The Road to Ruin 94
Holt, Richard, on organization and regulation of sport 7–8
Homer
    Byron's allusion to his "broad Hellespont" 189–90
    Odyssey story of Trojan horse 126
Hone, William, series of books on popular customs 30
Horace, on Young Romans swimming near military training ground 183
Horse Whisperer, The (Evans), *see* Evans, Nicholas
horses
    dangers of riding in fact and fiction 133–5, 148n23
    horse racing received most media attention 10
    "horse whisperer," *see* Sullivan, Daniel
    Houyhnhnm equine society 127–8
    literary depictions of horse culture 13, 125–50
    Swift's portrayal of authors as horsemen 126–7
Hours of Idleness (Byron), *see* Byron, Lord
how-to books on archery 120
Hoyle, Edmond, gambling associated with card games more than horse racing 133
Hoyle's Game Improved 94
Humphries, Richard 5, 154, 156, 159
Hunt, Leigh, on Byron rehearsing the part of Leander 179–81
Hutton, Ronald, on John Aubrey 25

identity, *see* nationalism/national identity
internationalism, Asian and African influence on ancient Olympics 36
Island, The (Byron), *see* Byron, Lord

Jackson, John
    and Byron 179–80, 182, 185
    and Mendoza 153, 173n3
James Boswell wrote *The Cub at Newmarket* 116
James I (king)
    Book of Sports 4, 40, 85, 169

enjoyment of sports 3–4
politicalization of sport 40
James Street Theatre, history of two tennis courts 97
Jenkins, David, on history of James Street Theatre 97
Jews/Judaism; *see also* race and national identity
    blamed for disorder in Old Price Riots 171
    Mendoza and anti-semitism 13, 153–7, 167, 171–2
Jockey Club
    antedating 13, 136–41
    members during Brereton's expulsion 144
    and *The New Foundling Hospital for Wit* 141–5
Jockey Club and its Founders in Three Periods, The, *see* Black, Robert
"Jockey Club, The" (frontispiece in Ward's book) 137, **138**
"jockey-ship" 129, 147n11
John, Anne and William Orde (portrait by Devis), *see* Devis, Arthur
Johnson, Christopher, on boxing 160, 162
Johnson, Samuel
    on classical precedents for combat 175n41
    close calls getting off a horse 134
    on temporary decline of boxing 158–9
Johnstone, Charles, race-fixing in novel *Chrysal* 131–2
Jones, Mr., description of Miss Littledale's match 116
Jonson, Ben
    Bartholomew Fair 179
    uninspired lines in *Annalia Dubrensia* 43
Journal of a Tour in the Levant (Turner), *see* Turner, William
Jovial Crew or The Merry Beggars (Brome), *see* Brome, Richard
Joys of the Chase, or The Rising Woman and Falling Man, The (Collet), *see* Collet, John
Juel-Jensen, Bent, on Cotswold games 42
Julius Caesar (Shakespeare), *see* Shakespeare, William

Kauffman, Angelica, portraits of women in Turkish trousers 71
Kemble, John Philip, hired Mendoza to squelch Old Price Riots 171
Kennett, White 20, 25
Killigrew's King Men performed in Gibbon's Tennis Court 97
Killing no murder (Cruikshank), *see* Cruikshank, George
Kilwinning (Scotland) papingo shoot 106, 122n7
Kit-Cat Club 137

Ladies' Pocket-Book, illustration of Lady Salisbury at targets 116
Lady Worsley, *see* Reynolds, Sir Joshua
Lancashire Bowmen 114
landscapes by Collet 65
Laroon, Marcellus, drawing of sportsman offering pheasant 64
Lawful Amusements (Burder), *see* Burder, George
"lawful" and "unlawful games" 4, 23, 85
lawn tennis born at end of nineteenth century 83, 98
Leander, *see* Byron, Lord; Marlowe, Christopher
"Learning to Swim" (Franklin), *see* Franklin, Benjamin
Lee, Sir Sidney, letter from Theodore Cook on Shakespeare 41
Leeds Mercury, *see* Baines, Edward
Leeds Races, dispute between newspapers regarding 28–9
Leeuwen, Thomas A.P. van, on swimming as part of military training 192n18
legitimate vs. illegitimate theater 169–72
Lesage, Alain-René, reference to tennis in *Gil Blas* 93
lesbian relationship suggested of Misses Wicket and Trigger 63–4
Lever, Sir Ashton, archery activities 106–8, 117, 121
Levi, David, "Levi's theological victory over Priestley" 157
libertine attitudes, changes from mid- to late eighteenth century 72, 75
Licensing Act controlling theaters 169–70
Life in London, *see* Egan, Pierce

Litchfield Squabble, The 133
literacy, increase and spread of sport culture 1
Littledale, Miss, victory over men at private archery match 116
London Magazine
freedom of women's fashion as cause of divorce 71
on regulating pleasure of the people 21–2
London Olympic games, 1908, 1948, and 2012 49–50
Long, Edward Noel, Byron's memories of 185
Long, Henry, on Byron's swimming ability 181
Louis XIV (king), preference for billiards over tennis 95
Love, James, poem praising cricket 90
"Love Match, A" (Collet), *see* Collet, John, *Modern Love*
Lukin, Robert, *A Treatise on Tennis* 87, 88–9, 95, 99
Lust's Dominion, *see* Dekker, Thomas
L'Utilité qui provient du Jeu de Paume au corps et à l'esprit, *see* Forbet l'Aisné
Luze, Albert de, on Louis XIV's preference for billiards 95

Macaulay, Aulay, desired suppression of wakes 29
MacNally, Leonard, *Robin Hood; or, Sherwood Forest* 118
Magnificent Amersons, The (Tarkington), *see* Tarkington, Booth
Maison académique, frontispiece showing enclosed space for tennis and other games 95, **96**
Making of the English Working Class, The (Thompson), *see* Thompson, E.P.
Malcolmson, Robert
argued industrialization undermined recreational calendar 19
Popular Recreations in English Society 1700–1850 11, 31
Manevieux, M. de, *Traité sur la connaissance du royal jeu de paume* 87, 94–5

Marchand, Leslie, on swimming near Grantchester 184
Marlowe, Christopher, "Hero and Leander" 179
Marriage-a-la-Mode (Hogarth), *see* Hogarth, William
Marshall, Julian, *The Annals of Tennis* 87, 98
masquerades and cross-dressing 71
mass marketing, *see* advertising/adverts
Measure for Measure (Shakespeare), *see* Shakespeare, William
mechanical arts, tennis construed as one of the 88
medical benefits of tennis 90; *see also* Galen
Meditations, see Pseudo-Bunyan
Memoirs of the Life of Daniel Mendoza, The, see Mendoza, Daniel
Mendoza, Daniel; *see also* Jews/Judaism
  The Art of Boxing 153–6, 159–62
  fight with Humphries in Odiham 159
  The Memoirs of the Life of Daniel Mendoza 153–7, 160–62, 168
  references in plays, poems and songs 163
  Regency Crisis satirized in print of Humphries and 5
  role in Old Price Riots 167–8, 170–72
Merry Sherwood; or Harlequin Forester (O'Keefe), *see* O'Keefe, John
Merry Wives of Windsor (Shakespeare), *see* Shakespeare, William
metaphor
  tennis as metaphor of life and love 83, 84, 91–2, 93, 97, 99
  use of sports as 5–6
Middleton Archers 107
Middleton, Thomas, *The World Tossed at Tennis* 92
military dress worn by women 71
Milton, John, "Sabrina fair" from his masque *Comus* 185, 186
Miss Tipapin Going for All Nine (Collet), *see* Collet, John
Miss Wicket and Miss Trigger (Collet), *see* Collet, John
Modern art of boxing, The (Mendoza), *see* Mendoza, Daniel, *The Art of Boxing*

Modern Love (*Courtship, Elopement, Honeymoon, Discordant Matrimony*) (Collet), *see* Collet, John
Molineaux, Tom 163–7
Montagu, Elizabeth, on Chudleigh's Iphigenia costume 72
Montaigne, Michel de, use of tennis metaphor 99
Monthly Magazine
  evangelical hope for innocent diversions 29
  music recommended as amusement suitable for poor 33n58
Moody, Jane, on connection between generic and cultural (il)legitimacy 169–70
Moor, Edward, on recreations in Suffolk 27
morality; *see also* sexuality
  assignment of values to sporting activity 39, 45–7
  "Olympian" festivals connected spiritual and moral values 35–7
  vagueness of antiquity allowed reinterpretation of ancient Olympics 37
Mores, E. Rowe, questionnaire sent to Berkshire parishes 25–6, 30
Morning Chronicle, on Leeds Races 28–9
Morning Frolic, or the Transmutation of Sexes, A (Collet), *see* Collet, John
Morning Herald, The, on Royal British Bowmen marriages 113
Moseley, Walter, *An Essay on Archery* 120
Muir, David, presentation of silver arrow 106
"Muse and the Horse-Race, The" 141–2
musket replaced arrow as weapon of choice 105
Musselburgh Arrow 106

nationalism/national identity; *see also* Jews/Judaism
  and boxing 13, 160, 163–5, 167, 170
  English masculinity vs. French or Italian effeminacy 8
  and horse racing 125
  longbow as symbol of British character 120–21

sport as foil for French/Italian
effeminacy 8, 160
and theater 170–71
natural law according to Pope 161
Neave, Oliver, letter from Franklin on
"Learning to Swim" 184
Nelson, William, *William Nelson Letter
Book, 1766–1775* 65
neoclassical ideals manipulated by
Mendoza 156–7, 160–61
*New 18th Century: Theory, Politics,
English Literature, The* (Nussbaum
and Brown) 12
*New and Impartial Collection of
Interesting Letters, A, see* Almon,
John
New Foundling Hospital for Wit, The 125,
141–5, **146**
New Historicism 12
Newmarket
*Articles for the Newmarket Town
Plate* 125
Defoe's description of day at 131
fight attracted Prince of Wales 159
as site of Jockey Club Coffee
Room 141
where commoners could feel like
kings 133
newspapers; *see also specific newspapers
by title*
and anti-semitic pamphlets 171
one avenue of boxing's literary
popularity 159
references to Jockey Club 136–7
Newton, Richard
The Battle for the Breeches 75
Wearing the Breeches 75, **77**
non-textual physical entertainment used to
avoid censorship 170
North, Lord (2nd Earl of Guilford
[Frederick North]), accused of
neglecting duties while gambling
144–5
nostalgia for horses reflected by books and
films 145–6
Nussbaum, Felicity A., *see New 18th
Century: Theory, Politics, English
Literature, The*

"Observations on the Practice of Archery
in England" (Barrington), *see*
Barrington, Daines
*Occasional Issues of Unique or Very Rare
Books* (Grosart), *see* Grosart,
Alexander B.
Odyssey (Homer), *see* Homer
*Officer in the Light Infantry driven by his
Lady to Cox Heath, An* (Collet),
see Collet, John
O'Keefe, John, *Merry Sherwood; or
Harlequin Forester*, review used
archery language 119
Old Price Riots (1809) 167–8, 170–72
Old Vicarage, Grantchester, The (Brooke),
see Brooke, Rupert
Oldfield, Henry, *Anecdotes of Archery,
Ancient and Modern* 120
Olympism
ancient Olympics' legacy 35–7
British Olympism from the eighteenth
century 45–50
emergence of English sporting
literature and 12–13, 38–45
opera considered bad for England's social
health and autonomy 169–70, 171
opinions regarding people's pastimes,
writers careful in expressing
themselves 23–4, 29–31
O'Quinn, Daniel, on theater of public
opinion 165
Oracle or Bell's New World, The, on female
Archers of Blackheath 113–14
Orlando Furioso (Ariosto), *see* Ariosto,
Ludovico
Orme, Nicholas, on methods of training
Roman soldiers 183
Ormerod, George, on annual wakes in
Cheshire 27
Oudry, Jean-Baptiste, "Bataille Arrivée
Dans le Tripot," tennis racket used
as weapon 97, **98**
Oxberry, William
*The Boarding House, or Five Hours at
Brighton* 163
Pancratia, Or, A History of Pugilism
158, 159
Oxford, 17th Earl of (Edward de Vere),
quarrel with Sidney 93

Pamela (Richardson), *see* Richardson, Samuel
Pancratia, Or, A History of Pugilism (Oxberry), *see* Oxberry, William
Parkyns, Sir Thomas, on usefulness of wrestling 21
Parnasse satyrique (Viau), *see* Viau, Theophile de
"Parody on the Celebrated Soliloquy in Hamlet By a Boxer," *see* "To box, or not to box …"
Pars, William, travels with Chandler 47–8
pastoralism
    ancient Olympic games celebrated human interaction with nature 35–6
    context for tennis 90
    in English sporting literature 38–45
    reflected in Olympic symbols 49–50
Pausania, *Description of Greece* 37
Pembroke, Earl, *see Encyclopedia Britannica*
Penny Brooks, William, Wenlock Olympian Society 49
Pepys, Samuel, on renovation of tennis court at Hampton Court 85
periodicals; *see also specific periodicals by title*
    cross-class market for sporting intelligence 48–9
    facilitation of debate about sports and culture 1–2
"PETITION *of Justice* Boden's *Horse to the Duke of* Newcastle," *The* 133–4
Piggott [*sic*], Lester 148n21
Pigott, Charles
    Piggott's New Hoyle 133
    satirical works on Jockey Club 135–6
Pilkington, James, on wakes in Derbyshire 28
Pinchbeck, Christopher, musical clock exhibit 97
Pindar
    opening line of Olympian odes as motto of first Swimming Society in England 184
    poems 37
Place, Francis, on ill-treatment of Jews 155
Plain-Truth, Peter, verses on local horse race in political buffoon 133

Plot, Robert, cursory interest in popular custom 25
politics
    boxing as allegory for debates 5
    political satire in *New Foundling Hospital for Wit* 141–5
    political uses of tennis 92–3
poor, *see* social class; social regulation
Pope, Alexander
    attendance at match between Figg and Sutton 2–3
    The Dunciad 163
    "Epistle to Miss Blount, on her Leaving the Town after the Coronation" 128
    Essay on Criticism 161, 163
    nearly drowned when coach overturned 134
    translation of Homer's *Odyssey* 126
popular customs, accounts in early histories 25–7
Popular Recreations in English Society 1700–1850 (Malcolmson), *see* Malcolmson, Robert
Porter, Endymion 42
Porter, Roy, on horse culture 131, 136
Post-Fandom and The Millennial Blues (Redhead), *see* Redhead, Steve
press, *see* print culture; *specific journals by name*
Prince of Wales, *see* George IV (as Prince of Wales)
print culture; *see also specific periodicals by title*
    expensive magazines focused on spectators more than the sport 48–9
    and spread of sport 1–2, 10–11
prizes for archery 105–8, 116, 117, 122n7, 122n16
prostitutes
    Collet's paintings of 74–5
    likened to horses 128–30
    slang and animals associated with images of 72
protests, use of football matches to mask public 4–5
Prynne, William, complaints against sports and theater 4
Pseudo-Bunyan, *Meditations*, allusions to tennis 92

Public Advertiser, deemed Collet worthy successor to Hogarth 68
public sphere, and sports' expansion 1
pubs, connection between pugilism and 162
pugilism, *see* boxing
Pulteney, William, *see* Bath, Earl of (William Pulteney)
Puritans
  Christian perceptions against study of sport in antiquity 35
  moralist attitude toward sport and recreation 3, 4, 5, 29, 40, 85, 169
  writers considered games less harmful than zeal of 20

Quiet Husband, The (Collet), *see* Collet, John

race and national identity 163, 164, 165, 167
race-fixing 132–3
Racing Calendar, first official sporting release 2
racquets (game) 98
Rake's Progress, A (Hogarth), *see* Hogarth, William
Rakewell, Tom 137
Rapin, Rene 6–7
Ravenna Journal (Byron), *see* Byron, Lord
recreation; *see also* Sunday
  perceptions of 3
  social elites and popular 1, 19–34
Redgrave, Richard, on Collet 64
Redhead, Steve, on "literaturisation" of British football image 50
Reflections on the Revolution in France (Burke), *see* Burke, Edmund
Refusal, The (Collet), *see* Collet, John
Règles et principes de la Paume (Barcellon), *see* Barcellon, Pierre
religion, *see* Puritans
respectability conveyed by various "Olympic" descriptors 47
Restoration, *see* Charles II (king)
Revett, Nicholas, travels with Chandler 47–8
Revolutionary War, *see* War of American Independence
Reynolds, Sir Joshua, *Lady Worsley* 59–60, 63

Richardson, Samuel
  letter against lady's "affecting manly arts" 60
  Pamela as "mere Tennis-ball of Fortune" 91
Richmond Archers 106
Richmond, Bill, trainer and patron of Molineaux 164
riding habits 56–60, 71
Ritson, Joseph, collection of Robin Hood ballads 119–20
Rival Milliners, The (Collet), *see* Collet, John
Road to Ruin, The, *see* Holcroft, Thomas
Roberts, Thomas, *The English Bowman; or Tracts on Archery* 120
Robin Hood
  in archery literature 118–21
  England's medieval folk hero and master archer 105
  Hainault Foresters posing like merry band 112
  Robin Hood Society ball 117
Roman Comique, Le (Scarron), *see* Scarron
Roman Empire, antipagan laws crucial in demise of ancient Olympics 36
Roman Generals, or the Distressed Ladies, The (Dover), *see* Dover, John
Rosinante (*Don Quixote's* horse) 129, 147n12
Rousseau, Jean-Jacques, Byron compared himself to 180
Royal British Bowmen 110–12, 113
"Royal Cockpit" 97
Royal Company of Archers in Edinburgh 106
Royal Kentish Bowmen 110, 120
Royal Newfoundland Constabulary 46
Royal Society, founding 5
Royal Surrey Bowmen, Duke of Clarence a member of 110
Royal Veterinary College 135
royalty
  English kings and tennis 85–6
  relationship to sport and theater 1, 3–5
  tennis originally a royal game 83, 88, 90, 97
Rule Britannia, *see* Thompson, James

Sabie, Francis, "Second Eclogue" 90
"Sabrina fair" and Byron's memories of Cambridge 185, 186
Salisbury, Marchioness of **115**, 116
Sambrook, Sam, satirical compilation of 32 clubs 137
Sauer, K.C., on Dawes and Collet 65
Sawyer, Tom
    on aristocratic patronage of boxing 159
    on sword ceasing to be dress accessory 173n23
Sayer, Robert, *The Draughtsman's Assistant; or, Drawing Made Easy ...* 68
Scaino da Salo, Antonio, on tennis 84, 86, 91–2
Scarron, *Le Roman Comique* 97, **98**
Scorton Archers 105–6
Scott, Sir Walter 134
Scrivener, Michael, on writing by British Jews 156–7
Sea Biscuit (film) 145–6
Second Stage of Cruelty (Hogarth), *see* Hogarth, William
Secret History of Clubs, The 137
sexuality
    Byron on swimming and lovemaking 188–9
    exchanging male and female clothing as erotic sport 75, **76**
    horses used to symbolize war and 125
    love in Byron's life and writing 181, 189–90
    opportunities to meet prospective spouses 21, 113, 114
    Pope's warning about choosing horse-mad mate 128
    in popular literature 46
    and riding horses 128–30
    in Shakespeare's interpretations of sport 41
    "sporting girl" slang for promiscuous woman 45
    and women's dress 60, 71, 77, 78n9
Shakespeare, William
    Egan's allusion to regarding Mendoza 156
    works
        Hamlet 163

Henry V 84, 92–3
Henry VI, Part 3 41
Julius Caesar 182–3
King John 165
Measure for Measure 162
Merry Wives of Windsor 43–4
Troilus and Cressida 41
Shaw, Stebbing, on "Whitsun bower" 27
Sheridan, Richard Brinsley, turned down comic opera on William Tell for political reasons 119
Sheridan, Thomas, Apollonian trope in compliment to Swift 126
Shield, William, composer of music for archery plays 118–19
shooting; *see also* archery
    Collet's pictures of shooting sportswomen 70–71
    musket replaced arrow as weapon of choice 105
Sidney, Sir Philip
    allusions to tennis in *Arcadia* 92
    quarrel with Earl of Oxford 93
    sport abilities 183
silver arrows, *see* prizes for archery
"skewer one's opponents," origin of phrase 95
skill and fortune in archery 106, 108, 116
Slack, Jack, fight with Broughton and shift in legal standing of boxing 158
Smith, Adam, suggested promotion of public diversions 24
Smith, John, published *Designs by Jn. Collet* 68
Smollett, Tobias
    The Adventures of Roderick Random, dream about tennis ball 91, 99
    description of 'bathing machine" 181
soccer, *see* football
social class; *see also* recreation
    clothing and 75, 77
    Collet's freedom of movement across 64, 68, 74
    cross-class aspect of Cotswold games 43
    sports associated with 41
    sports writing linked upper classes with masses 47

social regulation
    allowing poor to enjoy traditional recreation 21–2
    football matches as form of 4–5
Society for the Reformation of Manners 7
songs
    about archery 117, 118, 119
    about boxing 163, 165–7, 168
    ballad on *Swimming Lady* … 46
    Rule Britannia 165, 170
    "Sabrina fair" 185, 186
Southey, Robert, on recreation for laborers 28
Spectator, Steele's invocation of Rapin 6–7
Spenser, Edmund, on Sidney's sport abilities 183
spirituality
    benefits of fishing for body and soul 38–40
    "Olympian" festivals connected physical to ethic values and 35–7
sport; *see also* clothing; Jews/Judaism; Olympism; recreation; theater; *specific sports by name*
    as academic field of study 11–12
    athletics foster literary arts 161
    participation by text contributors 13
    playing by the rules 1–16
    use of tennis courts for billiards or bowls 83
Sport and the Literary Imagination (Hill), *see* Hill, Jeffrey
Sporting Magazine, The
    definition of sport very wide 55
    illustration of Lady Salisbury at targets **115**, 116
    letter from Duke of Dorset on women's cricket 10
    Mendoza's frequent appearances in 163, 167
    poem: "A Boxing We Will Go" 164, 166–7
    pride in national language 7
Sports and Pastimes of the People of England, *see* Strutt, Joseph
sports writing; *see also specific publications by title*
    development of genre 10–11
    Mendoza's refashioning of traditional literary principles 156, 167

Oxberry's play pitting ancient vs. modern boxing champions 163
    shaped popular ideas about nationalism, theater, and sport 172
Sprawson, Charles, on swimming 181, 184, 189
sprezzatura 182, 184
St. James's Chronicle, exchange of letters on Collet's works 69–70
status; *see also* social class
    as ancient Olympic athletes' goal 36
    of boxing 172
    horses representing 126, 130
    of Jews 155
    of sports elevated by literature 50, 93
stays and body molding as form of sexual assertion 60, 78n9
Steele, Richard
    critique of generic adulteration 170
    invocation of Rapin 6–7
    quote from Virgil in Bickerstaff essay 5–6, 8
Steevens, G., on Collet 64
Stephen, J.K., poem on superiority of tennis 90
Sterne, Laurence, *The Life and Opinions of Tristram Shandy, Gentleman* 128–9
Stot, Joseph, response to Clayton's *Friendly Advice* 24
Strickland, Sir William, gain when Frampton's race-fixing backfired 132–3
Strutt, Joseph
    notion that Collet engraved his own works 65
    Sports and Pastimes of the People of England 30, 47
Stuart, John, *see* Bute, 3rd Earl of (John Stuart)
Stukeley, William, on loss of sports due to religious zeal 20–21
Suicide, The (Colman) 60
Sullivan, Daniel ("horse whisperer") 135
Sunday
    Puritan objections to recreation on 4, 40
    sports publications 10
Surtee, Kate Convetry, advice on maternal pedagogy 45

Sutton, Ned, fight with James Figg 2
Swift, Jonathan
    allusion to *Odyssey* in "A Description of a City Shower" 126
    attendance at boxing match 2–3
    Battle of the Books 126–7
    Gulliver's Travels 127–8
    imagined better world governed by horses 145
swimming; *see also* Byron, Lord
    abilities of Julius Caesar, Sidney and Orlando 182–3
    literary context of organized 184
    as part of military training 183, 192n18
Swimming Lady or a Wanton Discovery, The (ballad) 46

Tagus River, Byron's swim across 188
Talbot, Sir Gilbert, presentation of silver arrow 106
Tam O-Shanter (Burns), *see* Burns, Robert
Targets (formal archery matches) 107–10, 113–18
Tarkington, Booth, *The Magnificent Amersons* 145
Tatler, Steele as Bickerstaff's essay on blood sports 5–6, 8
tennis
    background and origins 83–5
    celebrations of 88–93
    Garsault's description of court and racket 87–8, **89**
    nature of 13, 84–8
    transformations and decline 93–9
theater
    archery portrayed on stage 118–19
    relationship with boxing 156, 157, 167, 170–71
    relationship with sport 1, 6–7
    tennis courts used/converted for 84, 95, 97, 99
Thelwall, John, on seeing lodge of Royal Kentish Bowmen 120
thieves, Collet's protected but Defoe's Moll Flanders deported 56
Thompson, E.P., *The Making of the English Working Class* 11
Thompson, James, *Rule Britannia* 165, 170
Thornton, Henry 156, 173n15

"Thought on Seeing Races Advertised for Runney-Mead, A" 143–4
Thrale, Hester, on Lady Worsley 63
Throsby, John, descriptions of traditional festivities 26–7
Tillemans, Peter, *View of a Horse-Match over the Long Course at Newmarket, from the Starting Post to the Stand* 139
time, criticism of recreation as wasting laborers' 24–5
Tom Jones (Fielding), *see* Fielding, Henry
Tour through the Whole Island of Great Britain, A (Defoe), *see* Defoe, Daniel
Town and Country Magazine, on women dressed in male clothing 71
Toxophilite Society 106–10, 113, 116–20, 124n76
Toxophilus (archer's bible), *see* Ascham
Traité sur la connaissance du royal jeu de paume, *see* Manevieux, M. de
Tranter, Neil, on sport as means of social regulation 4
Trattato del Giuco della Palla, *see* Scaino da Salo, Antonio
Treatise on Archery; or The Art of Shooting with the English Bow, A, *see* Waring, Thomas, Jr.
A Treatise on Tennis, *see* Lukin, Robert
"Treatise Upon the Useful Science of Defense", *see* Godfrey, John
Treatyse of Fysshynge wyth an Angle (Berners), *see* Berners, Dame Juliana
Tricks of the Town Laid Open, The, warning about cheating in horse racing 133
tripot, French word for tennis-court used to describe gambling halls 102n48; *see also* Oudry, Jean-Baptiste
Tristram Shandy (Sterne), *see* Sterne, Laurence
Troilus and Cressida (Shakespeare), *see* Shakespeare, William
Trojan horse or mare, *see* Homer
Troops Fording a Brook (Collet), *see* Collet, John
trousers, *see* breeches worn by women

Troy, Byron's apparent exploration of 189–90
Troyer, Howard William, on Ward's imaginary Atheistical Club 137
truce, Olympic 36
Turner, James G., maximalist definition of libertine 72
Turner, William, and Byron's swimming the Hellespont 188–9, 190
Two Foscari, The (Byron), *see* Byron, Lord

Universal Magazine, The, poem on Kitty Fisher falling from horse 134
Universal Spectator, The, proclaimed sexes should wear different dress 77

Vaughan, Anne, husband spent more time with his horse 128
Vegetius, *Epitoma Rei Militaris* 183
Venice, Byron's swim from the Lido to Grand Canal 188
Vere, Edward de, *see* Oxford, 17th Earl of (Edward de Vere)
veterinary schools 135, 148n29
Viau, Theophile de, erotic poem *Parnasse satyrique* 92
"Vicissitudinarius," alarmed by horse racing and gambling 143–4
View of a Horse-Match over the Long Course at Newmarket, from the Starting Post to the Stand (Tillemans), *see* Tillemans, Peter
View of Calais; taken from the side of the canal leading from thence to St. Omer's (Collet), *see* Collet, John
Virgil
    quoted by Broughton 157
    quoted by Steele 5–6, 8
Vivès, Juan-Luis, tennis illustrated rules of sociability 91

wakes 20, 21, 22, 23, 28
Walbancke, Matthew, *see Annalia Dubrensia*
Walpole, Horace, on Chudleigh's Iphigenia costume 72
Walpole, Robert 2–3, 5, 169
Walton, Izaac, *The Compleat Angler* 39–40, 46
war, horses used to symbolize sex and 125

War Horse (film) 146
War of American Independence, and gambling English politicians 145
Ward, Ned, *History of the London Clubs* frontispiece "The Jockey Club" 137, **138**
Waring, Thomas
    archery warehouse and shop 120
    co-founder of Toxophilite archery society 106–9
    prize won at 1782 Annual Target 117
    on women's targets 114
Waring, Thomas, Jr.
    on miles walked by archers in course of a Target 114
    takeover of father's business 122n25
    A Treatise on Archery; or The Art of Shooting with the English Bow 120
Watt, James, engine improvements changed nature of horse power 145
Weatherill, Lorna, on women's ownership of art 68
Webster, John, *The Duchess of Malfi*, allusions to tennis 92
Weekly Dispatch 10
Wenlock Olympian Society 49
West, Michael, on Digby's *De Arte Natandi* and swimming 183–4
Whale, John, on martial prowess of England due to sports 160
Wharton, Thomas, note on Cotswold Hills 44
"When for Air I take my Mare," *see* D'Urfey, Thomas
Whitaker, John, on "contagious viciousness" of crowds 29
Whitehead, Paul, tribute to pugilism 162
Whitsuntide festivals 27, 40, 42, 47
Wilkes, John
    Collet's possible support of 72, 75
    exaltation of English liberty 71
    Hogarth's 1763 engraving to satirize 145
    notoriety assisted political satire 141
William III (king)
    death said to be caused by horse accident 134
    restoration of tennis court at Hampton Court 85

Williams-Wynne, Sir Watkin 110
Winterson, Jeanette, on Swift's Gulliver 127–8
Wodehouse, P.G., quote on tennis as metaphor on love and life 83
women; *see also* sexuality
    advice to send lovers off to play tennis 90
    Collet's pictures of women shooting 70–71
    as purchasers of art 68
    roles in all-male archery societies 113
    and slaves excluded from ancient Olympics 36
    in sports 9–10, 35–6, 55–80, 111–16
Wood, Anthony, on maypole dancing 20
Wood, Sir William, *The Bowman's Glory or Archery Revived* 105
Woodmen of Arden of Meriden, marriages with fellow Woodmen's daughters and sisters 113
World, coverage of Mendoza and Humphries 154–5
World Tossed at Tennis, The (Middleton), *see* Middleton, Thomas
Worsley, Lady 59–60
wrestling, *see* boxing
"Written after Swimming from Sestos to Abydos" (Byron), *see* Byron, Lord
Wybergh, Thomas, defeated at archery by Miss Littledale 116